Scottish Birds

Culture and Tradition

In memory of my father, Edward Hull,
who taught me to see birds.

And for his great grandchildren
Hannah, Edward, Hamish and Isobel
hoping that they will learn and take pleasure from birds
as much as their grandsires.

SCOTTISH BIRDS
Culture and Tradition

Robin Hull

MERCAT PRESS
EDINBURGH
www.mercatpress.com

First published in 2001 by Mercat Press
James Thin, 53 South Bridge, Edinburgh EH1 1YS
www.mercatpress.com

ISBN: 184183 0259

The illustrations used to decorate the text are taken from
An Illustrated Manual of British Birds *(London, 1899) by Howard Saunders*
and are by G. E. Lodge and others

Set in Ehrhardt at Mercat Press
Printed and bound in Great Britain by
Bell & Bain Ltd., Glasgow

Contents

Preface

Birds have been in existence for 150 million years, man for a mere six million; birds are our seniors by 25-fold. The first men appeared in Scotland less than 10,000 years ago, after the retreat of the ice. Though birds must have been in Scotland before the Ice Ages, and during warm interglacials, they too only arrived in Scotland in any numbers when the sterilising deep freeze of the Pleistocene ended. This book tells how the class Aves has influenced the species *Homo sapiens sapiens* in the last 10,000 years.

On holiday in Arran and growing bored of the beach I walked by myself to a Neolithic burial site near Torrylin. Over a century before human remains had been discovered in the one chamber of this tomb undamaged by vandals. I stood in the chamber wondering at the people who made it. I noticed that its long axis pointed straight at the enormous phallus of Ailsa Craig. It seemed that the builders of this monument to death also had ideas of reproduction and birth in mind. The boulders of the tomb were huge and, as many must have done before me, I marvelled at how they were manipulated into place. I bent to examine them, mindful of the huge stones I had unearthed from my garden in Perthshire with pick and crowbar. Suddenly I was startled by a loud call and, straightening my back, I saw a Curlew fly over me.

At that instant I had a spine-tingling moment of *déjà-vu*. A man working in this barrow some 5,000 years ago might well have heard the same eerie call from exactly the same species. I suddenly felt a tremendous link with that man, so different from myself. The millennia were bridged by the call of a Whaup.

This book explores the relationship between man and birds and how, like the slow maturation of a good malt whisky, this has evolved with the flavours of time.

Scottish Birds sets out to be a companion to the many excellent field guides that are available to those who watch, try to identify and understand birds. It came about because of a lifelong interest in birds and a deep love of Scotland, the country of my mother's birth. The book was also influenced by what my partner in a Warwickshire General Practice called 'my little weakness'.

My English father was fascinated by natural history. He taught me to use my eyes and to question what I saw. He was a reasonable, kind but somewhat Victorian man, and, when I was seven, I was astonished at his sudden atypical criticism. It was in 1938 when war seemed a possibility and there were army manoeuvres near our Hertfordshire home. I was puzzled by the browns and greens of the soldier's vehicles and asked my father why they were painted in such funny colours.

'It is called camouflage, Robin, it makes them more difficult to see.'

'But it makes them easier to see,' I burst out, only to be reprimanded with 'Don't be silly, boy.'

I remember that episode clearly for it rankled, but it was not until many years later, when I experienced difficulty working with microscopes on stained material as a preliminary to medicine, that I discovered I was severely red-green colour blind.

Colour blindness is an inherited condition, usually affecting males, in which the cellular structure of the retina differs from the norm. The affected may see better at night but have impaired perception of colour.

Colour blindness is a great drawback for a birdwatcher. Excellent though modern Field Guides are, they are often of little help to me, for birds never really look like their portraits in the book. This problem is not limited to the colour blind, for many people with normal vision also experience difficulty. A single, rather stereotyped, pose does not convey the real bird as a living creature, even if you can appreciate its colour.

It became necessary for me to study birds in a different way, looking at their behaviour, their history and nomenclature in order to understand more about them. As a boy I was fascinated by country names for birds, which are so often descriptive of shape, sound or behaviour. Thus 'Jack-o-bo-peeper' or 'Tom Pudding' said more to me about the Long-tailed Tit or the Little Grebe than their standard English names. I was encouraged in this approach by Geoffrey Grigson's splendid book *The Englishman's Flora*[81] in which he described the history, nomenclature and medicinal use of many wild British plants. He supplemented this with wide-ranging botanical and general references from Pliny, through Shakespeare, to the present.

This led me to making a collection of vernacular names which, when put together, often spelt out the Jizz of a species. Jizz (originally Giss) is a bird-watcher's acronym derived from aircraft recognition during World War II, and stands for General Impression of Size and Shape. Since popular names, like human nicknames, reflect behaviour as well as appearance, they were helpful in dealing with my 'little weakness'.

Vernacular names reflect many attributes of a species, including its history, man's attitude towards it, as a benefit or a pest, and the folk belief that has grown up round it. The more names I found for a bird the better I came to know it.

This book has grown from the distillation of a lifetime of looking at birds all over the world and being dissatisfied with what I found in books. In retirement I realised a lifelong ambition of moving to my mother's country, where she had brought her family for so many wonderful holidays. Since living in Perthshire there has been more time for birds and at the same time my wife and I have steeped ourselves in Scottish history, its culture and its wildlife. Recently the acquisition of Tess Darwin's *The Scots Herbal, The Plant Lore of Scotland*[50] suggested the idea of this book.

How to use this book

As a companion to available Field Guides I hope this work will be as helpful to normal-sighted individuals as writing it has been to me.

The first part of the book consists of a chronological account of the ever-changing relationship between man and birds in Scotland since the end of the Ice Age. It also examines how birds have influenced human history and culture.

The second part deals in turn with the commoner birds found in Scotland. It collects together the names, history and other attributes of 195 species, that are not to be found in field guides, but which shed light on the jizz of each bird. The epilogue speculates briefly on the ecological future of Scotland.

The notes throughout the text are keyed to the Bibliography, p.283.

Abbreviations used in the text

Aber	Aberdeenshire	Lan	Lanarkshire
Arg	Argyllshire	Lin	Linlithgow
Ayr	Ayrshire	(lit)	literary
Banf	Banffshire	Loth	Lothians
Bas	Bass Rock	Low	Lowlands
Berw	Berwickshire	(m)	male
Bord	Borders	Mor	Morayshire
Cai	Caithness	N	North
(child)	children's name	NE	Northeast Scotland
Clack	Clackmannanshire	NS	Northern Scotland
Crom	Cromarty	Ork	Orkney
Dumb	Dumbartonshire	OutH	Outer Hebrides
Dumf	Dumfriesshire	Peeb	Peeblesshire
E	East	Per	Perthshire
EC	East Coast	Renf	Renfrewshire
Far	Faroes	Ros	Rosshire
(f)	female	Rox	Roxburghshire
Fif	Fifeshire	S	South
For	Forfarshire	Selk	Selkirkshire
Fou	Foula	Shet	Shetland
Gall	Galloway	SS	Southern Scotland
Har	Harris	StK	Saint Kilda
Heb	Hebrides	Stir	Stirlingshire
(imm)	immature	Suth	Sutherlandshire
Inv	Invernessshire	SW	Southwest Scotland
InH	Inner Hebrides	W	West
Jed	Jedburgh	WI	Western Isles
Kinrs	Kinross	Wig	Wigtownshire
Kirk	Kirkudbrightshire		

Acknowledgements

I am indebted to many friends for their help in providing advice and hosts of books and references, which have helped to combine a wealth of disparate information in *Scottish Birds, Culture and Tradition*. Among these I would particularly mention:

Peter Danks for climatological advice.

Jeremy Duncan, Librarian A.K. Bell Library, Perth, for finding references for me.

David Fletcher of David Fletcher Associates who put me in touch with the publishers.

Felicity Given, Archivist of Glenalmond College, for help in tracing Dr C.L. Williams.

Sandie Goodyear, Broadcaster at Heartland FM for 'mistressminding' Birds and Words.

James Holloway, Keeper of the Scottish National Portrait Gallery, Edinburgh.

Tom Johnstone of Mercat Press for being brave enough to publish the book.

Dr. Sheila Kidd (of the Department of Celtic, *Roinn na Ceiltis*, University of Glasgow) and her mother Norma Kidd, for help with Gaelic.

Brendan Murphy of Wordwright Communications, Aberfeldy, who galvanized me into broadcasting Birds and Words on Heartland FM and so started the book off.

James Irvine Robertson, for literary examples and many references.

Henry Steuart Fothringham, for allowing me free range in his extensive library.

Janet Henderson for advice on cooking Capercaillie.

Jimmy Knox, for listening to my ideas for hours spent in a boat as we fished together.

Campbell Steven, a great writer, natural historian and friend who kept me on the right path and criticized my style. To his wife Maisie Steven, for encouragement and dietary information on eighteenth-century Scotland, and to their son Ken for allowing me to quote his poetry.

Helen Watson, Librarian of the Scottish National Portrait Gallery, for patiently searching her archives for bird references in paintings

Ann Wyllie for a recipe for Solan Goose.

And to Gillian, my wife, for reading, re-reading and checking proofs and the drafts of the manuscript with her customary constructive criticism.

I am also indebted to many people who have allowed me to quote from copyright material. Thanks to:

John Kerr for allowing me to quote from his book *Queen Victoria's Scottish Diaries.*

Mr Angus MacDonald-Lockhart and Neil Wilson, publisher, for use of quotations from Paul Seton Gordon's works.

Catherine Proudfoot for references from Alexandra Stewart's *Daughters of the Glen.*

Random House, for the use of poems. 'Greenshank', 'Dipper', 'Puffin' and 'Ringed Plover' are from *Collected Poems* by Norman MacCaig published by Chatto & Windus, and are used by permission of the Random House Group Limited.

Every effort has been made to reach other copyright holders. I, and my publishers, apologise if there has been any inadvertent infringement of copyright.

Robin Hull
Strathtay, Perthshire and Paphos, Cyprus, September to December 2000

PART ONE: BIRDS IN SCOTLAND FROM THE ICE AGE TO THE PRESENT

1
Prehistory

The first known bird appeared during the Jurassic Period, which started about 195 million years ago. A fossilised feather of an extremely ancient bird was discovered in limestone deposits at Solnhofen in Bavaria in 1861. Later four complete fossil specimens were found, one of which was purchased by the British Museum in 1862. This creature was named *Archaeopteryx lithographica*. 'Archaeopteryx' means 'early winged one' and the specific name 'lithographica' was added because the very fine-grained limestone in which the fossil was discovered was used for lithography. *Archaeopteryx* was about the size of a present pigeon and it had many reptilian features including a long tail, a bill with teeth and a forelimb with three clawed digits. It also had feathers, which, though they had evolved from reptilian scales, mark it out as being avian.

From then things happened relatively quickly. By 130 million years ago in the Cretaceous Period of the Mesozoic Era, the great land mass of Pangea was breaking up. First, a cleavage parallel to the equator separated Laurasia in the north from Gondwana in the south. The latter was to form the continents of Africa, Australasia, South America and Antarctica and also the subcontinent of India. Laurasia later divided to form Eurasia and North America. Before this division, the biggest mountain chain the world has ever known formed in its north-western part. When Laurasia divided these mountains were split to form the ranges of Scandinavia, the Torridonian hills of northwest Scotland and the Appalachian chain in America. In the Cretaceous these mountains were far higher than the present day Himalaya, but subsequent erosion has reduced them to between 1,000 and 2,000 metres. In the Cretaceous birds were developing rapidly. Predecessors of the Divers were present in primitive birds such as *Ichthyornis* and *Hesperornis* and some early Penguins had appeared.[191] Some Penguins were as much as five feet five inches in height (today's largest Penguin, the Emperor, is just over three feet in height).

In the early Cenozoic Era there was again massive volcanic activity in Scotland, especially in the west, giving rise to massive shield volcanoes, floods of basalt lava with huge granite intrusions and swarms of dykes along a belt running from the Inner Hebrides to Northern Ireland. It was then that the hexagonal basalt columns of Staffa and the Giant's Causeway, the lava terraces of Mull and the plug of Ailsa Craig were created. The Dinosaurs had gone and life on Earth was beginning to be dominated by the latest arrivals, the mammals. Among birds *Diatryma*, a gigantic running ground bird, seven feet tall, found in America, has been called a landmark of avian palaeontology. This bird did not occur in Britain, though *Gastornis*, a creature as large as an Ostrich, has left remains in Eocene deposits in England and Belgium.

By the Eocene period of the Cenozoic the continents, as we know them today, were moving towards their present-day locations. They were increasingly populated with mammals and 14 of the present 31 orders of birds are known to have been in existence. These early birds were divided into those that flew, the Carinates, and those that were flightless and ran, the Ratites. Among the Carinates, the best preserved specimens are water birds, such as Divers, Rails, Herons and Gulls, which were preserved in the mud of water margins. The early Ratites include predecessors of the Emus and Moas. The Moas of New Zealand lingered on until they were killed for food by Maori and European settlers; the last had disappeared by the eighteenth century. Among the Ratites were the huge Elephant birds, the largest of which, *Aepyornis titan*, was over ten feet high. Its eggs have been found in Madagascar and measured 2.5 feet in girth with a capacity of over 2 gallons.

The Pliocene saw the arrival of early hominids such as *Australopithecus* of some 7 million years ago, followed by *Homo erectus* at the beginning of the Pleistocene.[104] It was at this point in earth's history when the avifauna burgeoned. Passerines, including the pigeon family, which included the Dodo, were present in the Pleistocene. In Scotland this was a period of great landscape change. The period is known as the Ice Age, but in fact was a succession of seventeen alternating ice ages and relatively warm interglacial periods, each lasting some 100,000 years. Scotland was covered by ice, and huge glaciers, appropriately called 'God's ploughshares', gouged out the glens and lochs we know today. For much of this time Scotland was sterilised by the deep freeze though, in warmer periods, birds must have migrated north from ice-free southern England to prospect during the brief summers.

However, in other parts of the Palaearctic, bird evolution was progressing apace, so that by the arrival of the warm, wet Holocene, about 10,000 years ago, all the 31 orders of birds known today were in existence.

The Paleolithic or Old Stone Age began about 300,000 years ago when the first archaic *Homo sapiens* appeared. From this species two distinct races of early humans evolved, *H. s. neanderthalensis* and *H. s. sapiens*. The former, Neanderthal man, was specially adapted to cope with the cold steppes of Ice Age Eurasia and he gradually disappeared. *H s. sapiens* first appeared in the south of Britain about 30,000 year ago in an early warm interglacial. Although man may have been present in Scotland during warm interglacials, there are few palaeolithic remains to confirm this.

One effect of the enormous sheets of ice, some as much as 1,000 metres thick, was to press down the land by its weight. At the same time so much water was locked in the ice that sea level was much lower.

The Mesolithic, or Middle Stone Age, began 10,000 years ago when the ice retreated. About 9,000 years ago, Man first appeared in Scotland either from the south or by crossing the land bridge from Europe formed by the lowering of sea level. Some of the earliest human settlements appear to have been in the Inner Hebrides, particularly Rum. From about 8,500 years ago the climatic change produced a warm wet climate when colonisation by plants and animals developed rapidly. Trees were first, with the development of extensive forests of birch, hazel, and a little later elm, oak and pine. Birds must have been present in Scotland at this period but there is no clear evidence of them. During this period, with the melting of the ice, the sea level rose again. One effect of this was to produce raised beaches which are visible today in many Scottish islands, notably Arran. This raising of sea levels cut Ireland off from Britain and, a little later, the English Channel flooded to separate Britain from the Continent. This explains some difference in species between Britain and Ireland on one hand and Britain and the rest of Europe on the other. Birds, though they do show such regional variation (for example the White and Pied Wagtails), are not as circumscribed as less mobile species. At about the same time *H. s. sapiens* gradually came to dominate and replace Neanderthal man across Europe. The Mesolithic lasted until farming began about 5,500 years ago.

The Neolithic, or New Stone Age, began with a change from the old hunter-gathering society of the Mesolithic to the introduction of farming in a much more populated Scotland, where most of the ancient forest had been cleared. The centres of population were in the islands and in the fertile crescent from what is now southern Perthshire, extending north and east into present day Aberdeenshire.

A great deal of what we know about the early history of birds in any part of the planet has been discovered through archaeology. One aspect of this burgeoning science is Palaeo-osteology, the study of old bones.[154] But bone is easily destroyed; it may be weathered, frost-shattered, scavenged or smashed by man or other predators, all affecting its survival. Throughout history, man has discarded his unwanted rubbish into refuse heaps or middens, and this is the source of much animal bone. These middens prove a treasure-house for archaeologists, one of whom, Stuart Piggot, is said to have defined his subject as the 'Science of Rubbish'! Survival of bone depends much on pH of soil. Acid soils, as found in much of Scotland, destroy the inorganic structure of bone. Bone evidence will be referred to in discussion of the history of many species mentioned in Part Two of this book, so an explanation of the subject is appropriate here.

Taphonomy (Greek *Taphë*, Burial, or *Taphos,* grave and -*nomia*, area of knowledge) is the study of how and why bones and other buried material arrived in archaeological deposits and how material moves from the biosphere (living) to the lithosphere (fossil). Modern techniques allow recognition of quite small fragments of bone, so allowing indentification of the species to which they belong. DNA fingerprinting based on minute samples of DNA retrieved from bones allows precise identification of species. Much else can be learned about the original living, individual animal.[154] For example, female bird bones become more heavily calcified before breeding, as the bird stores calcium for egg production (at other times this would be a hindrance by increasing weight). This can be demonstrated in ancient bone, radiologically or by drilling.

Bones may arrive in deposits in many ways. They may be carried by flood-water and deposited in silt or gravel. The creatures from which the bones originated may have walked or flown into their own graves, fallen into crevices or bogs or have been drowned in water. They may be carried there by other predators than man, such as wolves, and also by birds. Owls were particularly helpful to archaeologists because they swallow prey whole and regurgitate pellets of indigestible material especially bone. Because Owls, especially the larger species have favourite roosting sites their discarded pellets are often concentrated, providing large deposits below favoured perches in caves. Bones may be related to man at kill sites, by cooking or in middens.

Small bones, especially those of fish and very small birds, may be missed or damaged at excavation, but these have much information to give and new techniques involving washing deposited material through fine sieves allow collection of such bones.

Bones may also provide clues to climatic change; for example the presence of an arctic species in dated archaeological strata in close proximity with tropical species in another indicates change of climate. Indeed this is how much of the succession of glacials and interglacials of the Pleistocene was

4

originally worked out. (More recently analysis of ice cores from Antarctica has been used instead).

Much of our knowledge of the Neolithic inhabitants of Scotland has been acquired from excavation of their homes, their refuse dumps and the structures which they built for spiritual or funerary purposes. Disposal of the dead has long been a feature of a people's culture. In many cases it appears that the period between death and decomposition of soft tissues has been regarded as potentially evil since it was thought that the spirits of the dead were active. It was thus important to hasten this process and the dead were exposed on racks for defleshing by birds. There are sites in Perthshire of burial mounds in which defleshed bodies were buried. In some places in Perthshire post holes have been discovered. These allow partial reconstruction of the Neolithic wooden buildings used for exposing bodies for excarnation by birds. Some more or less articulated skeletons lack fingers and toes suggesting that these were removed by scavenging birds. In some cases defleshing was performed by dogs, and a few human bones bear obvious canine tooth marks. In Orkney, the presence of talons and bones from White-tailed Eagles in the Tomb of the Eagles raises the possibility that these birds may have been instrumental in excarnation, and so their relics were buried with the human bones. Noticeably talons, and even bones, of this Eagle accompany some interred bones, suggesting the individual's importance (see p.132).

Even as long ago as the Neolithic, birds played a part in culture. The round-bottomed pots of the period (made that way because round pots stand better than those with flat bases when there are no flat surfaces) show incised decorative patterns. Dorothy Liddell (sister of Alexander Keiller the Dundee marmalade manufacturer and archaeologist) working at Avebury, made the chance observation that many small bird bones were mixed with broken pottery. She matched the imprints of epiphyses of bones made on plasticene with the incised patterns on the pots, proving their use in ceramic decoration. At some time a man sucking marrow from a bird's thigh bone noticed that it emitted a sound and his curiosity led to experiment and discovery of the first flute. Some of the earliest known instruments were made from Eagle wing bones and these, because of the awe in which the Eagle was held, would have had special significance.

The warm wet forests, lakes and coasts of the early Holocene must have abounded in birds and these undoubtedly featured commonly in the diet of Neolithic man. Even as early as the Paleolithic, there is evidence from the south of England that birds contributed to diet. Bones found at Kent's Cavern, Torquay, show that Grouse, Ptarmigan, Greylag Goose and Whooper Swan were being hunted for food.[157]

Coastal sites were particularly important because of the wealth of seabirds.

At Morton, in Fife, midden remains have yielded birds such as Guillemots in addition to shellfish and mammalian bones. Evidence from Oronsay shows that the hunting of marine birds and mammals was especially important as a source of fat and oil. At Skara Brae and Rousay in Orkney, evidence of Gannets, Eider (and their eggs) with Pink-foot Geese and Whooper Swans was found in middens. In 1913, Solan Goose (Gannet), Great Auk, Razorbill, Guillemot, Cormorant, Shag, Swan, Wild Goose, Merganser, Gull, Tern and Water Rail were found in Mesolithic middens dating from 7,500-3,500 BC. Shell mounds at Caisteal-nan-Gillean on Oronsay have yielded bones of Red-breasted Merganser, Shelduck, Shag, Cormorant, Gannet, Ringed Plover, Auks and unidentified Gull and Tern species.[82]

As human technology progressed through the Bronze and Iron Ages, man's ability to modify habitat increased at a time of climate change. From about 7,000 to 5,000 years ago, the climate in Britain became warmer and drier. This period, known as the climatic optimum, coincided with extensive clearance of the primary forests to make room for agriculture and to provide fuel. Such habitat change in the early Holocene had profound effect on the distribution and ecology of birds in Scotland. Many of these are referred to under individual species in Part II of this book.

2

From Early Times to the Middle Ages:
AD 0-1600

This has been called the Legendary or Credulous Period of Natural History. Much of Celtic history in general and Scottish early history in particular is intertwined with the supernatural, with tales of Tir nan Og, the mythical land of perpetual youth, of the Celtic hero Cú Chulainn and of fairies. This Celtic spirituality, first expressed in Druidism and the occult, led on to a religious fundamentalism, which sometimes amounted to fanaticism such as that which led to the persecution of innocent women as witches. Much of this twilight knowledge of ghoulies and ghosties persists in present-day bird nomenclature and association.

The veracity of what was written, or more often passed down orally, is highly questionable. Despite this, some early beliefs are interesting partly for their bizarre nature and also because many have persisted to dog scientific ornithology, which did not begin until the seventeenth century.

The early history of birds in Scotland depends largely on records of their use for food or sport. Because documents of the time are scant, and references to birds within them even scarcer, some of this history has to be inferred from records outwith Scotland.

During the Roman period, 52BC–410AD, traces of birds have been found in a cave in Somerset considered to be late Celtic but, since Roman coins were found as well, this is not certain. Identifiable bones include those of Geese, Duck, Crows, Capercaillie and Pigeons. Roman remains near Haddington, in East Lothian, have yielded Buzzard bones.[82] Raven bones are common among Roman remains; this may have been because they were caged and hung at doors as guards to salute visitors, just as the Magpie was in Rome.

The Romans not only left written evidence of life in the early centuries, but also brought with them the classical natural history of Aristotle and Pliny, which were to influence thinking for many centuries to come, not least in Scotland.

The Venerable Bede (673-735) wrote of four peoples inhabiting Britain: the Britons, the Picts, the Scots and the Angles, who were a German speaking people from northern Europe. The Britons were Celtic-speaking people who had colonised Britain in a number of archaeologically recognisable invasions up to, and probably after, the arrival of the Romans in 55 BC.[14]

The Picts are shrouded in mystery since they left no written account of themselves, though they left numerous examples of their intricate and beautiful art. They may be seen as the true aboriginals of the country now called Scotland.[98] For the purpose of this book, the Picts are the people who inhabited part of Scotland up to the ninth century and were known to the Romans as the *Picti*, the painted ones. This name probably came about as a soldier's nickname for the denizens of the land north of Hadrian's Wall. The Picts, by Bede's time, occupied lands north of the Forth-Clyde line. Their history is obscure but they must have been there well before the Romans reached Britain. It is likely that they too were Celtic in origin though this is not universally accepted. By the seventh century they had formed a single people strong enough to defeat the Northumbrian Angles whom they had thrown back south of the Forth.[14]

The Scots originally came from Ireland in successive migrations, and are called by Roman writers both the *Scotti* and the *Hiberni*. These people grew in number and in strength, in approximately what were to become the counties of Bute and Argyll. In about 500 they formed the Kingdom of Dalriada, in western Scotland. In 563 Columba, a prince of the royal house of Dalriada, established a Christian monastery at Iona. Columba consolidated the Christian faith in his new country, spreading the Gospel from the already established Church at Whithorn, where St Ninian had introduced Christianity to Scotland at the beginning of the fifth century.[62] St Ninian's conversion was not unopposed; for instance at Caerlaverock where, legend says, that 'for a Lark's nest' the battle of Arthuret was fought in 573. Caerlaverock means the fort of the Lark, and it is suggested that Merlin of Arthurian Legend was present at this battle and fled from it to take refuge in the Caledonian Forest.

Birds began to creep into poetry as early as the fifth or sixth century. The first mention of the Solan Goose comes in a section of *The Romance of Beowulf*, of about 600AD, which, in translation, reads: 'Many a one shall greet the other with benefits, over the gannet's bath; the ringed ship shall bring over the deeps offerings and tokens of love.'

A little later the Gannet is again mentioned in an Anglo-Saxon song 'The Seafarer', which also refers to Swan, Starling (stearn in the original, which some believe to have been a Tern), Eagle and the Cuckoo. The 'note of Huilpe' is also mentioned, an unidentified bird, though the description suggests a Curlew.

St Cuthbert (?653-687) was an ascetic who spent much of his life in a hermit's cell on the Farne Islands and is reputed to have been very fond of the Eiders who shared his solitude. He is reputed to have restored to life an Eider, which had been killed—and even eaten—by a man called Leving. The miracle was faithfully recorded about 500 years later! To this day his name is remembered in the vernacular name for the Eider, St Cuthbert's Duck.[82]

Pagan Celts had enormous respect for the natural world of trees and birds, which became even more marked with the spread of Christianity. Columba taught the monks of Iona to show hospitality to both humans and birds. He told one of the brothers to watch for a crane flying over from Ireland. The bird was to be carried up from the shore, taken to a house and fed and looked after for three days. This was done and Columba commended the monk for tending their brother pilgrim. Even today, though most of the originals have gone, two early columns of Iona cloister sculpture remain with floral carvings on them. The missing pillars have been replaced and their capitals have been sculpted to recreate the concept of flowers, trees and birds believed to have been in the originals. (See p.68.)

Another saintly legend tells that Kevin of Glendalough was once engaged in a vigil with his hands outstretched in the form of a cross, when a blackbird laid its eggs in the palm of his hand. Not wishing to disturb the bird he remained in this uncomfortable position until the brood hatched.[82] Birds figured frequently in Celtic Christian art, such as the illumination of *The Book of Kells* and the cross dedicated to St Martin at Iona Abbey, both of which display birds.

By the seventh century the Scots were gradually establishing themselves in the south-west of the country. Despite their crushing defeat at Degsastan (dubiously identified as Dawston in Liddisdale), they gradually recovered to unite the Pictish and Scottish peoples in 843 when Kenneth Mac-Alpin became King and set up his throne at Forteviot. Despite this union the separate cultures persisted. There is archaeological evidence from excavations of Pictish sites in Orkney of about 900-1100 AD of the bones of Gannet, Cormorant, Great Northern Diver, Whooper Swan and Great Auk. Similar remains have been found in Ayrshire and in East Fife, with traces of Geese, Gulls and Divers.

The ninth century was dominated by the Vikings. Though they have a reputation as rapists and pillagers, many of them were peaceful pastoralists who settled around the coast of Scotland, leaving an influence through their genes and language.

The remarkable Archbishop Aelfric, called the Grammarian (c. 955-1022), was a prominent figure in Old English literature, celebrated for his stylistic excellence and breadth of learning. Though writing chiefly on religious matters, he also recorded the rustic life of shepherds, hunters and ploughmen. Aelfric[1] was one of the first to write about birds and listed nearly a hundred species, including Swans, Eagles, Herons and some passerines. He also wrote dialogues between a teacher and pupils; one of which is concerned with the capture and training of falcons. *Domesday Book*, at end of the eleventh century, also mentions many birds in England, which are likely to have been extant, if unrecorded, in Scotland.

In the twelfth century there are wonderful records from Ireland by Gerald de Barri, also known as Gerald of Wales. Born in Pembrokeshire, Gerald took Holy Orders in 1172 and though he was elected bishop of St David's, Henry II refused to confirm him in this post. He travelled widely through Ireland and Wales writing extensively about his observations on everything he saw, including natural history. In his *History and Topography of Ireland* he recorded some astute, and some quite astonishingly bizarre, accounts of birds, listing raptors, waterfowl, Woodpeckers, Corvids, Capercaillie and other game. He called Herons Cranes and perpetuated Pliny's tale of the birds' vigilance:

> Cranes are so numerous that in one flock alone you will often see a hundred or about that number. These birds, by a natural instinct, take their turns by night in watching for the common safety, standing on one leg only, while in the other featherless claw they hold a stone. They do this so that if they should go to sleep they will be wakened again immediately by the fall of the stone and continue their watch.[65]

By the fourteenth century, there were more reports of birds in Scottish records, for example Capercaillie were mentioned as occurring in tracts of forest in 'Gallowedia, Argyle and Scotia'. In ancient Scotland, venison was the prerogative of the upper classes. When the pursuit of lesser game threatened extermination of the deer, an Act of 1367 prohibited the striking down of game 'with culverings, crossbows, and hand-bows'.[159]

By the fifteenth century references to birds increased rapidly. Storks were recorded breeding on the top of St Giles Church, Edinburgh, in 1416. In 1424 an Act of James I stated: 'Therefore as men consider that Rooks building in churchyards, orchards, or trees do great damage upon corn, it is ordained that they whom such trees pertain to, do let them build, and suffer on no wise that their young ones fly away, and where it be proved that they and the young ones be flown, and the nests be in the trees at May-day, the trees shall be forfeit to the King'.[159] Another act of 1457 proscribed Eagles, Buzzards, Kites and some hawks.

'Solan Geese breed at the Bass Rock in great abundance' wrote Walter Bower, Abbot of Inchcolm, in *Scotichronicon*, his massive history of the Scottish nation, written in 1447.[22]

In 1453 Sir Richard Holland[90] wrote a satire on James II of Scotland. It was called 'The Howlat' (The Owl or Owlet), a reference to the King, whose face was somewhat deformed and said to resemble an Owl. Though later writers dismissed this as 'an elaborate and dreary allegory of alliterative verse'[159] several birds are mentioned including Solan Goose, Bittern, Starling, Corncrake, Cuckoo, Lapwing and Swallow. Sixteenth-century Privy Purse accounts show that in 1511 Solan Geese were bought at one shilling Scots each for the court of James IV.[82]

John Major or Mair[123] was born at Glegharnie less than four miles from the Bass Rock, and lived near Berwick. He taught at the Universities of St Andrews and Paris, where he was considered the most eminent exponent of medieval learning. In *De Gestis Scotorum* of 1518 he wrote: 'Near to Glegharnie, in the Ocean, at a distance of two leagues, is the Bass Rock, wherein is an impregnable stronghold. Round about it is seen a marvellous multitude of great Ducks (which they call Sollends) that live on fish. These fowl are not of the very same with the common wild duck'. Major describes the breeding and fishing of the Gannets, the young of which were sold in the neighbouring country: 'if you eat of these birds twice or thrice yearly you will find them very savoury. For these birds are extremely fat, and the fat skillfully extracted is very serviceable in the preparation of drugs; and the lean part of the flesh they sell... The produce of these birds supports thirty or forty men of the garrison upon the rock; and some rent is paid by them to the lord of the rock.'

By 1525 the household of James V was buying Moorfowls, Partridges, Wild Geese, Swans, Teal, Plovers, Herons, Cranes, Dotterel, Redshanks and Larks for food. Also mentioned in royal accounts of the time were Water Rail and Quail, but no Ptarmigan or Capercaillie.

Hector Boece (?1465-1536) was a Dundonian who became a professor, with Erasmus, at the University of Paris. Later, in 1498, he became Principal of the newly founded King's College Aberdeen (later to become part of the University of Aberdeen) and published a history of Scotland up to the reign of James III. This included fabulous narratives (including that of Macbeth, which passed via Holinshead to Shakespeare). In 'Cosmographe and Description of Albion'[20] he wrote 'of Fowlls, such as live by plunder, there are many kinds in Scotland; as Eagles, Falcons, Goshawks, Sparrowhawks, Merlins, and such-like fowls. Of waterfowls there is so great a number, that it is a wonder to hear'. He goes on to list Capercaillie, 'a fowl larger than a Raven which lives upon the buds of trees' and Black Cock, 'not unlike

11

a Pheasant both in quantity and savour of their flesh, but they have black feathers and red eyebrows.'

Dean William Turner (1508-68) has been described as the father of British ornithology. He was sometime Dean of Wells Cathedral in England but, as a reformer, was frequently in trouble with the established church and this led to his imprisonment in 1540, after which he travelled widely on the continent. He was the first to publish and describe British birds in his illustrated *Avium precipuarum, quarum apud Plinium et Aristotelem mentio est, brevis et succincta historia* ('A short and succinct history of the principal birds noticed by Pliny and Aristotle'[195]) which was printed in Cologne in 1544. In this, Turner wrote that the Solan Goose 'looks to its young with so much loving care that it will fight most gallantly with lads that are let down in baskets by a rope to carry them away, not without danger of life. Nor must we fail to mention that a salve, most valuable for many diseases, is made by Scots from the fat of this Goose, for it is wonderfully full of fat.'

Richard Hakluyt wrote of the 'Penguin' or Great Auk: 'Havoc was soon made among them because these simple birds could be driven into boats with the natural result that they were speedily wiped out.'[83]

Konrad von Gesner published *Historium Animalium*[66] between 1551-58. In this he attempted to bring together all then known about the animal kingdom. He wrote of the Solan Geese at the Bass Rock, quoting a learned Scot to the effect that 'they lay their eggs on rocks; and with one foot placed upon them.' From this he suggests a possible derivation of the name from the sole of a foot.

Birds and Belief

Early beliefs had developed from the various cultures which had combined to make up the spiritual life of early Scotland. Such beliefs crept into folklore and, as shown in Part II, frequently influenced the way people related to birds.

One of these was the belief in the Gabble Ratchet or the Seven Whistlers, which has coloured the mythology of many species of birds such as Wild Geese, Plovers and Curlews. The legend of the Seven Whistlers is widespread in various forms throughout Europe, where the Whistlers are believed to be the souls of unbaptised children wandering through the air till the day of judgement, or those of the Jews who crucified Christ, and also known as the Gabriel Hounds. All these versions are remnants of the ancient belief in the 'Wild Hunt' in which a spectral hunter, in some legends Odin, and his dogs frequent certain forests and occasionally appear to mortals. In response to the call of ravens accompanying the hunt the spirits of the dead rise up to join in the chase while earthly hounds give tongue in response to the ghosts. One belief held that the hunter was a Jew who would not suffer Jesus to drink except from a puddle good enough 'for such an enemy of Moses'. Another explanation is that six whistlers search for the missing seventh and that when they are reunited the World will end. This legend appears in differing forms in many countries. In Scotland it gave rise to many bird names and beliefs; in England it led to the legend of Herne the Hunter, who so tormented Falstaff in *The Merry Wives of Windsor*.

In Celtic mythology there was a terrifying Goddess referred to as the *Cailleach* (Gaelic, literally meaning an old woman, but also used of a witch or other malign female spirit). The *Cailleach* was thought capable of transmuting herself into any creature, particularly a hare but also many birds, especially Ravens and Crows. She also appeared at streams washing clothes which turned out to be the shroud, complete with death wounds, of any human who saw her (see pp.226-7).

In pre-Christian times Druids kept wrens as pets and used them in ritual. Later the wren was persecuted and a legend grew up that it was responsible for the betrayal of Christ to Roman soldiers. These associations may account for the name Jenny, which was also used for a witch.

According to another tale Christ, pursued by enemies through Scotland, hid under seaweed where he was guarded by two black birds with long red bills. When the pursuers had gone Christ emerged from the seaweed and gave the birds a white cross to wear for their service. So Oystercatchers earned the Gaelic name *Gille Brighde*, the servant of St Bride the foster-mother of Christ.[10]

Sigurd the Viking, Earl of Orkney in the tenth century, was the son of a Christian princess. When threatened by the Pictish leader Finnleik he sought his mother's help. She gave him a Raven banner on which the bird would raise its wings when Orkney was to win. It did so and the Picts were defeated.[10]

St Servanus of Culross had a pet Robin which perched on his shoulder. Ruffians killed the Robin much to the distress of the saint, but St Kentigern (who became patron saint of Glasgow) brought the bird back to life and it now takes a proud place in the coat of arms of Glasgow.[10]

The Yellowhammer or Yorling was associated with the Devil. Its egg was 'gouted with the De'il's blood' and every first of May (Beltane, the morning after the German *Walpurgisnacht*, Satan's birthday) it is said to drink a drop of Old Nick's blood. The Yorling was thought to be hatched by toads and to be a friend of the snake. Its association with snakes, which were symbols of the Devil, came about because of the herpetiform markings on its eggs.

Almost all black birds were associated with the Devil. Swifts, often known as Devilins for this reason, were referred to as the souls of the damned,

13

destined to haunt the places where they lived. Swallows too were devilish, carrying a drop of satanic blood under their tongues, which, if they fell down a chimney in a shower of soot, they might spit out to bring misfortune.

Another devilish bird was the Wheatear, also supposedly hatched by toads, with whom a meeting carried a prophecy of imminent death. Magpies too were 'De'il's Birds', since they refused to join Noah in the Ark, choosing to remain outside to scoff at the flooded world. Worse still, at the crucifixion, a Magpie refused to don full mourning and so was obliged to be black and white until the end of time.[10]

The Curlew was associated with the Gabble Ratchet and in Scotland it is called the Whaup, which is partly onomatopoeic, but also refers to the hook-nosed goblin that infested the gable ends of houses.

Birds and Language

The mixture of peoples which occurred during early Scottish history intro-duced many languages. The Celtic languages fall into two groups. The P-Celtic or Brittonic was that spoken in Brittany, Cornwall and Wales. The Q-celtic was spoken in Ireland and the Isle of Man. The language of the Picts, presumed to be an early P-Celtic dialect, must have influenced the Q-Celtic Irish of early Scots from Northern Ireland, leading to the evolu-tion of Gaelic. This incredibly rich language has survived orally in countless stories, songs and prayers. Thr oral tradition has produced a complexity of spelling and wealth of synonym that has enormous regional variation. The multiplicity of synonyms is especially apparent in bird nomenclature, some species having as many as ten Gaelic names. The Viking invaders spread by sea, settling in the good agricultural land of the east coast and in the Hebrides. They introduced many Norse words to the evolving languages of the Scots. In Orkney and Shetland, where Gaelic was not spoken, the unique language of Norn developed as a dialect of Norse. It was still spoken as late as the nineteenth century. In southern Scotland English was being melded into Lallan Scots (see p.77). It was from this linguistic crucible that bird names evolved and then, in turn, influenced further development of language. Many words, phrases and expressions used today derive from this evolution. Words become birds and birds make words, combining as two strands, to be braided into a single rope by time. Examples of sixteenth-century bird names include:

Bussart	Buzzard
Corbie	Crow or Raven
Cushat	Wood Pigeon
Mavis	Song Thrush
Merl	Blackbird

Muircock	Red Grouse
Paitrick	Grey Partridge
Specht	Woodpecker
Thristle	Song Thrush

Many of these names survive to this day, especially in poetry.

Birds and the Arts

Pictish art is difficult to put in chronological order, but it appears that symbols incised on more or less undressed stone date from the seventh and eighth centuries, whereas symbols carved in relief and often accompanied by a cross on a carefully shaped monument are from the ninth and tenth centuries.[156]

Many symbols involve stylised birds: for example, on a fine stone at Rossie Priory a man holds two birds and, at Brechin Cathedral, the Mary Stone of the late ninth century shows an Eagle, the symbol of St John, which also appears in the *Book of Kells*.[24] An interesting discovery was made in Orkney. About sixty years ago, children found a Pictish stone of about the seventh century depicting an Eagle, which is now in the Tankerness Museum in Kirkwall. A Northumbrian illuminated missal of slightly later date was found to have an identical Eagle. At the time Northumberland was extremely powerful, and it appears that the link between the two identical Eagles was a third effigy, made of silver and used as a diplomatic gift to the Nothumbrians by a Pictish Orcadian ruler.

Among over 200 records of Pictish symbol stones, several depict birds.[156] There are nine or ten showing the typical stylised Eagle of the Picts, four with a Goose and others showing a predatory bird, a bird with a loaf, an exotic bird and a man drinking from a horn whose base is a bird.

It seems likely that the fine illuminated manuscript, the *Book of Kells*, was begun in Iona. In the early ninth century, when the threat of Viking attacks was severe, the treasure was removed for safety and taken to Kells in County Meath, Ireland. It may not have been completed before it went to Ireland, but probably was mainly designed in Iona and it shows much Pictish influence.[98, 24] The manuscript is embellished with superb ornamentation, including Pictish designs and symbols, but with many stylised creatures such as fish, birds and beasts. The most common bird is the Eagle, the symbol of St John. Another eagle-like bird clutches a fish and may represent the Osprey.

Among early pictures of birds, the commonest relate to falconry, or feature in the ceiling decoration of old castles. In most of these pictures the bird species is not identifiable, in keeping with the characteristics of the legendary or credulous period of natural history. Gurney[82] shows a picture of James I holding a Falcon. Many copies of pictures from the library of the National Portrait Gallery of Scotland show similar fifteenth and sixteenth century hawking portraits. Eleanor of Scotland, by an unknown artist, holds a hawk with a barred tail. James IV of Scotland, in a copy of a lost original, which is the best extant image of this king, holds a very dark Falcon. A portrait of James VI, painted in 1574 by an unknown artist, shows the king as a boy with a falcon at his wrist.

Ceiling paintings were a feature of sixteenth-century Scottish castles and mansions. At Prestongrange House, a ceiling dated 1581 has many designs of animals, fruit, snakes and human figures. Amongst these are recognisable birds such as the Peacock and the mythical Phoenix. Others may be Swans and Herons, and one large bird with a forked tail could, with a stretch of imagination, be a Red Kite. The sixteenth-century ceiling at Crathes Castle has two recognisable Ravens.

William Dunbar (1460-1520) from East Lothian has been called the chief poet of early Scottish literature. He wrote of birds in the 'The Thrissil and the Rois' ('Thistle and the Rose'):

> The lork hes done the mirry day proclame,
> To rais up luvaris with confort and delyt...
> The restles suallow commandit scho also
> To feche all fowll of small and greit renown...
> Syne crownit scho the Egle King of Fowlis...
> And bawd him be als just to awppis and owlis
> As unto pacokkis, papingais, or crennis
> And mak a law for wycht fowlis and for wrennis

The same poem also mentions the Mavis, the Merle and the Nychtigall. Dunbar also described the noise of seabirds:

> The air was dirkit with the fowlis
> That cam with jammeris and withyowlis
> With shrykiking, shrieking, skryming scowlis
> And meikle noyes and showtis.[54]

In a long poem about the Eagle and the Robin Redbreast Alexander Scot (c1515-c1583) describes how the Eagle called all birds to a meeting:

> Thither the valiant Tersals doup,
> And heir rapacious corbies croup,
> With greidy gleds and slie garmahs,
> And dinsome pyis and clatterin daws
> Proud pecocks and a hundred mae...

At this meeting the 'canty' Robin sang so well that the Eagle sent a 'buzzart' to reward him, but the Judas of a Buzzard castigates poor Robin with:

> Ah! ye ring sae dull and ruch
> Ye haif deirt our lugs mair than enuch

16

The Robin, in despair, decides to sing no more.[164]

The Ayrshire poet Alexander Montgomerie (?1555-1598) in 'The Cherrie and the Slae' referred to the legend of Philomel and Progne, who were two sisters in Greek mythology. Progne was married to Tereus, King of the Thracians, by whom she had a son, Itys. Tereus was in love with Progne's sister Philomel and told her that Progne was dead and so seduced her. He tore out Progne's tongue to prevent her reporting his unfaithfulness, but Progne wove a message into tapestry informing her sister. In revenge the sisters killed Itys and served him to his father for dinner. The king was about to have both sisters slain when they were turned into birds, Progne to a swallow and Philomel to a nightingale. This classical legend recurs in bird poetry through many ages and cultures.

'The Cherrie and the Slae' mentions many birds:

> About a bank with balmie bewes,
> Where nightingals their nots renews
> With gallant goldspinks gay,
> The mavise, mirle and Progne proud,
> The lintwhite, lark and laverock loud,
> Saluted mirthful May:
> When Philomel had sweetly sung,
> To Progne she deplored,
> How Tereus cut out her tongue
> And falsely her deflorde...
>
> The cushat crouds, the corbie cries,
> The cuckow couks, the pratling pyes
> To geck hir they begin
> The jargoun of the jangling jayes
> The craiking craws, the keckling kays
> They deav'd me with their din.[134]

Birds and Economy

Falconry was introduced into England by the Saxons. In about 750 AD Archbishop Boniface of Mons presented Ethelbert II, King of Kent, with a hawk and two falcons.[82] Falconry was first mentioned in Scotland at the Battle of Luncarty in 980. The Danes, in one of their hostile incursions, penetrated from Montrose to the vicinity of Perth where they were met by Kenneth II at Luncarty. The right and left wings of the Danish army were scattered after the King's victory and fled. The fugitives got into a narrow lane bounded by a bridge and a mud wall. A farmer named De Luce, with his two sons and

17

armed only with spades and a ploughshare, compelled them to return to the battle.[159] De Luce galloped to report to the King, to whom his first words, presumably addressed to his horse, were 'Oh, Hey'. King Kenneth replied: 'henceforth that shall be your name.' (Hay changed his name but Mrs De Luce did not agree to this change so the hero of Luncarty had her drowned!). The King rewarded Hay by giving him as much land as a hare could run on or a hawk could fly over. Hay chose the latter and his hawk flew from St Maddoes on the west to the village of Erroll on the east. Boece[20] records this 'als mekil therof as ane falcon flew of ane man's hand or scho lichtit'.[130] The stone where the falcon landed still stands at a village called Hawkstane:

> Still stands the ever famous stone
> The good gyr falcon perched upon.

Pennant[147] also mentions the exploits of Hay on the field of 'Lengcarty, where the Scots obtained a great victory over the Danes by means of the gallant peasant Hay and his two sons. The noble family of Hay descended from this rustic hero'. Indeed one of Hay's descendants became the first Earl of Kinnoul. This was by no means this family's last association with birds, for Charlotte Elizabeth Hay married a Capt. Drummond in 1859 and took the name Drummond-Hay (see p.51).

Falconry was popular and there are other early references in Scotland. During the reign of William I 'The Lion' (1143-1214) falcons were held in high value. There was a dispute over hawks in Eskdale between the Abbey of Melrose and Robert of Avenel. Alexander III (1241-86) kept falcons at Forres and Dunipace. Robert I, the Bruce (1274-1329), had a falcon-house at Cardross and in 1342 John of the Isles sent a gift of falcons to David II (1324-71). In these early days a special annual tax, called in Gaelic *Cearcseabhag*, of a fowl was paid by each tenant to the 'falconer of the lord of the soil'.[56] Tax (*cain* in Gaelic) was often paid in birds. The legal term 'kain' referred to the best fowl exacted as rent by a landlord. This was a common method of paying rent in St Kilda. A similar tax was called a 'reek hen', when a bird was paid from every house with a smoking lum or chimney.

In many early accounts the Goshawk and the Sparrowhawk are mentioned, but, after the fourteenth century, the peregrine was the popular falcon and in 1489 James IV (1473-1513) sent a trained falcon to the English court as a gift to Henry VII (1457-1509). In the fifteenth century, hawks were procured from the forest of 'Athole', from Orkney and Shetland, from Abbey Crag near Stirling and from the Ochils. The best hawks came from northern counties and falcons from Caithness were sent by James V (1512-42) to the King of France. James VI (1566-1625) was a keen falconer as was Charles I who had falcons brought to him 'from the northerne parts of the kingdome'. Peregrine Falcons were highly priced. James IV paid £189 to the Earl of

Angus for one, and in the reign of James VI, a pair of falcons was valued at £2,000.[159]

Turner, writing in 1544, said of the Osprey 'it is much better known today to Englishmen than many who keep fish in stews would wish: for within a short time it bears off every fish.'[195] It appears to have been tried by falconers with little success, though there are records of the capture of young Ospreys which were tied to posts: when their parents brought fish to them, this was taken for human food.

As early as the beginning of the fifteenth century, the rarer birds were preserved to the sportsman, or rather the sovereign and his court. In 1427 a law was passed that partridges, plovers, black game and muir-cocks be not killed from the beginning of Lent until August, under penalty of 40 shillings. And in 1551 the shooting of wild fowl was prohibited under pain of death. It was ruled in 1555 that partridges were not to be killed before Michaelmas, under the penalty of £10, and barons and freeholders were empowered to enforce this within their bounds. An Act was passed in 1567, whereby it was provided that the shooting of herons and 'fowls of the revar' (sic = river) with gun or bow be forbidden, under penalty for the first offence of forty days' imprisonment, with forfeiture of movables.

Birds and Food

The evidence that the Picts of early Roman times were great hunters, as well as farmers and fishermen, is clearly shown in the South Uist and Benbecula wheel-house middens where there are considerable numbers of bird-bones.[183] Excavations of middens in the vicinity of ancient earth forts include recognisable remains of Solan Goose, Swans, Great Auk, Cormorants, Divers and other seabirds.[82]

The Swan was domesticated in England since the end of the twelfth century and was a Royal Bird from the thirteenth to eighteenth centuries. However no such domestication occurred in Scotland where they were not crown property. In 1274 swans cost three shillings, Geese 5*d*, Capons 2½*d* and pheasants 4*d*.

Many bizarre birds were eaten in the past, even Divers. Leonardo da Vinci gave a recipe for the Red-throated Diver, which modern experimenters have pronounced quite inedible.[160] Leonardo added: 'His Holiness The Pope, in Lent, eats little with a pious look upon his face but then he leaves the table early and journeys to that other table which he keeps within his private quarters and there he fills himself with capon, Quail and Coot.' As we shall see the Catholic Church found many ways round the Lenten proscription of meat.

In 1529 The Earl of Atholl gave a feast for James V when he was hunting in Perthshire. The feast, according to the chronicler Robert Lindsay of

Pitscottie, included Crane, Swan, Partridge, Plover, Blackcock, Muirfowl and Capercaillie.[82]

In *The Scots Kitchen* Marian McNeill[127] quotes William Dunbar's 'Dirge to the King at Stirling' in which he invites James IV to return to the festive halls of Holyrood:

> To eit swan, cran, pertrik and plever,
> And every fische that swymis in rever,
> To drynk with ws the new fresche wyne,
> That grew upon the rever of Ryne...

Sir Walter Scott, in *Marmion*, describes the kitchen of a sixteenth-century inn in the Lammermoors

> ...in dark nook aloof
> The rafters of the sooty roof
> Bore wealth of winter cheer
> Of sea-fowl dried, and solands store
> And gammons of the tusky boar.[165]

A Heron was regarded as being lighter of digestion than a Crane, but a Bittern was not so hard of digestion as a Heron. Certainly Herons figure frequently in many household accounts of the sixteenth century when the birds, though not always young, were considered good to eat (cf W.H. Hudson's view, p.75).[82]

Most people in Scotland ate very frugally. For the poor the diet consisted of vegetables with little meat other than blood from cows,[183] but for the rich and powerful things were different. Pennant enumerates birds mentioned in the Household Regulations of the Earl of Northumberland, begun in 1512. This 'will shew not only the birds then in high vogue at the great tables of those days, but also how capricious a thing is taste, several then of high price being at present banished from our tables; and others again of uncommon rankness much valued by our predecessors. Thus Wegions [I give the spelling of the time] Sea-pyes, Sholardes, Kyrlews, Ternes, Cranys, Hearon-sewys, Bytters, See-gulles and Styntes were among the delicacies for principal feasts, or his lordship's own mees... Those excellent birds the Teylles were not to be bought except no other could be got. Fesauntes, Bytters, Hearon-sewys and Kyrlews, were valued at the same price twelve pence each.'[147]

Although the above record is from England, Scottish gourmandizing was much the same. During the fifteenth and sixteenth centuries, the abbot and monks of Cupar, through fowlers 'secured for their larder the wild-geese, the crane or swan, the partridge, the plover, the dottrel, the curlew, the wild-duck, the red-shank, the lapwing, and the teal... The bittern, heron, solan-goose, and other coarse birds, were allowed to the peasant and the wayfarer.' In 1541

John Soutar was fowler of Cupar Abbey, when he became bound to deliver to the cellarer of the monastery such fowls as might be slain by himself or his assistants. He was paid for a crane or a swan 5 shillings, a wild goose 2 shillings, a partridge 8 pence and for 'a plover, dottrel, curlew, wild duck, red-shank lapwing, teal, and other small birds, fourpence each.'[159]

Such high living incensed John Knox, and in 1581 a law was passed against 'superfluous banqueting' with much wine, meat and game. Senior clerics and Earls were forbidden to have more than eight 'dishes of meat while lesser men such as burgesses nor other substantious men, spiritual nor temporal, bot three dishes and bot ane kinde of meate in everie dish.'[183]

Birds and fashion

Primitive man was fond of dressing up in feathers; sometimes they were the only things he wore. Though in Ancient Greece the Ostrich plume was a popular adornment and Peacock's plumes traded for large sums, it was not until much later that they became important in Scotland.

3
The Seventeenth Century

This century saw the beginning of the progression from the period of legendary or mythological bird knowledge towards scientific ornithology. It was marked by religious controversy, which on one hand led to civil unrest and war and on the other to the beginning of conflict between scientific and Biblical concepts of creation. There was still very little in the way of systematized understanding of birds, but this was beginning to filter in from academics abroad such as Aldrovandi, Gesner and Belon, whose writings were to have much influence on British ornithologists of the late sixteenth and early seventeenth centuries.

Ulisse Aldrovandi (1522-1605) lived in Bologna, and his three volumes of *Ornithologiae hoc est de avibus historiae*[3] were published between 1599 and 1603. Aldrovandi included more fable and mythology in his writing than contemporaries such as Belon and Gesner and his accounts of some birds are rather strange. Among his splendid illustrations is one of Barnacle Geese hatching from shellfish.

Konrad von Gesner, 1516-65, was a naturalist from Zurich who became professor of Greek at Lausanne in 1537 and professor of Physics and Natural History at Zurich in 1541. He corresponded with scientific scholars throughout Europe including Dr William Turner of Wells in England. He published, between 1551 and 1558, his *Historium Animalium*, in which he attempted to bring together all that was known about the animal kingdom.[66] Pierre Belon (1517-64) wrote *L'Histoire de la Nature des Oyseaux* in 1555.[17] He died aged 47 at the hand of murderers in the Bois de Boulogne.

In Scotland, learning was well developed; the early universities, St. Andrews (1412), Glasgow (1451), Kings College (the forerunner of Aberdeen) in 1495, and Edinburgh (1583) had established the tradition of scholarship. In those early days learning was predominantly theological but gradually, first medicine and later general science, began to assume greater importance.

In 1603 the crowns of Scotland and England were united by James VI and I, and the Scottish court moved to London. This brought respite from recurring wars with the south and encouraged exchange of ideas between the countries. One effect of this was to hasten scientific development in Scotland, then less advanced than London where scientists were already moving towards the foundation of the Royal Society in 1660.

But, if actual war was over, this was to be a century of religious conflict between an increasingly Catholic England, ruled by Charles I, and a staunchly Protestant Scotland. On 23 July 1637, the first Sunday after the *Book of Common Prayer* had been imposed on Scotland by Charles I, an outraged old woman, Jenny Geddes, shouted out at a service in Edinburgh's St Giles Cathedral 'Dost thou say mass at my lug?' and she threw her stool at the Dean. The outcry that followed led to the National Covenant of 1638 in which people from all over Scotland protested to defend Protestantism. Meanwhile The English parliament was increasingly at odds with Charles I, leading to civil war in 1642. The Covenanters sided with the Parliamentarians and it was to them that the King ultimately surrendered in 1646. Three years later he was executed and England and Scotland were without a king. Charles II was proclaimed King of Scotland on condition he upheld the principles of the Covenant. He eventually conceded to the demands of the Covenanters and was crowned at Scone in 1651, a decade before the restoration of the monarchy in England. For much of this time Cromwell fought the Scots while Charles II was in exile. Following Cromwell's death in 1658, the monarchy was restored in England in 1660 and Charles II was declared head of both Church and State. But the King reneged on his pledge to the Covenanters and restored the episcopacy. This immediately opened old wounds in Scotland and the Covenanters flocked to hear the illegal preaching of priests at gatherings called 'conventicles' in remote glens. During the period 1661 to 1688, some 18,000 people were killed in persecutions and encounters between the Covenanters and the King's forces, leaving a bitter memory to taint Church and civil history.[99]

The death of Charles II led to the brief reign of James VII and II who attempted to re-establish Catholicism. This caused further outrage and James was deposed in favour of the Protestant William of Orange and his queen Mary II, who became joint rulers. This exacerbated conflict between the Catholic and Protestant churches, culminating in the Scottish Parliament passing an act abolishing bishops and establishing the Presbyterian Church of Scotland. In turn this ignited the smouldering fire of a Catholic group who supported James VII (or Jacobus as he was called in Latin), thus sowing the seeds of later Jacobite risings.

Birds and Belief

The religious turmoil of the seventeenth century tore Scotland apart; such religious differences were to become reflected in beliefs associated with birds. Bishops, hated by the Presbyterians, were derisively called Magpies because of their black and white vestments.[61] This was a double insult, for the Magpie, having scorned the crucifixion by refusing to take on mourning weeds, was believed to hold the Devil's blood under its tongue. It was from thence that ranting bishops were supposed to derive their heresy.

Lapwings earned opprobrium for betraying the secret conventicles when devout Covenanters held illegal meetings in the hills. The Teuchits, disturbed by the clandestine meetings near their nesting sites, circled round them, crying their haunting pee-wit calls. This alerted searching soldiers to the *al fresco* services.

The Swans which lived on Linlithgow Loch are said to have deserted it when Cromwell's army arrived there and occupied the Royal Palace. They did not return to the Loch until the restoration of Charles II.[10]

Birds and Language

The language of Lowland Scotland, variously called Lallan, Lalland, Lallans or Lowlands, gradually evolved from Northern English, Gaelic and other sources. It had replaced Gaelic south of the Highland Boundary Fault by the fourteenth century. When Scotland gained independence from England in 1328 the language, then called 'Scottis', became distinct from 'Inglis'. Gradually growing in usage and importance, Lallans replaced Latin as the official language of record keeping and literature by the sixteenth century. From the eighteenth century it became the vernacular, sometimes called the Doric to distinguish it from the Attic, the more refined speech of Edinburgh, which was then called the 'Athens of the North'. Still present as a dialect of English, Lallans persists in many place names and, particularly, bird names into the present century.

Some examples of sixteenth century Lallans bird names:[37]

Fasian or Feesant, the Pheasant.
Gled, the Red Kite.
Gormaw, the Cormorant.
Gowdspink, the Goldfinch.
Groose, the Red Grouse.
Merlzeo or Marlzeon, the Merlin.
Piet, Pyat or Pyot, the Magpie.
Pliver or Pluvar, the Golden Plover.
Titlin or Titling, the Meadow Pipit.

The names Merlzeo, or Marlzeon, and Capercailzie are interesting since there is no z in Gaelic. Some Gaelic sounds are difficult to represent in letters, this particularly applies to the pronunciation of the letter combination 'ng' as in the surname Mengies. Printers introduced a symbol rather like a subscript three (thus ƺ) to represent this sound. So Mengies became Menƺies. In the course of time, this has resulted in the introduction of the letter z into many names (e.g. Menzies or Mackenzie, which derived via Mackenƺie from MacConnich, meaning son of Connich or Kenneth). The use of the letter z leads to considerable Sassenach difficulty with place names such as Culzean!

Birds in Art and Poetry

Painting in Scotland advanced a great deal in the seventeenth century and recognizable birds were portrayed more often. There was still much lavish decoration of the wooden boards between rafters which comprised ceilings of important chambers. Near Grandtully in Perthshire there is the tiny village of Pitcairn, which has an unusual church. The little low whitewashed church of St Mary was built in the sixteenth century, but refurbished in 1636 at a time of great religious turbulence. Half the vaulted ceiling is covered in renaissance-style painting. A central panel depicts a deathbed scene surrounded by scrolls, which include a number of birds and armorial designs. Most of the birds are allegorical, but clearly recognizable are Peacocks, Doves, Turkeys and what may be Herons. Turkeys had been introduced into Europe from North America late in the sixteenth century. An extraordinary feature is that all the angels appear to be in a late stage of pregnancy.

At Dean House in Edinburgh, panels painted by the Scottish School of about 1630 labelled 'Taste' and 'Hearing' show ladies with Swans in the background. John Knox's House in Edinburgh has a surprisingly sexually explicit ceiling decoration which also shows Swans, and another panel is full of flying birds, possibly Herons, and unidentifiable waterfowl.

At Pinkie House in Musselburgh, a painted ceiling features an old man surrounded by barrels inscribed *Dives inops ratio Antichyrum destruit* (Antichyra was a town in Phocis important for growing medicinal hellebore). Two falcons stand beside an illuminated panel below this picture, other panels have a Stork and two Parrots and several small birds; one perched is probably a Turtle Dove, one shown on ground with a crest could be a Lapwing and a dark bird with a cere could be a Rook.

At the garden house at Traquair a pre-1750 ceiling depicts Swans flying with Cupids.

In a seventeenth century painting by Jacob de Wet (1640-1697) in the chapel at Glamis Castle, depicting the Baptism of Christ, a Dove, symbol of the Holy Spirit, hovers over Christ as he is baptised by St John.

Rossend Castle has a painted ceiling showing many stylised birds; one has a horseshoe in its bill, some look like doves, one has a bifurcated curved tail and might be a Blackcock.

At Largs there is the Skelmorlie Aisle erected by Sir Robert Montgomery in 1636 and painted in the Scottish Decorative style in about 1638. This shows a complex series of seasonal paintings labelled *Ver, Aestas, Autumnus, Hyems*. Each has a curved panel containing the main painting with two orna-mented semilunes below. The semilunes hold texts with surrounding illu-minations, often with birds. *Ver* (spring) is a bustling river scene. The left semilune has the text 'Blessed are they that mourn' surmounted by two birds which look like Crows. The other semilune has the text 'The Day of the Lord will come as a thief in the night' and is surmounted by a Magpie and an Owl. *Aestas* (summer) has no birds in the main picture but Peacocks and Pheasants appear in the semilunes. *Autumnus* (autumn) includes an inn with a Swan as its sign and there are possible Eagles in the semilunes. *Hyems* (winter) shows a winter skating scene with many flying birds. The semilunes show farmyard Cocks and more Peacocks.

Among portraits there are increasingly identifiable bird species. William III, painted by Jan David de Hem in about 1662, has recognisable Golden Eagles, and in another picture his Queen, Mary II, as a child, holds a Dove. A painting of John, 4th Lord Cranstoun, in a portrait attributed to Abraham Hondius of about 1675, includes a Mallard. Sir Alexander Abercromby of Birkenbeg, Grand Falconer to Charles I, was painted by an unknown artist in about 1661; he bears a large hawk, possibly a Goshawk. Clearly Scottish painters were becoming much more observant about birds and painted them with increasing accuracy.

Many Scottish ballads refer to legends about birds. These are often diffi-cult to date, but for the most part are probably from the fifteenth or sixteenth century, though rarely much later.

'The Earl of Mar's Daughter' tells the story of a damsel who fell in love with a Turtle Dove—'O Coo-me-doo, my love sae true'—and took him to her home in the castle where, in her locked room, he was transformed into a beautiful young man. He remained with her for ten years during which she bore him many sons, which the Turtle Dove took away to his mother to look after. When a suitor appeared the Earl's daughter rejected him in favour of her Dove. The Earl then swore to kill the bird and force his daughter to wed the suitor. But the Dove escaped and flew to his mother who turned four-and-twenty 'wall-wight' (strong) men into 'storks in feathers grey' and the Dove was changed to a Goshawk, 'a bird o' high degree', who led the storks to the bridal feast. There they bound the groom to an oak tree, seized his men and flew away with the Earl of Mar's daughter. (The 'Storks' were probably

Herons, which unlike white Storks have grey feathers and were often confused with them.)

Perhaps the most famous of all Scottish ballads is 'Twa Corbies' (see p.279). The Goshawk figures in another ballad in which a maid sends the hawk to her fled lover:

> O well's me o' my gay Gosshawk,
> That he can speak and flee!
> He'll carry a letter to my love,
> Bring another back to me.[8]

John Cleveland (1613-58) likened the Rebel Scot to a Gannet:

> A Scot, when from the Gallows-tree got loose,
> Drops into Styx, and turns a Soland-Goose.[39]

Birds and Economy

During the seventeenth century, birds were to become of increasing economic importance. Elizabeth I had made a law for the destruction of 'noyfull fowls and vermin' including Cormorants and Shags, and authority was given to churchwardens to pay a bounty for the destruction of these birds. Cormorants had been trained to fish in fifth century Japan and China. This knowledge reached Britain in the seventeenth century when both James VI and I and Charles I employed a 'Master of the Cormorants', a position of some importance. The Master carried his birds hooded, as falcons were, and a band fastened round the bird's neck prevented them swallowing their prey. As soon as the pouches above the band were full of fish the birds returned to the Master who extracted the catch.

Wild birds had materially diminished in number in Scotland, when in 1621 an Act was passed forbidding all persons, save landowners, from destroying them. The Act was renewed in 1685, and in 1707 it was ruled by statute that no one should 'kill, sell, or eat moor-fowl from the 1st March till the 20th August, under penalty of £20.'

In many parts of Scotland birds have been, and in some cases still are, an essential part of rural economy. This was particularly true of the Northern and Western Isles, reaching its peak in the St Kildan Islands of Hirte, Boreray and Soay.[120, 85] From the time of the earliest settlement of these islands, birds, which breed there in vast numbers, were an important source of food, clothing, lighting fuel and even medication. Sir Donald Monro, High Dean of the Isles, visited St Kilda in 1549 and painted a word picture of Hirte in *A Description of the Western Isles of Scotland*, which however remained unpublished until 1774. 'This ile is maire nor ane mile lange, and narrest als meikle in braid... The inhabitants thereof are simple poor people, scarce

27

learnit in aney religion...'. Monro also mentions payment of rent with roast and dried birds: 'the said stewart receives thir dewties in miell and reistit mutton, wyld foullis reistit, and selchis'.[133]

After Monro, a anonymous writer in 1595 described work on St Kilda 'Taking of foullis and gaddering their eggis, quhairon they leif for the most part of their fude.'

Birds' eggs and fledglings were collected by climbing the stupendous cliffs of the St Kildan Islands, some of which are well over 1,000 feet high. This was extremely difficult and often very hazardous. Robert Moray, in a paper published by The Royal Society in 1678,[136] described how birds were 'stolen' (as the islanders put it) from one of the stacks near the island of Hirte.

> After they have landed with much difficulty, a man having room for but one of his feet, he must climb up twelve or sixteen fathoms high. Then he comes to a place, where having but room for his left foot and left hand, must leap from thence to another such place before him; which, if he hit it right, the rest of the ascent is easie: and with a small cord, which he carries with him, he hales up a rope, whereby all the rest come up. But if he misseth that footstep, (as oftentimes they do) he falls into the sea, and the company takes him in by the small cord, and sits until he be a little refreshed, and then he tries again; for every one there is not able for that sport.

Seabirds and their eggs were jealously guarded. In 1685, a boatload of strangers attempted to steal some eggs from the cliffs. The St Kildans fought off the intruders and put the precious eggs back in the nests. For good measure the islanders confiscated the pirates' trousers before sending them on their way.[179]

Writing in the 1850s, Edward Stanley, Lord Bishop of Norwich, gave an account of how a man caught sea fowl in St Kilda:

> Several ropes of hide and hair are first tied together... one extremity of these ropes... is fastened like a girdle round his waist. The other extremity is then let down the precipice to a considerable depth, by the adventurer himself, standing at the edge: when, giving the middle of the rope to a single man, he descends, always holding by one part of the rope, as he lets himself down by the other, and supported from falling only by the man above, who has no part of the rope fastened to him, but holds it merely in his hands, and sometimes supports his comrade by one hand alone, looking at the same time over the precipice, without any stay for his feet, and conversing with the other as he descends to a depth of nearly four hundred feet.

As a former rock climber, this account makes me almost as breathless in its danger as it makes me to read the Bishop's long sentences! These climbs often ended in accidents, as two other accounts by Stanley show:

Many bird-catchers go on these expeditions without any companion to hold the rope or assist them. It was on such a solitary excursion, that a man, having fastened his rope to a stake at the top, let himself down far below; and, in his ardour for collecting birds and eggs, followed the course of a ledge, beneath a mass of overhanging rock: unfortunately he had omitted to take the usual precaution of tying the rope round his body, but held it carelessly in his hand; when, in a luckless moment, as he was busy pillaging a nest, it slipped from his grasp, and after swinging backwards and forwards three or four times without coming within reach, at last became stationary over the ledge of projecting rock, leaving the bird-catcher apparently without a chance of escape, for to ascend the precipice without a rope was impossible, and none were near to hear his cries, or afford him help. What was to be done? Death stared him in the face. After a few minutes pause, he made up his mind. By a desperate leap he might regain the rope, but if he failed, and, at the distance at which it hung, the chances were against him, his fate was certain, amidst the pointed crags ready to receive him, over which the waves were dashing far, far below. Collecting, therefore, all his strength, with out-stretched arms, he sprang from the rock, and lived to tell the tale—for the rope was caught![178]

A father and two sons went out together, and, having firmly attached their rope at the summit of a precipice, descended, on their usual occupation. Having collected as many birds and eggs as they could carry, they were all ascending by the rope—the eldest of the sons first, his brother a fathom or two below him; and the father following last. They had made considerable progress, when the elder son, looking upwards, perceived the strands of the rope grinding against a sharp edge of rock, and gradually giving way. He immediately reported the alarming fact.

'Will it hold together till we can gain the summit?' asked the father.

'It will not hold another minute' was the reply; 'our triple weight is loosening it rapidly!'

'Will it hold one?' said the father.

'It is as much as it can do', replied the son—'even that is doubtful.'

'There is then a chance, at least of one of us being saved, draw your knife and cut away below!' was the cool and intrepid order of the parent;—'Exert yourself,—you may yet escape, and live to comfort your mother!'

There was no time for discussion or further hesitation. The son looked up once more, but the edge of the rock was cutting its way, and the rope had nearly severed. The knife was drawn, the rope was divided, and his father and brother were launched into eternity.[178]

Bird harvesters at St Kilda, Ness and other sites in Scotland, sought birds of several species. The Fulmar, especially when young, was the favourite bird of the St Kildans, and harvesting young Fulmar and Gannets was as important as grain harvests in other economies. In addition a number of Auks and Shearwaters were eaten. St Kilda is now uninhabited, but in other parts of Scotland, notably at Ness in Lewis, such harvesting of seabirds still continues.

Up until 1878 Fulmar only occurred at St Kilda, and even today the island holds the largest colony of Fulmar in Britain. However Sula Sgeir, in Lewis, and Mingulay now both hold colonies of over 5,000 pairs.[153] While Hirte was inhabited, this species was always the most important food source because, as Martin Martin observed in 1698, 'the inhabitants prefer this, whether young or old to all other; the old is of a delicate taste, being a mixture of fat and lean; the flesh white, no blood is to be found but only in its head and neck; the young is all fat, excepting the bones, having no blood but what is in its head; and when the young fulmar is ready to take wing, it being approached, ejects a quantity of pure oyl out of its bill, and will make sure to hit any that attacks it, in the face, though seven paces distant... This oyl is sometimes of a reddish, sometimes a yellow colour, and the inhabitants put great value on it, and use it as a catholicon for diseases, especially for any aking in the bones, stitches etc.'[126]

Giben, which was the fat of sea-fowls made into a pudding in the stomach of the fowl, was regarded as a good 'vulnerary' or wound healer in men and beasts, as Turner, the sixteenth-century writer on the use of birds in medicine, described: 'Nor must we fail to mention that a salve, most valuable for many a disease, is made by Scots from the fat of this Goose (for it is wonderfully full of fat) which deservedly rivals the Commagemme vaunted much by Pliny in its virtue and the number of its cures.'[195]

This giben, gioban or giblion probably gave rise to the modern word 'giblets' for bird offal (though an alternative etymology suggests that it comes from the Old French for game stew). The habit of using fulmar oil as a cure-all was later to play a part in the failure of the community. Fulmar oil, contaminated with bird dung, was used to anoint the umbilical cords of the newborn. As a result neonatal tetanus was a great scourge among St Kildans though the connection was not realised.[120]

The Gannet was also an important food source. In 1549 Sir Donald Monro[133] described the collection of Guga, immature Gannets, from Sula Sgeir by the men of Ness:

> Be sexteen myle of sea to this ile, towards the west, lyes ane ile callit Suilskeray, ane myle lang, without grasse or hedder, with highe blacke craigs, and black fouge thereupon part of them. This ile is full of wylde foulis, and quhen foilis hes ther birdes, men out of the parochin of Nesse in Lewis use to sail ther, and stay ther seven or aught dayes, and to fetch hame with them their boitt full of dray wild foulis, with wyld foulis fedders.

The Gannet or Solan Goose was the principal food source in St Kilda from earliest times, but gradually became replaced by the Fulmar. By 1698 Martin described the Fulmar as the choice eating bird but Gannets were still an important part of the menu both as eggs, Guga or young birds, and as adults. They were so common at breeding sites among the stacks of St Kilda that he wrote: 'The heavens were darkened by those flying above our heads; their excrements were in such quantity, that they gave a tincture to the sea, and at the same time sullied our boat and cloaths.'[126]

Hunting wary Gannets was a difficult task, best attempted on windy days when the birds 'took a vacation from fishing', or at nights. 'The solan geese have always some of their number that keep centinel in the night-time... if the centinel be awake at the approach of the creeping fowlers, and hear a noise it cries softly, grog, grog, at which the flock move not; but if the centinel see or hear a fowler approaching, it cries quickly, bir, bir, which would seem to import danger, since immediately after, all the tribe take wing, leaving the fowler empty on the rock to return home *re infecta*, all his labour for that night being spent in vain.'[126]

The Gannet was not only taken at St Kilda. John Ray (1627-1705) wrote mostly about birds in England but in 1661 he travelled to Dunbar with friends and 'went to Leith, keeping all along the side of the Fryth.* We viewed Tontallon Castle, and passed over to the Basse Island, where we saw, on the rocks, innumerable of the Soland Geese. The Soland Goose called here Anser baffinus. In the Bass Island in Scotland lying in the middle of the Edinburgh Frith and nowhere else that I know of in Brittany a huge number of these birds doth yearly breed. Each female lays only one egg. Upon this island the birds being never shot at or frightened are so confident as to alight and feed their young ones close by you. They feed only upon filth yet are the young geese counted a great dainty by the Scots and sold very dear so that the Lord of the Isles makes no small profit of them yearly.'[155]

* 'Fryth' or 'Frith' was the common seventeenth century spelling of what is now called a 'Firth'.

Apart from providing food and medication, the Gannet's feathers were sold for stuffing bedding and their skins were used for clothing. Martin describes how this was done: 'The women inhabiting this isle wear no shoes nor stockins in the summertime; the only and ordinary shoes they wear, are made of the necks of solan geese, which they cut above the eyes, the crown of the head serves for the heel, the whole skin being cut close at the breast, which end being sowed, the foot enter into it, as into a piece of narrow stockin. This shoe doth not wear above five days, and if the down side be next the ground, then not above three or four days; but however, there is plenty of them; some thousands being catch'd, or, as they term it, stolen, every March.'[126]

Among the Auks young Puffins were considered good, but Razorbills and Guillemots were tough and only eaten when better birds were unavailable. The flightless Great Auk was present at St Kilda where Martin described it as the 'stateliest as well as the largest of the fowls of St Kilda'.[126] It was eaten regularly by mariners and was likely to have figured in the St Kildan diet. The Great Auk, with a white marking on its head, was named by Welsh seamen *Pen Gwyn* (whitehead) and later gave rise to the name Penguin for members of the order *Spheniscidae*. Certainly the eggs of the 'Garefowl' or Great Auk, being much larger than those of Auks, Gannets and Fulmar would have been harvested and this inevitably contributed to the species' extinction. In fact it is remarkable that more species were not lost when the harvest of birds or eggs is examined. The daily allowance for each St Kildan was eighteen Guillemot eggs, and Martin Martin calculated that he and his companions between them consumed sixteen thousand eggs in three weeks! They were not altogether to his liking, for he found them 'astringent and windy'. Some of his men became costive and some 'had the hemorrhoid veins swell'd'. Martin also records 29 baskets, each with 400-800 eggs of various species, taken in a single expedition.[126] However the St Kildans managed their birds carefully, always ensuring that breeding stocks were maintained despite this high cull.

But it was not just in Scotland that egg collection reached these levels: 'Huge baskets of their eggs are sometimes brought to the markets of seaport towns, and sold for a price exceeding that of domestic fowls, for they are much larger, and are said to afford good eating.'[97] Eggs were so important that a report from the Privy Council of 1615 proscribed the trade of collecting eggs in Scotland for export to the south.

The Guillemot or Lavy, though often eaten, was regarded as poor fare and better kept as an egg producer. 'The lavy, so call'd by the inhabitants of St Kilda; by the Welch, a guillem; it comes about the bigness of a duck; its head, upper side of the neck all downwards of a dark brown, and white breast, the bill strait and sharp pointed; the upper chop hangs over the lower; its feet and claws are black.'[126]

A visiting poet in 1618 described the food of Scottish nobles as including 'partridge, moor-cocks, capercailzies and termagents.' The Capercaillie was found in Perthshire until 1651, but soon thereafter disappeared.[159] Gannet, as mentioned above, was widely eaten and Charles II commented that there were two things he disliked in Scotland, Solan Goose and the Solemn League and Covenant.[183] John Taylor, the Thames Water-Poet, accompanied the Earl of Mar in 1618 on a shooting expedition numbering about 1,400 people in the Highlands, and mentions among other viands 'pidgeons, hens, capons, moor-cootes, heath-cocks, capperkellies and termagents'. John Taylor also commented on the Solan Goose: 'The soleland goose, a most delicat fowle, which breeds in great abundance in a little rock called the Basse, which stands two miles out to sea. It is very good flesh, but is eaten in the forme wee eate oysters, standing at a side-board, a little before dinner, unsanctified without grace: and after it is eaten, it must be well liquored with two or three good rowses of sherrie or Canarie sacke.'[183]

Birds and fashion

In the seventeenth century there seems to have been little call for feathers for dress though some plumage was used in headgear, especially for military bonnets. The main commercial use for feathers was for insulation and mattresses. 'Feathers were used for bedding and were sold dearly in Edinburgh'.[74]

4
The Eighteenth Century

The early eighteenth century brought the 1707 Union of the Scottish and English parliaments under Queen Anne. When Anne died in 1714, the Jacobites were united in opposing the succession of 'The wee German Lairdie', George I, leading to the rising under the Old Pretender in 1715. By the time the would-be James VIII landed in Scotland from Dunkirk, the rising had been quashed.

The Old Pretender's son, Charles Edward Stuart, Bonnie Prince Charlie, tried once more to regain the crown but this, after much adventure, came to grief on the murderous field of Culloden in 1745, when 'Butcher' Cumberland, later called 'Stinking Billy', inflicted appalling massacre on the Scots. Culloden marked the beginning of repression of the Highland way of life. An Act of 1747, proscribing Highland dress, the bagpipes and the right to bear arms, was harshly enforced by the English troops. Worse still, many estates in the Highlands were owned by absentee landlords who sought to maximise their income by banishing the peasantry. During the last third of the century, sheep increasingly ousted the Highlanders from the glens in clearances, which were to increase in the nineteenth century.

Despite political and religious unrest, the academic life of Scotland was burgeoning, leading to what later became known as the Scottish Enlightenment. Edinburgh, under the influence of the charismatic Dutch professor of Medicine, Boerhaave, based its medical school on Leyden. This Dutch influence brought with it a religious freedom within higher education. The absence of such freedom still fettered the development of thought at Oxford and Cambridge. This meant that natural philosophy, as science was then known, could begin to question Biblical concepts of creation. Scotland,

34

which hitherto had lagged behind England in science, took a great leap forward. Great names appeared. Among these leaders of their fields were David Hume the philosopher (1711-76) and the Hunter brothers, William (1718-83) and John (1728-93), in medicine. James Hutton (1726-97) was pre-eminent in geology and Joseph Black (1728-99) in chemistry. Nor were their developments limited to Scotland; the Glaswegian James Watt (1736-1819), whose name became synonymous with the steam engine, carried ideas to Birmingham where the influential Lunar Society, founded by William Small (1734-75) from Aberdeen University, was to become a hothouse of new scientific ideas. Previously William Small had been professor at Williamsburg in America where he exerted great influence on the young William Jefferson.

Scotland was also opening up for travellers from the south. Thomas Pennant (1726–98) made two tours in Scotland in 1769 and 1772.[147] He published these as *Tours in Scotland 1771-76*. Though these writings were much more travelogues than records of natural history he amassed much Scottish data, which he subsequently used in *British Zoology*.[148] In 1773 Boswell accompanied Dr Johnson on a tour of the Hebrides when, unfortunately, he says little about the countryside and its avifauna apart from comments on Raasay and a few entries on birds as food.[21]

In the last years of the eighteenth century, the unique work of Sir John Sinclair produced the *First* or *Old Statistical Account* of Scotland.[145] The word 'statistical' was then used to mean 'of or pertaining to the state' rather than its modern mathematical sense. Sinclair (1754–1835) was a lawyer who established the Board of Agriculture in 1793 and served as lay member of the Assembly of the Church of Scotland. He conceived the idea of getting the incumbents of all the 938 parishes in Scotland to respond to a list of 166 queries and from these amassed the *Statistical Account*. He hardly edited the material at all and it provides a fascinating record of many aspects of Scottish life at the end of the eighteenth century. Sinclair managed, not without some difficulty, to get a staggering 100% return. He was a hard taskmaster; in July 1793 he asked the remaining recalcitrant clerics to turn their responsibility for the *Statistical Account* over to others and slowly he neared completion. In only twelve instances did he have to send out what he called his 'statistical missionaries' to the delinquent parishes to gather information and themselves to submit an account of the parish. Most of the 166 questions dealt with parochial and social matters together with farming, lists of historical sites and famous people in each parish. Question 39 was of interest to natural historians and read: 'What birds are there in the parish? What migrating birds? and at what times do they appear and disappear?' This led to the accumulation of a great deal of information about the avifauna of the time, varying from parish to parish according to the interest of the individual incumbent. From these records one may deduce how the Scottish avifauna has changed over the last two centuries. References to migration are also of great interest since that phenomenon was poorly understood and in some cases not accepted. Many birds such as the Cuckoo and Swallow were still believed to sleep with the fairies or disappear into the bottom of ponds.

Birds and Belief

Burying a Black Cock alive in the floor at the centre of a house was thought to be a cure for epilepsy, but digging the bird up would cause its recurrence.[119]

Crows, though associated with Odin in Scandinavian mythology, were generally considered of ill-omen. If two crows fly above a house, a birth or a wedding is forecast. In Shetland, a young spinster would follow the first crow she saw on Candlemas morning (2 February) in the hope it would lead to her destined husband, but if the crow flew to the kirkyard she was destined to be an old maid. Peewits were believed to hold the departing soul of the dead.[10]

It was believed that Adam and Eve were transformed into Eagles and lived in the Shiant Islands off the Isle of Lewis. Swans were believed to be devout women under enchantment. In the Hebrides, to harm a Swan was evil.

Birds, Science and Language

By the eighteenth century, Scots were beginning to interest themselves in Natural Philosophy, the forerunner of biological science. In London, Sir Hans Sloane (1660-1753), the son of an Ulster Scot, was a physician and naturalist who became at first secretary and, later, president of the Royal Society. His natural history collection formed the basis of the British Museum.

Another Scot, Francis Buchanan-Hamilton (1762-1829), was born in Callander, the son of Thomas Buchanan of Spittal and Elizabeth Hamilton, heiress of Bardowie in Stirling. Francis qualified in medicine at Edinburgh and travelled extensively in India as surgeon to the Hon. East India Company, but was soon fully employed working on the natural history of the Subcontinent. He contributed enormously to the knowledge of Indian avifauna and had one species, the Grey-necked Bunting (*Emberiza buchanani*) named after him. When he returned to Scotland to inherit his mother's estate, he added Hamilton to his name and became head of Clan Buchanan a year before his death.

Birds and the Arts

In the eighteenth century, Scottish painters often included birds in portraits, though as yet there were no artists in Scotland who concentrated on bird portraiture. Many recognisable species now featured in portraits. In about 1710, Richard Waitt depicted John and Alexander Birnie of Broomhill as children and one is holding a probable Song Thrush. Sir William Murray of Ochentyre and James Moray of Abercairney, in portraits painted by Jeremiah Davison in 1735 and 1717, each hold a Peregrine.

The portrait of Prince Charles Edward Stuart as a boy by Philip van Dyck (1740) features a Jay, and that of William, 1st Earl of Fife, by William Mosman (1741) is painted with a Magpie. Both these birds are rich in folklore and the symbolism in these pictures is fascinating. Despite an association between the Jay and vainglory, in the case of Prince Charles' portrait it symbolises J for Jacobite.

Other species include Blackcock, in a portrait of John, 4th Duke of Atholl, with family by David Allan, and Gray Partridge in a rather poorly preserved painting from about 1742 of George Lindsay, 21st Earl of Crawford, by Chamberlain.

Owls feature in at least two portraits. Charles, 4th Duke of Buccleuch, painted by Sir Joshua Reynolds in 1777, is pictured with what looks like a Tawny Owl, and in George Willison's 1765 portrait of James Boswell a Little Owl, with typical staring yellow eyes, sits on a branch above his head. This is particularly interesting as the Little Owl was only a vagrant in Britain at the time (see p.205), the first having been found at the Tower of London in 1758. The inclusion of this Owl may be a compliment to the sitter since it is a symbol of wisdom. On the other hand it may have been a double entendre, since Owls can also represent folly and Boswell's career was sometimes impetuous.

William Mosman in 1741 painted Jean, Countess of Fife, with her son sitting beside her. The little boy has let go of a string attached to a House Sparrow's wing and the bird has flown to a window. This picture seems rich in obscure symbolism. Raeburn painted William and Charles Thorold Wood as children showing one holding a Goldfinch, the symbol of Christ's Passion. Reynolds painted a Robin in the foreground of his 1777 portrait of the three-year-old Lady Caroline Scott, later Marchioness of Queensberry.

The greatest Scottish bird artist of this period, Alexander Wilson, was perhaps better known in the Scotland of his day as a poet and is included among them (see p.41).

In the eighteenth century Scottish literature was developing fast and poets were particularly active in writing about birds. Robert Crawford (1690-1733) from Renfrewshire wrote on 'Tweedside':

> The warblers are heard in the grove
> The linnet, the lark and the thrush
> The blackbird and sweet caring dove
> With music enchant ev'ry bush.[45]

James Thomson (1700-1748), describing Winter in *The Seasons*, wrote:

> Retiring from the downs, where all day long
> They pick'd their scanty fare, a black'ning train
> Of clamorous rooks thick-urge their weary flight,
> And seek the closing shelter of the grove.
> Assiduous, in his bower, the wailing owl
> Plies his sad song. The cormorant on high
> Wheels from the deep, and screams along the land.
> Loud shrieks the soaring hern; and with wild wing
> The circling sea-fowl cleave the flaky clouds.[193]

John Logan [1748-88] greeted the Cuckoo:

> Hail, beauteous stranger of the grove,
> Thou messenger of Spring!
> Now Heaven repairs thy rural seat,
> And woods thy welcome ring.[110]

Poets often write about birds and Rabbie Burns was no exception. However, unlike Shakespeare, he was not much of an ornithologist. Nevertheless there are some twenty species listed by name in the complete works, though it must be said of this Lothario of a poet that most of his references to birds are in likening them to some young woman who had caught his eye, or to sympathetic birdsong which soothed or echoed his frequently broken heart.

Burns was born in 1759 near Alloway in Ayrshire, and as the son of a farmer must have known the countryside well. Depressed by poverty and injustice, he became an ardent supporter of the French Revolution and this coloured his writing. But he drew on many bird images in his love poetry. Many of his poems include references to the birds of his native Lowlands, for example 'Composed in August':

> Now westlin winds and slaught'ring guns
> Bring Autumn's pleasant weather;
> The moorcock springs on whirring wings
> Among the blooming heather...

> The Partridge loves the fruitful fells,
> The plover loves the mountains;
> The woodcock haunts the lonely dells,
> The soaring hern the fountains,
> Thro' lofty groves the cushat roves,
> The path of men to shun it;
> The hazel bush o'erhangs the thrush,
> The spreading thorn the linnet.[25]

From 'Composed in Spring':

> The wanton coot the water skims,
> Amang the reeds the ducklings cry,
> The stately swan majestic swims,
> And everything is blest but I.[26]

In the last line of this we begin to hear the dejection that creeps into so much of Burns' poetry; sometimes because of the hard life he led as a ploughman and labourer, but more often because of his rejection by one of his 'dearly loo'ed lasses'. This becomes apparent in an 'Address to a Woodlark':

> O stay, sweet woodlark, stay,
> Nor quit for me the trembling spray!
> A hapless lover courts thy lay,
> Thy soothing, fond complaining.
> Again, again that tender part,
> That I may catch thy melting art;
> For surely that wad touch her heart
> Wha kills me wi' disdaining.
>
> Say, was thy little mate unkind,
> And heard thee as the careless wind?
> Oh, nocht but love and sorrow join'd
> Sic notes o' woe could wauken!
> Thou tells of never-ending care;
> O' speechless grief, and dark despair:
> For pity's sake, sweet bird nae mair!
> Or my poor heart is broken.[27]

This is interesting, since the Woodlark (see p.218) does not now occur in Scotland, but only in southern Britain where it is uncommon (indeed I saw my very first Woodlark in Cyprus as I was finishing this book). This species was often confused with the Tree Pipit, but the detailed description of the song suggests that Burns really did hear a Woodlark.

The sadness evoked by the Woodlark is echoed in Burns' 'Lament of Mary Queen of Scots on the Approach of Spring':

> Now laverocks wake the merry morn
> Aloft on dewy wing;
> The merle, in his noontide bow'r,
> Makes woodland echoes ring;
> The mavis wild wi' mony a note,
> Sings drowsy day to rest
> In love and freedom they rejoice,
> Wi' care nor thrall opprest.[28]

Sometimes Burns tells us quite a lot about the behaviour, particularly the sounds of birds, as in his 'Elegy on Captain Matthew Henderson'. The poet adds to this title that Henderson was 'A gentleman who held the patent for his honours immediately from Almighty God!'

> Mourn, ye wee songsters of the wood;
> Ye grouse that crap the heather bud;
> Ye curlews, calling thro' a clud;
> Ye whistling plover;
> And mourn, ye whirring paitrick brood;
> He's gane forever.
>
> Mourn, sooty coots and speckled teals;
> Ye fisher herons, watching eels;
> Ye duck and drake, wi' airy wheels
> Circling the lake;
> Ye bitterns, till the quagmire reels,
> Rair for his sake.[29]

Also mentioned in this poem are cushats, craiks and houlets.

In another elegy, this time for Tam Samson, who was obviously a great hunter, Burns wrote:

> Rejoice, ye birring paitricks a';
> Ye cootie muircocks, crousely craw;
> Ye maukins, cock your fud fu' braw
> Withouten dread;
> Your mortal fae is now awa;
> Tam Samson's dead![30]

Despite having been brought up to hear my Scottish mother recite Burns by the hour, I sometimes have to take recourse to a Scottish dictionary to find out what he is on about. In Tam Samson's elegy 'paitricks' are partridges, 'cootie' means feathered at the ankles, as indeed muircocks are, 'crousely craw' is to crow boldly; 'maukins' are hares and their 'fuds' are their tails.

Perhaps my favourite Burns bird is the Mavis described in 'On hearing a thrush sing in a morning walk in January':

> Sing on, sweet thrush, upon the leafless bough,
> Sing on, sweet bird, I listen to thy strain,
> See aged Winter, 'mid his surly reign,
> At thy blythe carol, clears his furrowed brow.[31]

Writing on his 'favourite things' in a letter to Mrs Dunlop he said: 'I never hear the loud solitary whistle of the Curlew in a Summer noon, or the wild, mixing cadence of a troop of grey-plover in an Autumnal morning,

40

without feeling an elevation of soul like the enthusiasm of Devotion or Poesy.'

Another poet, Alexander Wilson, was to become as famous as Burns in a different way. Alexander, or Sandy, Wilson was born on 6 July 1766, son of a former smuggler from Paisley who had turned to weaving. Sandy was a clever lad and his mother wanted him to enter the church. However the boy was much more interested in fishing and hunting rabbits than in his divinity studies, and early theological aspirations were dashed. Sandy entered his father's weaving business, but the monotony of the looms irked him and he preferred to read poetry. Soon he was writing verse himself and he spent as much time as possible watching birds, but more as a poet than an ornithologist. He wrote of them in 'Lochwinnoch, a Descriptive Poem':

> Adjoining this, 'midst bordering reeds and fens,
> The lengthened lake its glossy flood extends,
> Slow stealing on with lazy silent pace,
> The Peel lone rising from its wat'ry face.
> Here stalks the heron gazing in the lake,
> The snowy swan and party-coloured drake;
> The bittern lone that shakes the solid ground,
> While thro' still midnight groans the hollow sound;
> The noisy goose, the teal in black'ning trains,
> And long-billed snipe that knows approaching rains;
> Wild fowl unnumbered here continual rove,
> Explore the deep or sail the winds above.[199]

Unfortunately some of Wilson's verse was libellous; he was clapped into the tolbooth and his poetry was publicly burnt by the official hangman at Paisley's market cross. But he was not entirely unsuccessful; while in jail his 'Watty and Meg' was published and sold more than 100,000 copies. Unfortunately the public believed it was the work of Sandy's contemporary Robert Burns and he never received the acclaim he deserved. Out of jail in 1794, depressed and broke, he sailed with a friend to America with nothing but 'a flute, a fowling piece and a few shillings'.

Between 1804 and 1810, in order to realise his ambition of painting all the American avifauna, he walked thousands of miles along the great rivers of America, from New York to New Orleans. On one of these journeys, in 1810, he chanced to call at a grocery in Louisville on the Ohio River. There he showed his portfolio to the man behind the counter who was also an amateur bird painter. That man was John James Audubon, who became inspired by Sandy Wilson to extend and publish his own paintings. Audubon, who was to become the greatest name among bird artists, influenced the world of birds but also Scottish ornithology through his friendship with MacGillivray in the early nineteenth century (see p.52). Audubon's magnificent volumes of *The*

Birds of America are the most expensive books in the world, reaching record auction prices at over two million pounds ($3.96 million).

Wilson completed his 3,000 mile journey to New Orleans in less than six months, during which he had discovered a dozen birds unknown to science. He then returned home to work on his eight volume *American Ornithology*, which was completed just before his death from dysentery in 1813 at the age of 47.

Though Wilson's poetry was overshadowed by his contemporary, Burns, and his painting by Audubon, he left an enormous legacy. He was first to describe 48 new species, many of which, including Wilson's Phalarope and Wilson's Storm Petrel, bear his name. The latter is now believed to be the most abundant bird in the world. Both Wilson and MacGillivray, two great Scottish bird artists, are linked by the famous name, but much lesser man, John James Audubon.

Few birds seem to have influenced Scottish music but there is a link through the Golden Plover. This bird, called *Feadag* in Gaelic, is often simply called the Plover in the Highlands. It is renowned for its whistle and the Gaelic word *fead* means a whistle. The same root gives feadan, the bag-pipe chanter, which, in skilled hands, can be as evocative as the early summer call of the Golden Plover. There is also a Pipe March called the Curlew.

Birds and Economy

Writing about the Bass Rock on his first tour, Pennant[147] noted that 'various sorts of water fowl annually repair to the rock to breed, particularly the Soland Geese and Kittiwakes. The profits arising from the young are farmed out, and produce no inconsiderable revenue, though a Gannet or Soland Goose, is still sold for twenty pence; the very price it fetched in the time of Ray.' At the Bullers of Buchan 'as well as in the neighbouring cliffs, breed multitudes of Kittiwakes. The young are a favourite dish in the north, being served up, a little before dinner, as a whet for the appetite.'

In Perthshire on 'the vast hill of Laurs... the country abounds with game, such as Grouse and Ptarmigan.' These species were also mentioned at Braemar where 'Eagles, Falcons, and Goshawks breed. These birds are proscribed, and a particular bounty is paid for the destruction of each.' On his second tour Pennant[147] returned to Tayside where he noted 'It is not known if the Fieldfare or Redwing ever breed in this country... Sea Eagles breed in the ruined towers, but migrate in winter. The Black Eagles continue all the year round and are so numerous, that a reward of five shillings has been given for the destruction of each.'

Pennant also visited several islands including Ailsa Craig (which he called Alisa). 'Marine birds are very numerous. The Earl of Cassilis is the proprietor of Alisa, who lets the whole for £33 a year. The rent is made of young Gannets, which are taken for the table, and of the feathers of other birds.' On Jura, Pennant observed that birds were plentiful and included Blackcocks, Grouse, Ptarmigans and Snipes, and near Mull he delighted in watching Gannets precipitate themselves from a vast height to plunge on their prey.[147]

Boswell had little to say about birds but does mention them in Raasay where he had a day's hill walking apart from Dr Johnson. 'There are black-cock in extraordinary abundance, moorfowl, plover and wild pigeons, which seem to me the same as we have in pigeon-houses, in their state of nature. Raasay has no pigeon-houses.'[21]

As we have seen in the previous chapter, sea fowl were as essential to life on St Kilda as reindeer to the Laplanders. As early as 1758, the island-ers claimed that the Fulmar had begun to replace the Gannet as the staple of their diet. The reasons for the change were probably many. There was a sharp increase at that time in the number of Fulmars breeding upon St Kilda, and the feathers and oils of the bird were of great value to the proprietor. The amber oil of the fulmar was said to have many of the properties of cod liver oil; rich in vitamins A and D, it was sold on the mainland as medicine. Indeed in the eighteenth century St Kildans claimed the Fulmar was a most useful commodity which 'furnished oil for the lamp, down for the bed, the most salubrious food, the most efficacious ointments for healing wounds and a thousand other virtues.'[179]

But all was not well in Hirte; an old man went from St Kilda to Harris in 1726 and there caught smallpox and died. The following year relatives col-lected his belongings including his clothes. The effect was disastrous: almost everyone contracted the disease and 94 died leaving only four adults to care for many orphans. Of the few that survived, 11 had gone to the stacks fowl-ing and nobody was fit enough to get them back, so they remained there for several weeks and escaped infection.[85]

The slaughter of birds was not confined to St Kilda. By the eighteenth century it was customary to shoot auks at their nest sites, as the Minister for Coldingham in Berwickshire described in the *Old Statistical Account*:

> There is also a prodigious number of sea-fowl, known by the names of scouts and kittywakes, with a mixture of sea-gulls, that arrive in the spring yearly, upon the high and inaccessible rocks on the south side of St Abb's Head. They breed incredible numbers of young; and about the end of May, when the young are said to be ripe, but before they can fly, the gentlemen in the neighbourhood find excellent sport by going out in boats, and shooting great numbers of them; when they are killed or wounded, they fall from the rocks into the sea, and the rowers haul them into their boats. Their eggs are pretty good, but their flesh is very bad; yet the poor people eat them.[145]

The *Old Statistical Account* makes clear that the same carnage occurred near Duncansby Head, in Caithness:

> The Stalks of Dungisbay, as they are called, are two piramidal pillars of naked freestone rock. They are frequented in summer by innumerable sea-fowls, who hatch and bring forth their young about their sides, while the eagle sits in royalty upon their summits. The coasts, throughout the year, abound in multitudes of sea-fowl. In the summer months, the swarms of scarfs, marrots, faiks, etc. that come to hatch in the rocks of Dungisbay and Stroma, are prodigious. They in a manner darken the air, when, on any sudden alarm, they take wing in a body from their nests. The gun makes frequent and bloody havock among them. They are shot for amusement from boats, and the common people appropriate their flesh and feathers to their own use. The sport is cruel and unprofitable, as numbers die upon their young in the nest.[145]

And, near Thurso:

> The Clett is an insulated rock ...supposed to be about 400 feet above the surface of the sea. It is well worth the visiting, particularly in the months of May, June, and July, when it is frequented by immense flocks of sea fowls chiefly gulls, cormorants and marrots, which come there to nestle. The marrots range themselves in regular lines on the shelves of the rock, and being rather a silly unsuspecting bird, they frequently fall in dozens to the shot of the cruel sportsman, who reaps no other advantage from his prey, except the savage pleasure of destroying it. These birds have an excellent plumage, and their feathers might be turned to good account; but as yet no attempts to that effect have been made. Their flesh is eat only by the fishermen, who indeed value it so much, that, with a tolerable marksman, they will pass a day at the Clett shooting, without asking any other consideration for their trouble.[145]

But harvesting, though not always so cruel, must have depleted stocks of seabirds sorely. In Orkney:

> on the sand and shores of Deerness are seen miriads of plovers, curlews, sea-larks, sea-pies, ...and the lofty rocks of Copinshay are covered with wild-fowl of various kinds, without name, and without number. The taiste, or black guillemote, builds her nest in the cliffs; the kittewakes are by themselves, in the east end of the rock, the whole surface of which they render white, as that of the other end is mottled black and white, by the auks, the scouts, the cormorants, the shags, the gulls, etc., which crowd upon every shelf. The people of this island

44

get vast quantities of sea-fowls, eggs, and feathers; which last they sell for 9*d.* per lb.

In The Western Isles to Barray, and to the island of Bernera, great numbers of sea-fowls resort every year in the month of May, the same with those in St Kilda, though not in such variety; they come in the latter end of April or the beginning of May to clean their nests from the rubbish of last year, then set off, and after some days return to lay their eggs and hatch, and so soon as the young are able to take the wing, they disappear, and are not to be seen till the same season next year.[145]

Handa must have been as good a place to see seabirds in the 1790s as it is today, for its minister noted in the *Old Statistical Account*:

Island Handa is remarkable for being the resort of vast numbers of sea-fowl of different kinds, which about the end of April every year come to it to breed and hatch their young. Their numbers are so great, that the whole face of these tremendous rocks, and the sea in the neighbourhood, appear covered with them. There they remain all the summer and harvest till the middle of September, when they migrate, nobody knows whither. Many of those who live nearest this island, as well as its inhabitants, make it their business, as often as they can, to come with boats to this place, and besides catching and killing great numbers of them, to the great benefit of their families in the way of provision, they make considerable profit of the feathers, bartering them commonly for an equal weight of wool. The flesh of the birds, (the young ones excepted), has a fishy taste, offensive to most palates. Three men, at different times, lost their lives by falling from the rocks, where they were unhappily scrambling in pursuit of them and their eggs, in the memory of the present inhabitants.

The rock Sulisker lies 4 leagues to the east of Rona... It abounds with a great variety of sea-fowl. The boat which goes to Rona, generally touches there for fowls and feathers, the men busy in taking the birds, who are so tame, that they knock them down with sticks; their feathers sell at Stornoway, at from 9 to 10s. per stone.[145]

These excerpts from the *Old Statistical Account* show how little has changed in 200 years despite the culling of so many birds. Throughout these accounts the privations of the fowlers are all too apparent and their expeditions were surrounded by hazard. Such danger is pointed out by a twentieth century writer:

From time immemorial the men of Ness have culled Gannets at Sulisgeir [Gannet Rock]. In the eighteenth century, every September they navigated 40 miles to the skerry in a small six-oared boat without a compass. Before a mooring ring was fixed in the rock some had to stay in the boat, ensuring safe escape, while the rest went ashore to collect the Gannets, which were easily killed with sticks. Many rituals were observed; the men could not relieve themselves on the skerries as this might bring misfortune, they were not allowed to kill birds with a stone before landing nor after evening prayers. They made a 'deiseil' turn [that is with the sun, not the widdershins turn of witchcraft] stripped themselves of outer clothing and prayed ritualistically before fowling.[117]

Surprisingly few St Kildans 'went over the rocks' as they called it; from 1830 to 1846 only two islanders died as a result of fowling accidents.[179]

Birds and Food

There are far more Scottish records of birds as food during the eighteenth century. Captain Burt, an engineer and surveyor in General Wade's service, wrote many letters to a friend in London in which he both complained of and extolled the food offered to him in Scotland.[33] 'They roast a fowl in the embers with the guts and feathers and when they think it done they strip off the skin, and think it fit for the table.'

On another occasion Burt had potted Pigeon set before him: 'Two or three pigeons lay mangled in the pot, and behind it were the Furrows, in the Butter, of those fingers that had raked them out of it, and the butter itself needed no close Application to discover its Quality. My Disgust at this sight was so great... I ate a crust of bread and drank a pint of good claret... and marched off.'[33]

Burt found game was cheap and plentiful: 'You can buy a partridge for a penny or less... not many brought to market except in snow and then indeed I have seen sacks-full of them.' 'Of the eatable part of the feathered kind peculiar to the mountains is, first, the cobberkely, which is sometimes called the wild turkey, but not unlike it, otherwise than in size. This is very seldom to be met with, being an inhabitant of very high and unfrequented hills, and is therefore esteemed a great rarity for the table.

Next is the black cock, which resembles, in size and shape, a pheasant, but is black and shining, like a raven; but the hen is not, in shape and colour, much unlike to a hen-pheasant... Lastly the tormichan, near about the size of the moor-fowl (or grouse), but of a lighter colour, which turns almost white in winter. These, I am told, feed chiefly upon the tender tops of the fir-branches, which I am apt to believe, because the taste of them has something tending to turpentine, though not disagreeable.'[33]

Harriet Glasse wrote *The Art of Cookery made Plain and Easy* in 1757. Though she sheltered behind the anonymity of calling herelf 'A Lady' she signed some copies, presumably for friends, H. Glasse.[67] She gave comprehensive recipes for birds, which adventurous readers could repeat nearly 250 years after they were written, were it not now illegal:

> Larks, roast them, and for sauce have crumbs of bread; done thus: take a sauce-pan or stew-pan and some butter; when melted, have a good piece of crumb of bread, and rub it in a clean cloth to crumbs, then throw it into your pan, keep stirring them about until they are brown, then throw them into a sieve to drain, and lay them round your larks.

Larks 'make a pretty good ragoo with fowls livers; first fry the larks and livers very nicely, then put them into some good gravy to stew, just enough for sauce, with a little red wine. Garnish with lemon.'

To roast snipes or woodcocks:

> Spit them on a small bird-spit, flour them and baste them with a piece of butter, then have ready a slice of bread toasted brown, lay it in a dish, and set it under the snipes for the trail to drop on; when they are enough, take them up and lay them on a toast; have ready for two snipes, a quarter pint of good beef gravy hot, pour it into the dish, and set it over a chafing-dish for two or three minutes. Garnish with lemon, and send them hot to table.

Ruffs and 'Reifs' should be fattened with white bread, milk and sugar but must be killed before they get too fat. Unlike Snipe and Woodcock they must be gutted before roasting on a spit and served with gravy thickened with butter.

Plovers, Wigeons and other ducks:

> To two plovers take two artichoke-bottoms boiled, chestnuts roasted and blanched, some skirrets* boiled, cut all very small, mix it with some marrow or beef suet, the yolks of two hard eggs, chop all together, season with pepper, salt, nutmeg and a little sweet herbs, fill the bodies of the plovers, lay them in a sauce-pan, put to them a pint of gravy, a glass of white wine, a blade or two of mace, some roasted chestnuts blanched and artichoke-bottoms cut into quarters, two or three yolks of eggs and a little juice of lemon; cover them close, and let them stew very softly an hour. If you find the sauce not thick enough take a piece of butter rolled in flour, and put it into the sauce, shake it round, and when it is thick take up your plovers and pour the sauce over them. Garnish with roasted chestnuts.

*Water parsnips, an aquatic plant with edible roots (which can be found now growing in the garden of Culross Palace).

To pot birds:

Season with salt and pepper and put them in a pot with as much butter as when melted will cover them, bake very tender. Leave the birds to drain then separate the butter from the gravy and remelt it pouring it over the birds in a pot, if necessary melting more butter so that it is near an inch thick above the birds.

If when you come to use the potted birds they smell bad each bird should be put into boiling water for half a minute, dry them and when they are quite cold return them to the pot and pour more clarified butter over them.[67]

Marjorie Plant[151] mentions interesting eighteenth century culinary devices such as serving oysters with Partridges and wildfowl, skewered on a spit, basted with butter and served with a sauce made from bread, claret, spice, nutmeg and sugar. Rich Highlanders could afford to be fastidious since their most plentiful provisions were those which Londoners considered luxurious, and they were often in glut. Indeed Partridge were so plentiful, especially when there was snow on the ground, that they were taken to market by the sackful and sold for a penny or less each. Eating in the eighteenth century was prodigious. In the Highlands the celebrated breakfast consisted of chops, fish and game. At a typical dinner in Edinburgh of 1745 the first course might consist of 15 dishes, the second of 18 dishes, with another thirty for dessert. A celebrated dinner at Foss, in Perthshire, given on a Sunday afternoon, was not finished until the bell was ringing for church the following Sunday... the diners did not realise how time had flown!

For the less well-off Pigeons provided most of the meat. They were kept in Doocots and Edinburgh had over 100 of them, but they fell into disuse by end of the eighteenth century because the birds were eating too much corn. Lesser mortals ate umble pie, the umbles being the offal of deer.[151]

Rural life was simple: looking after the beasts and making butter and cheese. In summer livestock was taken to high pastures where their owners lived in temporary huts or shielings. The diet consisted largely of oatmeal with dairy products, occasionally supplemented with game, hens and geese, which were always kept in agricultural Scotland. Eggs were seldom quoted in the menus of inland rural workers; they were sold to 'egglers', travelling hawkers who carried them in creels on their backs to town markets. In many places, especially the islands and around the coast, eggs of wild birds were commonly eaten. The practice of eating Lapwings' eggs was not uncommon in some Highland areas even into the twentieth century, but, more generally, it was eggs of Gulls, Guillemots, and Fulmars.[183]

Maisie Steven writes that for centuries 'In Orkney... the flesh of the Guillemot was considered a delicacy; young Cormorants, too, were eaten after first being buried for twenty-four hours to tenderise them.'[183] But an eighteenth century writer, Oliver Goldsmith, said that they were eaten by those with the grossest appetites, for this 'unclean bird has the most rank and disagreeable smell, and is more fetid than even carrion...'.[68] A piece of roast Gannet was considered a good appetiser. However a farmer attending a public dinner ate a whole Gannet beforehand and claimed his appetite 'was not a whit the keener for it'.[183]

Dr Johnson noted little difference between dinners in Scotland and London, but forgot to mention the enormous variety of fish and game, which were then very costly in London. Boswell and Johnson ate a fricassee of moorfowl at an inn near Fort Augustus and the Doctor commented 'At the tables where a stranger is received, neither plenty nor delicacy is wanting. A tract of land so thinly inhabited, must have much wildfowl, and I scarce remember to have seen a dinner without them. The moorgame is everywhere to be had.' Perhaps he preferred Scotch broth for, when asked if he had eaten it before replied 'No, sir, but I don't care how soon I eat it again.'[21]

Even the French were impressed at times by Scottish food. A visiting Frenchman described dining at an inn in Dalmally in 1797: 'Our supper consisted of two dishes of fine game, the one of heathcock, the other of woodcock.'[51]

5
The Nineteenth Century

The nineteenth century saw the flowering of the Scottish Enlightenment and brought industrialisation to the country. Transport was revolutionized first by the canals and, by mid century, the railways. In the Highlands the Clearances, started during the last decades of the eighteenth century, saw the depopulation of many glens with tens of thousands of clansmen evicted from their homes to allow room for the new immigrant *na caoraich mora*, the big Blackface and Cheviot sheep. This coincided with the collapse of many staple occupations of the Highlands and Islands. Fishing and kelping, for manure, declined and, in 1846, the plight of the poor was worsened by the potato famine. The face of the Highlands changed; where previously there had been thriving communities there were now roofless houses, deserted steadings and piles of stone. Amongst these the sheep grazed.

For the landowners this was a bonanza of wealth, and throughout Scotland big estates flourished, many new country houses were built and tourism commenced. Queen Victoria and her consort discovered Scotland, making the country and its fieldsports fashionable.

Birds and Belief

Now, when science was overtaking the legendary origins of ornithology, superstition was less common, though many of the old ideas died hard, especially in the Highlands and Islands. Schism beset the Presbyterian Church, when, in the Great Disruption of 1843, the Free Church of Scotland seceded. At this time in the Highlands the repetitive song of the Mavis was said, by some ardent members of what was to become known as 'The Wee Free', to chant the Gaelic equivalent of:

The Free Kirk's best by far,
The Free Kirk's best by far
The Moderates, the Moderates
Are worthless, are worthless.[61]

Birds and Science and Language

If Scotland had been slow to embrace science in the past it now rushed to do
so. Soon Scotland was to lead the world in many fields, not least ornithology.
Many Scots contributed to the science. Among them were Peter McDougall
(1777-1814) who was born in Kilsyth and read medicine at Glasgow before
entering general practice in Glasgow. He spent his leisure collecting birds
and, in 1812, when exploring Great Cumbrae in the Clyde, he and a friend
obtained Terns which were different from others he knew. He sent a specimen to Montagu (who was to give his name to Montagu's Harrier) in Devon
who named the new Tern *Sterna dougallii*.[129]

Sir John Richardson (1786-1865) was born in Dumfries, son of an inti-
mate friend of Robert Burns. He became a naval surgeon who explored the
Arctic with Franklin, writing extensively on Arctic ornithology. Richardson's
Skua, now known as the Arctic Skua, was named after him and the name did
not become obsolete until the 1950s.[129]

William Leach (1790-1836) was born in Plymouth but studied medicine
at Edinburgh, took an MD at St Andrews but returned to Natural History
and worked at the British Museum. At an important sale in 1819 Leach
bought a specimen of a Great Auk and 'an undescribed Petrel with a forked
tail taken at St Kilda'. This was subsequently examined by Temminck, who
named it *Procella leachii*. Since then the species has been known as Leach's
Petrel.[128]

James Clark Ross (1800-1862), whose picture hangs in the Scottish
National Portrait Gallery, was born in London, son of a Scot from near
Stranraer. He joined his uncle, John Ross, at sea when he was 12 and accompanied him for several years surveying the Arctic. In summer of 1823 he
shot a gull with a black ring round its neck. On his return home Richardson
examined the bird, naming it *Larus rossii*. It is now known as Ross's Gull.[128]

Henry Maurice Drummond (1816-?1890) later changed his name to
Drummond-Hay (see p.18) when, in 1859, he married Lady Charlotte Hay.
He was first President of the British Ornithological Union and Colonel of
the Black Watch. He lived at Megginch Castle in Perthshire, was president
of Perthshire Society of Natural Science and wrote extensively on Scottish
birds. His son, Colonel Drummond-Hay, was also a celebrated Scottish ornithologist until his death in 1928.

The collection of bird specimens in the nineteenth century was a bloody business. Audubon is renowned for remarking that it was a poor day when he did not shoot a hundred birds. An English collector who spent much time in Scotland coined the frequently used phrase 'What's missed is mystery, what's hit is history.' This was Edward Booth, who had such a bad name for his callousness in collecting that another saying of the time, 'B for Booth, B for Butcher' was commonly used of him. On one occasion he visited Scotland to acquire Peregrines for his collection. He killed three of four chicks in an eyrie and fastened the fourth on a rock surrounded by traps until he had caught both parents, in order that he could stuff the whole family. He visited North Berwick and wrote extensively of the Bass Rock.[129]

William MacGillivray (1796-1852) has been called the father of Scottish ornithology. He was born illegitimately and spent his boyhood in the Isle of Harris. He attended Aberdeen University, at first reading medicine but later changing to the discipline of Natural Science. In 1820 he transferred to Edinburgh under Jameson (Regius Professor of Natural History) and from 1831 to 1841 he was Conservator of the Museum of the Edinburgh College of Surgeons.[202] He was also a first rate painter and compiled a portfolio of fine bird pictures. While working on his *History of British Birds* he became acquainted with the American artist and ornithologist John James Audubon (1785-1841) whom he often quotes in his writing and to whose monumental *Birds of the United States of America* he made a considerable contribution. Audubon praised his painting as 'surpassing in splendour anything of that kind.' Audubon honoured the Scotsman when he drew a previously unidentified American Warbler and 'dedicated this pretty little bird to my excellent friend William MacGillivray, Esq.'[150]

Ironically MacGillivray's paintings have lain unacclaimed ever since and it is only recently that his ability as a bird painter has been acknowledged. An exhibition of his work was on show at the Natural History Museum in Kensington from April to June 2000.[202]

MacGillivray suffered ill health in his fifties, probably as a result of his privations when making field observations. He completed his *History of British Birds* shortly before he died in 1852. These five volumes are regarded as the most original account of British birds, but have been criticised because of MacGillivray's idiosyncratic classification, based on his own anatomical theories. He was also somewhat paranoid and, in the words of a biographer, 'scarcely disguised his contempt for triflers, blockheads, pedants, compilers and theorizers'. He indulged in long purple passages in his text where the patter of tiny avian feet rustles through his pages. To some modern readers this detracts from a scientific account of nineteenth century Scottish birds.

Birds and the Arts

The early tradition of painting ceilings continued into the nineteenth century. Phoebe Anna Traquair (1852-1936) was a mural painter who decorated the Catholic Apostolic Church in Edinburgh during the years 1893 to 1900. Her mural of the 'Second Coming' was an allegorical painting showing animals in Tree of Life including a white Dove with a halo. In a side chapel the ceiling shows Peacocks and Doves. At St Mary's Song School in Edinburgh she placed a symbolic Dove in a painted medallion. In both cases Peacocks and Doves were symbols of St Mary or of the Holy Spirit.

Sir Edwin Landseer (1802-73) in part of a mural at Ardverikie (now destroyed) portrayed an Eagle flying over a recumbent stag, and in a painting of Queen Victoria and Albert at Windsor he included game such as Curlew, Mallard and Pheasant. In 1826 Landseer painted George, 5th Duke of Gordon, with Blackcock and other game.

Nineteenth century ideas of sportsmanship were bizarre; Fisher[59] has a sketch by Henry Davenport, dated 1852, of shooting Kestrels at the Cathedral in Iona and there is a Scottish Naïve School painting of about 1800 illustrating the shooting of Crows in the grounds of St Andrews Cathedral. Similarly an engraving on wood by Richard Thompson depicting Charles St John shooting an Osprey in Sutherland in 1848[59] would not be acceptable in the conservationally minded twenty-first century.

Game featured increasingly in portaiture in parallel with its importance to the landed gentry. In 1801 Red Grouse feature in the picture 'Robert and James Smythe of Methven' by W.R. Begg. Curlew and Mallard accompany the MacLeod brothers in a painting by Kenneth MacLeary in 1868. But portraits were not all of the gentry: Mr Pattison, gamekeeper on the Dalhousie estate, was painted with a bag of Pheasants by William Douglas in 1822.

Up until the end of the eighteenth century bird illustration had been as much shrouded in myth as all ornithology. In 1797 Thomas Bewick of Newcastle published his *History of British Birds*[19] illustrated with his own woodcuts. Bewick (1753-1828) perfected a technique of producing woodcuts using hard woods incised with the grain to produce wonderful pictures of birds. He not only captured the bird's likeness but in many cases its habitat and behaviour as well. These are still widely used as illustrations for birdbooks. After Bewick many artists have produced black-and-white and colour illustrations for various texts on ornithology and the Field Guides which have burgeoned since he led the way.

James Grahame (1765-1811), described by Fisher[59] as 'the poet-ornithologist of Scotland' wrote *The Birds of Scotland* in 1806 and *Rural Poems of Scotland* or *Georgics* in 1808. His wife was very critical of his verses and it is suggested that this is why he published many of them anonymously. He must have been delighted when Mrs Grahame was full of praise for the unknown poet's work! Writing about the reclamation of marshland Grahame showed that habitat destruction has long been with us:

> No more the heath-fowl there her nestling brood
> Fosters, no more the dreary plover plains;
> And when, from frozen regions of the pole,
> The wintry bittern, to his wonted haunt,
> On weary wing, returns he finds the marsh
> Into a joyless stubble ridge transformed,
> And mounts again to seek some watery wild.[76]

Grahame also times the agricultural calendar to birds:

> Soon as the earliest swallow skims the mead,
> The barley sowing is by some begun;
> While others wait until her clay-built nest,
> Completed, in the window-corner hang:
> Or till the schoolboy mock the cuckoo's note.[76]

James Hogg (1770-1835) was born in Ettrick in the Borders where he worked with sheep, and this gave rise to his literary nickname of 'the Ettrick Shepherd'. He wrote extensively about the countryside, under the patronage of Scott, for *Blackwood's Magazine*.

'The Skylark'

> Bird of the wilderness
> Blithesome and cumberless,
> Sweet be thy matin o'er moorland and lea!
> Emblem of happiness,
> Blest is thy dwelling-place—
> Oh, to abide in the desert with thee.[88]

In his 'Lament of Flora Macdonald for Charles Edward Stewart' James Hogg used many bird images:

> The Moorcock that craws on the brows o' Ben Connal
> He kens o' his bed in a sweet mossy hame;
> The Eagle that soars on the cliffs of Clan-Ronald
> Unawed and unhunted, his eiry can claim.
> The Solan can sleep on his shelve of the shore,
> The Cormorant roost on his rock of the sea:
> But Oh! There is ane whose hard fate I deplore,
> Nor house, ha', nor hame in his country has he;
> The conflict is past, and our name is no more,
> There's nought left but sorrow for Scotland and me![89]

The great literary name of the period was Sir Walter Scott (1771-1832), whose Waverley Novels appeared, anonymously at first, between 1814 and 1831. Scott was a great nationalist who did much to reinstate old Highland traditions and costume. Much of the popular image of the 'Bonnie Scotland', beloved of tourists, can be laid at his door. Scott mentioned some 46 species of birds in his works but only by passing references, as in *The Heart of Midlothian*:

> Proud Maisie is in the wood,
> Walking so early,
> Sweet Robin sits in a bush
> Singing so rarely.
>
> 'Tell me, thou bonny bird,
> When shall I marry me?'
> 'When six braw gentlemen
> Kirkward shall carry ye.'
>
> 'Who makes the bridal bed,
> Birdie, say truly?'
> 'The grey-headed sexton
> That delves the grave duly.'[166]

Or in his description of Melrose Abbey by night from *The Lay of the Last Minstrel*:

> When distant Tweed is heard to rave.
> And the owlet to hoot oe'r the dead man's grave...[167]

In the 1820s Charles Spence wrote a lament over a unfaithful lover in a poem named after the Perthshire waterfall, Linn-ma-Gray:

> Linn-ma-Gray, high on thy crest
> The wagtail builds her felty nest,
> And down amid the misty spray
> The snipe finds home at Linn-ma-Gray.
>
> Linn-ma-Gray, the cushats cool
> Their pinions, fluttering in thy pool
> Where sunbeam never found the way
> Far ben the glack of Linn-ma-Gray. [glack = ravine]
>
> Linn-ma-Gray, thy hazels green,
> Lodge the thrush and finch at e'en
> Lodge me, too at close of day—
> I tune my harp at Linn-ma-Gray.[176]

In 1828 the Rev. David Landsborough (1779-1854) wrote a long poem about Arran in which he extolled Glen Sannox but, for some reason, phoneticised the Gaelic mountain name *Cir Mhor*:

> ...The glen to trace
> To mount the towering summits and return,
> Hours of laborious effort will require;
> Yet all the while, nor glimpse of face divine,
> Nor human habitation, wilt thou see.
> Yet think not tenantless this noble glen.
> Here with wild note the wheeling plovers rise;
> There whirring spring the snowy ptarmigan
> And eke the blackcock bold on glossy wing.
> High 'mong the cliffs abrupt of Kier-vore
> The screaming eagle flutters o'er her nest,
> And stirreth up her young.[102]

Mercifully Glen Sannox has changed little, though there are few, if any, Blackcock there now.

David Gray (1838-1861) wrote about the most loathed bird in Scotland with some affection:

> But this sweet day, an hour ago,
> A yellow-hammer, clear and low,
> In love and tender pity
> Trilled out his dainty ditty.[78]

Robert Louis Stevenson (1850-1894) was the best loved literary figure of his time and became famous for *Treasure Island*, *Kidnapped* and *Dr Jekyll and Mr Hyde*, the latter loosely based on Dean Brodie of Edinburgh. He also wrote poetry revealing his awareness of the birds of his country.

> So lying, tyne the memories of day [tyne = lose]
> And let my loose insatiate being pass
> Into the blackbird's song of summer ease
> Or, with the white moon, rise in spirit from the trees.

(Part of a sonnet written about the Ross of Mull in August 1870.)[185]

'Time to Rise'

> A birdie with a yellow bill
> Hopped upon the window-sill
> Cocked his shining eye and said
> 'Ain't you 'shamed, you sleepy-head'.[186]

In *Kidnapped* Alan Breck and David Balfour hid in the Heugh of Corrynakiegh (*Coire na Ciche*) where 'the burn was full of trout; the wood of cushat-doves; on the open side of the mountain beyond, waups would always be whistling, and cuckoos were plentiful.' Later the fugitives crossed Rannoch Moor 'lying as waste as the sea; only moorfowl and the peewits crying over it and far over to the east a herd of deer moving like dots.'[188]

And in part of a poem about the Pentland Hills:

> Frae the high hills the curlew ca's,
> The sheep gang baaing at the wa's
> Or whiles a clan o' roosty craws
> Cangle thegether.[187]

John Muir (1838-1914) was born at Dunbar, son of a domineering over-religious father with whom he emigrated to Wisconsin and become one of the world's leading conservationists, establishing some of the great National Parks of America. Now he is increasingly better known in his native Scotland, where his conservation work, through the aegis of the John Muir Trust, has come to the rescue of Ben Nevis and Schiehallion. In an exhibition about his life at Dunbar there appears the following quotation from Muir about the Dipper: 'The Water Ouzel's music was that of the stream itself... The deep booming notes of the falls are in it, the trills of the rapids, the swirling and gurgling of the potholes, low rushes of the levels, the rapturous bounce and dance of the rocky cascades, and the sweet tinkle of separate drops oozing from the ends of the mosses, and falling in tranquil pools.'[137]

The most famous diarist of the period was no less than Queen Victoria herself, and her journal entries for Scotland are collected in John Kerr's *Queen Victoria's Scottish Diaries*.[99]

Taymouth, Thursday, September 8.

Albert went off at half past nine o'clock to shoot with Lord Breadalbane... Albert returned at half past three. He had had excellent sport, and the trophies were spread out before the house—nineteen roe deer, several hares and pheasants, and three brace of Grouse; there was also a capercailzie that had been wounded, and which I saw afterward—a magnificent large bird.'

The following day the Queen recorded her Consort shooting on Drummond Hill near Taymouth Castle:

Albert set off again after nine o'clock, to shoot... Albert returned at twenty minutes to three, having had very hard work on the moors, wading up to his knees in bogs every now and then, and had killed nine brace of Grouse.

Birds and Economy

The Highlands were cleared so that absentee landlords could make room for sheep and game. By 1850 the letting of grouse moors was common practice, their rentals often being the principal source of a laird's income. David Craig, in *On the Crofters' Trail*,[44] faithfully records the stories from the descendants of those evicted. A crofter at Sleat in Skye: 'When the Victorian gentry were seized by the urge to kill everything that moved, they bagged thousands in a day, not only Grouse, Partridges and Pheasants but Curlew and Woodcock, Pigeons and Snipe... I remember between here and the road, you would start up a covey, and another one before you reached it, Grouse and Partridges and Blackcock—a beautiful bird—That tail! And when the shooters came down, it was bang-bang-bang.'[44] It is little wonder that the Grouse, which has been the cause of much misery to the Highlanders, is frequently referred to in their sayings and songs.[61]

The 'glorious twelfth' of August, the opening day of grouse shooting, has become a by-word. It is always slightly surprising that, while nearly all game seasons start on the first of a month, Grouse should come into season on the twelfth. The day has been the twelfth since 1752 when an Act of George III corrected an error in the calendar. The old calendar had managed to get eleven days ahead of itself. When these days were adjusted in 1752 what had formerly been the first of August became the twelfth.

Grouse numbers are partly determined by geology, with highest numbers occurring over basic rocks such as limestone, which increase soil fertility and therefore the nutritional value of the bird's food-plants, heather, vaccinia, bog myrtle and chickweed.

During Charles II's reign, it became more common, though not without much controversy, to shoot game-birds in flight instead of stalking perched birds or walking them up with dogs. Scots like Robert Burns or Alexander Wilson probably shot feeding birds on corn stooks. Grouse shooting as a sport is only about 200 years old, since in the nineteenth century it was not considered a fit sport for the aristocracy. Travel to the moors was arduous and tramping over them carrying a long, heavy, muzzle-loading gun was considered fit only for minor gentry. The invention of M. Houllier, a Paris gunsmith, of cartridge breech-loading shotguns in 1847 hastened the flocking of the aristocracy to the grouse moors. Shotguns, which until then were awkward and difficult to use, became lighter to carry and faster to load. The combination of the breech-loading shotgun and the advent of the railways providing easy access to the grouse moors produced enormous change in the avifauna of Scotland. From then on the twelfth became glorious indeed and gunsmiths had a heyday.

Grouse are generally short-lived. Nearly two out of three alive in August die within a year, irrespective of shooting, and some years are disastrous. 1872 was such a year when many birds died of starvation, but despite this shortage the season was extraordinary in the Tay valley with 220 brace falling to one gun in a single day at Grandtully. This record, held by Maharajah Duleep Singh, was somewhat contrived, much as if he had deliberately set out to get into an early version of the *Guinness Book of Records*. Riding from drive to drive with several shotguns, many loaders and scores of beaters, the Maharajah was determined to create a record.

A typical game record of the 1868 season shows 1,314 Grouse, 33 Black Game, 49 Partridges, 110 Golden Plover, 53 Snipe, 95 Woodcock among others. 'Now so many of these good birds are either quite extinct or on the verge of becoming so' observed the writer who recorded this festival of shooting.[81] It seems strange that nineteenth and twentieth century writers did not connect the size of bags with later scarcity.

The Capercaillie was once common throughout the Highlands. The first record of the species in Scotland comes from Boethius[20] who mentioned them at a feast in 1529 when James V ate 'black-cock, muir-foull and capercailles.' By an Act of 1621 provision was made against buying and selling of 'wyld foulles' including 'termigants, quails, capercailieis under penalty of a hundred pounds.' There continue to be sporadic records of Capercaillie which gradually fade away as the seventeenth century progressed. It is mentioned several times in the *Old Statistical Account*[145] as a once native bird of this country, now extinct. Harvie-Brown, in 1888,[87] devoted a whole book to it and told the story of its reintroduction between 1827 and 1840. The first attempt seems to have been made at Mar Lodge with birds from Sweden. However this venture ended in failure, possibly because the initial colony was so small and their confinement, designed to protect them from predators, prevented them finding the right food.

In 1836 Sir Thomas Fowell Buxton, who had been staying at Taymouth Castle wished to make some return to Lord Breadalbane for his kindness and instructed that the requisite number of Capercaillie be procured, at whatever cost, to establish the birds at Taymouth. Accordingly in autumn 1837 and the following spring some fifty birds were brought from Sweden. Sir Thomas sent his own head keeper from Norfolk to supervise the reintroduction. This time the experiment was successful and the birds were later released on nearby Drummond Hill where, within 25 years, the population was estimated at 1,000-2,000 birds.

The Capercaillie formerly abounded in Arran but had also become extinct there in the eighteenth century. Since the species was known to have done well there in the past and because of its isolated position, it was considered a good site for another experiment. Accordingly it was reintroduced in 1843 in the grounds of Brodick Castle, and over the next thirty years the birds did well, but were rarely seen away from Brodick. Unfortunately this venture did not succeed in the end and by 1880 all the birds had gone.

Drummond Hill near Aberfeldy used to be a sure place to find Capercaillie years ago, but by the late 1990s their numbers were down. The Capercaillie is threatened as a result of habitat degradation and injury caused from flying into deer fences. Since 1970 there has been approximately a 90% reduction in their population. The best chance of seeing the bird today is when a male becomes aggressive. He will then defend his territory against all comers, including man. You may not only see such a bird, but have to bid a hasty retreat from his apoplectic wrath.

Between 1837 and 1840 vermin destroyed in Glengarry included 15 Golden Eagles, 27 White-tailed Eagles, 18 Ospreys, 98 Sparrowhawks, 7 Peregrine Falcons, 11 Hobbies, 275 Kites, 5 Marshharriers, 63 Goshawks, 285 Common Buzzards, 371 Rough-legged Buzzards, 3 Honey Buzzards, 462 Kestrels, 78 Merlins, 63 Hen Harriers, 6 Gyr Falcons, 9 Montagu's Harriers, 1,431 Hooded Crows, 475 Ravens, 35 Horned Owls, 71 Nightjars, 3 Barn Owls and 8 Magpies.[94]

This is an amazing list for two reasons: firstly, it is hard to understand how we have any predatory birds at all today in view of such carnage; secondly, what a marvellous range of birds there were before the gamekeepers got to work.

There was a similar persecution of Raptors in Arran where the Duke of Hamilton ordered the annihilation of eagles. All but one of these splendid birds was killed and the sole survivor was kept in captivity. Fortunately they had returned when I climbed Goat Fell with my father (see p.134).

Birds and Food

Birds tasted good or bad according to palate. Smoked Solan Geese were well-known as contributing to the abundance of a Scottish breakfast, though too rank and fishy-flavoured for unpractised palates. According to Meg Dods (1826) they were eaten as whets, or relishes.[52]

In St Kilda June and July were lean months as far as sea birds were concerned. The Puffin was the only bird available for eating while the young Gannets and Fulmars fattened. The harvesting of Fulmars took place in August when the young birds would be killed in their thousands before they could leave the nest. The young brown-feathered Gannets, or Gugas as they were called, matured more slowly, and it would be a month later before men would take to the boats and rob the stacks of these birds.

The St Kildans used every part of the Fulmar; the feathers were graded by colour and packed into sacks. Once fumigated they were impervious to lice and bed-bugs and were popular in the army. The oil (about half a pint per bird) was poured into a Gannet stomach and later transferred into canisters to be bartered with the factor. The carcases were split down the back and packed with salt and stored like herrings in barrels. The guts were reserved for fishbait while the bones were used as fertiliser.[179]

The diet of the St Kildans was largely avian; breakfast consisted of porridge and milk with a Puffin boiled with the oats to give flavour. The main meal of the day at midday comprised potatoes and the flesh of Fulmars. Puffins were plucked and their carcases split down the middle before being hung on strings outside the houses to dry when they were ready for the pot. The St Kildans also fed these Puffins to their dogs and cattle. In the early nineteenth century they took about 25,000 Puffins a year; by 1876 this reached nearly 90,000.[179]

Gannets were salted down by the thousand; before being cooked they had to be steeped in water for a day to remove salt, then they were boiled with tatties, but they still tasted fishy. The Guga, regarded as a delicacy, was served on the steamers plying the Minch, but people lost the little taste they once had for its oily flesh and by 1900 Gugas began to disappear from shipboard menus. Guillemots were eaten in the spring and summer and their feathers kept for export.

Eggs were collected from below which involved carrying a large box up the cliff. The dangerous part was going down with a full box, weighing up to a hundredweight, on a man's back with minimal breakage. The eggs were eaten well into incubation and the islanders would say, 'if you don't like the young bird you can just throw it away and eat the rest'. St Kildans collected the eggs of some 14 species, most to be used for food but others, such as those of the Fork-tailed Petrel, were frequently requested by egg collectors. The most valued was the egg of the St Kilda Wren.

A late nineteenth century edition of Mrs Beeton[15] gives recipes for many birds. Snipe are not drawn, and after being plucked, only require wiping on the outside. 'One of these small but delicious birds may be given whole to a gentleman; but in helping a lady, it will be better to cut them quite through the centre and put only one half on the plate.' They cost 1/6–2*s* a brace, that is 7.5 or 10 pence today. Hanging birds was important. Blackcock, unless hung for a few days, would be tough and tasteless. Red Grouse too should hang as long as possible, 'pluck and draw them; wipe but do not wash them inside or out' and, she assures readers, 'the backbone of the Grouse is highly esteemed by many, as this part of many game birds is considered the finest-flavoured.' Grouse then were priced at 4 shillings (20 pence) a brace. 'Ptarmigan, when young and tender, are exceedingly fine eating, and should be kept as long as possible to be good. It feeds on the wild vegetation of the hills, which imparts to its flesh a bitter, but not altogether unpalatable taste, something of the flavour of the hare, and is greatly relished and much sought after by some sportsmen'. They cost two shillings and sixpence per brace (12.5 pence).

Pheasant cost about three shillings (15p) each. 'If eaten three days after it has been killed, it then has no peculiarity of flavour. Kept, however, a proper length of time—and this can be ascertained by a slight smell and change of colour—then it becomes a highly-flavoured dish, occupying, so to speak, the middle distance between chicken and venison. It is difficult to define any exact time to "hang" a pheasant; but any one possessed of the instincts of gastronomical science can at once detect the right moment when a pheasant should be taken down, in the same way as a good cook knows whether a bird should be removed from the spit, or have a turn or two more.'

Mrs Beeton[15] also gave recipes for small birds such as Larks and Wheatears. Larks (at 1/6-2*s* a dozen) 'are by many persons esteemed a great delicacy and may be either roasted or broiled. Pick, gut and clean them, brush them with egg yolk and roast them before a quick fire. Broiled larks are also very excellent. Wheatears, after they are picked, gutted and cleaned, truss them like larks, put them down to a quick fire, and baste them well with fresh butter. When done, which will be in about 20 minutes, dish them on fried bread-crumbs, and garnish the dish with slices of lemon. They are seasonable from July to October.'

Small birds such as Thrushes, Larks and Wheatear were trapped in huge numbers to satisfy the markets. Eggs, particularly those of Lapwings, were highly esteemed by Victorian epicures. Tens of thousands of eggs were sold throughout the country. For example one game dealer sent 600 dozen eggs to London in 1834 (many of these were the similar eggs of Redshank, Snipe, Reeve, Black-headed Gull and Black Tern). These 'Plovers' eggs commanded a price of 3 or 4 shillings a dozen and even eightpence each for early eggs. The sale of wild bird eggs as a delicacy continued sporadically until made illegal by the Lapwing Act of 1926. Mrs Beeton said of them 'Plover's eggs are served boiled hard and cold, the beautiful colour of the white being generally so much admired.'

Capercaillie seems to be an acquired taste: 'The delicacy of his flesh in some measure sets a high price upon his head' However this contrasts with a later view that the Capercaillie is 'A bird that tastes like a paint pot.'

Many unlikely birds found their way into Victorian cooking pots. Johns[97] records eating an Oystercatcher 'as an agreeable variation from the bacon and herrings which mainly constitute the dietary of a Scottish fishing-village inn. But I did not repeat the experiment, preferring fish pure and simple to fish served up through the medium of fowl.' Chough were plentiful enough to be eaten in Colonsay at the end of the nineteenth century.[143] One such unusual bird, the Great Auk, was to disappear forever.

> Though quantities are destroyed by the crews of vessels as well as by the Eskimos, their numbers never seem to decrease. Their flesh is both wholesome and delicate, and affords a welcome change of diet to the mariner weary of salt meat and pemmican. They are very tame and easily captured,—in some places being actually caught in hand-nets; they pass a great portion of their time on the ocean, where they disport themselves with equal grace and self-possession.[7]

(The last British Great Auk was killed about 1840 and the last of all in Iceland in 1844. Colonel Drummond Hay is reputed to have seen the very last Great Auk.)

But some of these bird recipes were clearly delicious: 'What grouse soup at Dalnacardoch ! You smell it on the homeward hill, as if it were exhaling from the heather.'[144] And at a dinner at an inn in Dalwhinnie: 'The accessories of the dinner were wretched, but the dinner itself, I remember was excellent with …salmon, …mutton and grouse, scanty vegetables, bad bread but good wine.'[77]

Birds and fashion

In Victorian times, after Prince Albert had made Grouse shooting so popular, many trophies of the sport became fashionable. Jewellers made fortunes from gold or silver brooches of game birds embellished with diamonds. At least these did not cause slaughter of birds though they represented the murder on the moors. A popular Victorian bangle was made from the foot of a Grouse with its feathered claws, which was mounted in silver with a cairngorm. My mother often wore one of these in her church-going hat before the Second World War, fascinating her very young son.

In the late nineteenth century birds were still in fashion, especially the Ostrich whose curved or straight plumes were used in fans. Before the First World War evening dresses were daringly low and huge boas of Ostrich plumes were worn across the shoulders to aid modesty or titillation. Hat feathers again became popular at that time, especially long straight feathers such as those from Pheasants worn in pairs set at different angles.

Egrets, during the breeding season, develop superb plumes as a form of sexual advertisement. The ladies of the nineteenth century copied the Egret's example by using its nuptial feathers to attract the attention of gentlemen. It must have worked, for so great was the slaughter of Egrets in America to satisfy the requirements of milliners that the bird's very existence was threatened. It was because of this that the Egret was adopted as the symbol of an American bird preservation organisation.

A similar thing happened in Britain. In the middle of nineteenth century 'grebe fur' became fashionable as millinery trimming for hats and coats. At first satisfied by imports from the continent, demand then turned on the British population of Great Crested Grebes, which, by 1860, had been reduced to a bare forty pairs. This trade gave rise to many of the vernacular names of the bird such as Tippet Grebe or Satin Grebe. Bird Protection Acts passed in Britain during the latter half of the nineteenth century improved the situation a little. Eventually, in 1889, a group of conservationally minded Victorian ladies formed a group calling themselves the 'Fur, Fin and Feather Folk'. This alliterative conservation society thrived and soon had a membership of over 5,000. In 1909 it changed its name to become the Society for the Protection of Birds, which later received the Royal Charter. Avian conservation today owes much to the Great Crested Grebe and to the RSPB.

6
The Twentieth Century

This was a century of two relatively short but very destructive European wars and one long and extremely cold war. It was a century of explosion in scientific knowledge, of emptying churches and burgeoning literature and art relating to birds. It was also the century of overpopulation, consumerism and despoliation of the ecosystem.

Birds and Belief

In the modern era of scientific ornithology many of the old legendary concepts were discarded as pure myth. Perhaps this was premature, for the ideas of former times, though now seen as nonsensical in themselves, shed light on the character and personality of wild species, particularly birds. Several of these old concepts are now embodied in literature and art.

Birds and Language and Science

As some of the old names of birds began to disappear, with them considerable insight into the character and jizz of species has been lost. Some of the old nomenclature persists in place names, for example: Caerlaverock is the fort of the lark and Roxburgh, formerly Rokesburgh, is the town of Rooks. The Isle of May comes from the Norse *Ma-ey* or Gull Island. Torphichen, from the Gaelic *torr phigeainn*, is the magpie hillock. Gowk's Hill is a tiny village near Penicuik in Midlothian; the two names are the same, for Pen-y-cuik is the Celtic name for the Cuckoo's Hill, which is Gowk's Hill in Lallans. In Islay, Beinn na Fithlach, and in Colinsay, Creag na Fitheach, refer to the Raven… and there are many more.

The twentieth century produced many ornithologists such as Sir Hugh Steuart Gladstone (1877-1949) of Dumfriesshire, son of the former Prime

Minister, who was Chairman of the Wild Birds Advisory Committee (Scotland) and wrote widely on birds and allied subjects. William Ogilvie-Grant (1863-1924) was educated in Edinburgh and later joined the British Museum of Natural History in charge of its ornithological section, where he catalogued the collection.

Anne Constance Jackson (1888-1928) spent most her early life at Swordale in Ross and Cromarty. She searched for rarities with the help of lighthouse keepers and published many papers in *The Scottish Naturalist*. She married Colonel Richard Meinertzhagen, also an ornithologist, in 1921, and together they explored extensively in the Middle East and Himalaya. She died after an accident with a revolver in 1928.

Known as the 'two ladies of Scottish Ornithology', Evelyn Baxter (1879-1959) and Leonora Rintoul (1875-1953) dominated Scottish ornithology from the 1930s until their deaths. They were both born in Fife and were encouraged by Dr Eagle Clark who, at the beginning of the century, had studied migration at Fair Isle and later made a study of the ornithology of lighthouses and small islands. Such was the enthusiasm of the two ladies ('Rintoul for rhetoric, Baxter for business') they were never seen without binoculars, even at church. In 1911, at the Isle of May, they recorded the first Nightingale in Scotland, (apart from the Sinclair experiment a century earlier, see p.234). They travelled throughout Scotland finding many other rarities and wrote the two volumes of *The Birds of Scotland* in 1953.[13] This book contained the fruits of almost two lifetimes spent observing and writing about birds throughout Scotland. It is a mine of historical and scientific data based on examination of old records and correspondence, combined with their own research.

Valerie Thom (1929-98) was Editor of *Scottish Birds* and President of the Scottish Ornithologists' Club. In his Foreword to her *Birds in Scotland* W.J.Eggeling wrote:

> It was always the hope of these two 'good ladies' [Baxter and Rintoul] of Scottish ornithology that their book would be continually up-dated, and they would have been glad indeed that this has been so competently done by Miss Valerie Thom to cover the past 30 years... We have now got two datum lines—the situation as described in *The Birds of Scotland* and the picture, 30 years later, as described for us... by Valerie Thom. An assessment again, possibly early in the next century, will undoubtedly reveal further change.'[192]

Birds and the Arts

By the twentieth century bird paintings had become accurate, if somewhat posed, depictions of real life. Many were painted for the huge output of reference books and Field Guides which became available during the century. In addition birds appeared as decorative art in sporting pictures and as part of landscapes. The latter was particularly true of Scotland which attracted artists from many parts of the world. Two British bird artists worked in Scotland. John Guile Millais (1865-1931) spent many years of his early life on the north-east coast of Scotland. As a boy he loved wildfowling, his weapon of choice throughout his life being a catapult, which had the advantage of causing minimal damage to the subjects he painted. He studied and painted ducks, contributing enormously to knowledge of their behaviour.[129]

The second was George Edward Lodge (1860-1954) (some of whose illustrations appear in this book) who began illustrating *The Birds of the British Isles* (1953-63) with David Bannerman. He had a nucleus of earlier paintings but he completed the series of 384 plates depicting 426 species by the time he was 91. He made many of these pictures from skins borrowed from Richard Meinertzhagen and the British Museum of Natural History.[129] Some of his paintings were published in his *Memoirs of an Artist Naturalist*; these included Crossbills at Fairburn in Ross-shire in 1907, a Great Skua with nest and eggs at Mid Yell, Shetland 1914, a Merlin with 4 chicks painted at Lerwick in Shetland, 1922, and a Capercaillie hen with nest and eggs in Ross-shire on 15 May 1927.[109]

The finest Scottish bird painter was Archibald Thorburn (1860-1935). He was born at Lasswade, Midlothian, the fifth son of the famous miniaturist Robert Thorburn. Archibald was well coached by his father and following schooling in Dalkeith and Edinburgh studied art in London, but is said to have learned more from his father than any other teacher. When the Dutch painter John Keulemans (1842-1912) fell ill in 1887 Thorburn completed the illustration of Lord Lilford's *Coloured Figures*,[107] producing 268 of the 421 plates in that classic work. He contributed watercolour paintings to a number of ornithological works of the late nineteenth century, including works by W.H. Hudson and Henry Dresser, and eventually wrote and illustrated several titles of his own including *British Birds* (1919) and *British Mammals* (1921). He continued to paint until his death and his last work was published posthumously in 1937. Since his death Thorburn's work has been published more often than any bird painter except Audubon. This is entirely understandable when one examines his work, which is not only anatomically accurate but somehow encapsulates the character of the birds he has portrayed. In the previous century Ruskin had set an example of meticulous detail in bird portraiture.[101] Artists of the late twentieth century preferred to show birds in their natural habitat; Thorburn marked a transition between the artists of the two centuries.[60, 101]

Among many talented present day Scottish bird painters the work of Donald Watson was used to illustrate James Fisher's *Shell Bird Book*,[59] and two modern Perthshire painters, Brockie and Hayman, are producing superb pictures. Keith Brockie's beautifully illustrated books such as *The Silvery Tay*[23] are outstanding for their accuracy and sensitivity. A visit to Glen Lyon is incomplete without visiting Alan Hayman's studio at Bridge of Balgie. He specialises in wildlife with superb pictures of Peregrine, Woodcock and the complex bird habitat of the Bass Rock, with a multitude of Auks, Gulls, Gannets and Ducks.

On a brief visit to Iona in October 2000 a Robin was seen flying free in the Abbey and singing loudly from the rafters. St Oran's Chapel had been renamed locally as 'the Chapel of the Swallows' since a pair had nested there in the summer; surely St Columba would have approved. In the cloister, carvings by the Glasgow sculptor, Chris Wood, display a Corncrake, a Diver, a drumming Snipe, a Gannet and a hawk, perhaps a Hobby, taking a Swallow. These are modern renovations copying, as far as possible, ancient crumbling pillars of the past (see p.9).

Though poetry flourished in the twentieth century, little was concerned with birds. Here very different Scottish poets paint verbal images of familiar Scottish birds.

Charles Murray, a homesick Scot, wrote his collection *Hamewith*[138] from South Africa, and it includes 'The Alien', 'The Whistle' and 'Spring in the Howe o' Alford' recalling birds of the poet's youth.

In 'The Alien', Murray yearns for 'hame':

> My trophies, I would freely give them all,
> To creep through mist an' heather on the great red deer—
> I want to hear the black cock call.

And in 'The Whistle' he remembers his Scottish boyhood of Lapwings and Herons:

> He cut a sappy sucker from the muckle rodden-tree
> He trimmed it, an' he wet it, an' he thumped it on his knee;
> He never heard the teuchat when the harrow broke her eggs,
> He missed the craggit heron nabbin' puddocks in the seggs,
> He forgot to hound the collie at the cattle when they strayed,
> But you should hae seen the whistle that the wee herd made!

And from 'Spring in the Howe o' Alford':

> The liftward lark lea's the dewy seggs,
> In the hedge the yeldrin's singin';
> The teuchat cries for her harried eggs,
> In the bothy window hingin'.

Violet Jacob, the poet and novelist, described the migration of the wild geese in *Songs of Angus* (1915):

And far abune the Angus straths I saw the wild geese flee,
A lang, lang skein o' beating wings, wi' their heids towards the sea,
And aye their cryin' voices trailed ahint them on the air—
'O Wind, hae maircy, haud yer whisht, for I daurna listen mair!'[95]

In a very different poem Norman MacCaig, who was born in 1910 and lived in Edinburgh but spent his summers in Sutherland, exactly captures the movement of a wader in 'Ringed Plover by a Water's Edge':

They sprint eight feet and—
stop. Like that. They
sprintayard (like that) and
stop.
They have no acceleration
and no brakes.
Top speed's their only one.

They're alive—put life
through a burning-glass, they're
its focus—but they share
the world of delicate clockwork.

In spasmodic
Indian file
They parallel the parallel ripples.

When they stop
they, suddenly,
Are gravel.[113]

Kenneth Steven in his evocative collection *Iona* describes 'A Lark':

A handful of lark
Buoyant on the strings of a summer morning
Twirling and spinning songs
Overtures and symphonies
Though it has learned no music
In the schools of London or Paris
But is sight-reading instead
The kettledrums of the Atlantic
The white bells of the orchids
The violins of the wind.[184]

An unpublished but meticulous recorder came to my notice by chance. Tom Johnstone of Mercat Press lent me a copy of Howard Saunders' *Illustrated*

Manual of British Birds of 1899.[162] When new this book had belonged to a Dr C.L. Williams of the Indian Medical Service who dated it *Madras August 1899*. Williams subsequently returned to Britain and made detailed notes, including post-mortem findings, on a number of the birds listed in Saunders' text. Between 1913 and 1915 he was Medical Officer and Bursar at Glenalmond School near Perth. During this period his notes show that he regularly visited exactly the same spots where I seek birds 85 years later and, in some cases find the same species. Some of Williams' original notes[198] are transcribed into Part II of this book.

Another twentieth century writer frequently quoted is Seton Gordon (1886-1977).[69-73] He was the only child of the town clerk of Aberdeen and was brought up in Aboyne where he roamed the hills, acquiring considerable knowledge of birds. He published the first of many books on Scottish natural history when he was 21 before starting at Aberdeen University and later moving to Oxford to read Natural Science. He became the epitome of a Highland gentleman and an expert on Highland wildlife. He was a friend of Lord Grey of Falloden[80] on whom he wrote extensively.

Campbell Steven,[181, 182] another writer about the Scottish countryside, its hills, islands and birds, is here writing of a hill climb on Scarba near the Gulf of Corryvreckan north of Jura:

> Towards the summit of Cruach Scarba we breasted a rock escarpment and saw, thirty feet below, a typical *dubh lochan* [small dark loch]. Almost before we had realized it, there was a Red-throat shuffling from its nest on the brink and swimming under water to join its mate at the far end of the pool. For several minutes the pair paddled about with ill-feigned nonchalance, then took off noisily, circled and sped away towards Corryvreckan. For our part, we lost no time in scrambling down to the nest-scrape and its two eggs, sited less than a yard from the water's edge.'[181]

Birds and Economy

When one ponders the huge quantities of eggs of many species taken all round Scotland it seems surprising that any birds survived at all. Hundreds of thousands of Guillemot eggs were harvested by the men of Faeroe alone. However natural wastage among the dense serried ranks of nesting birds was so high that the human contribution, except for the Great Auk, seems to have had little effect. Robert Atkinson[12] described the feckless breeding habits of the Guillemot which provided such meals for the piratical Skuas that the rocks below the cliffs were littered with eggs and young birds, some still alive, others half-eaten; casualties from the noisy nurseries above. Overhead in the crowd the parent birds went headlong into raising their own young while knocking their neighbour's eggs and chicks over the edge.

The 'glorious twelfth' of August, the first day of Grouse-shooting, has become a byword in the English language. In 1915 an effort was made by the House of Lords to start the season a week earlier on 5 August, as their Lordships found the demands of the war kept them in London too much. The idea was rejected by the Commons who said 'we want to shoot Germans not Grouse'.[125]

In the nineteenth century Grouse disease was responsible for many problems on the lucrative sporting estates of the North. In 1905 the Board of Agriculture set up an enquiry with Dr Edward Wilson (who was later to die with Scott on the ill fated South Polar expedition of 1910) as its principal field observer. Wilson visited almost every important Grouse moor in Scotland and many in England, quickly securing the respect and co-operation of moor-owners and keepers. He personally dissected 2,000 Grouse and recorded the physical and pathological condition of each. His field observations on the habits of Grouse were equally meticulous.[200] It was discovered that the disease was caused by a minute nematode, *Trichostrongylus tenuis*, which crawled up the fronds of heather and lay in the dewdrops on the ends of the young shoots on which the Grouse fed.

Decline in the Scottish Grouse population in the late 1970s was linked to severe weather, when excessive rain killed many young birds. Though there was some improvement in numbers between 1987-8, the population is now thought to be well below 500,000 pairs. Many factors contribute to this decline, including threadworms and the viral disease louping ill, which is carried by ticks and is often fatal to grouse. Louping ill has been known in Scotland since 1807 as a disease of sheep, and occasionally sheep handlers. It is so called because of the peculiar gait exhibited by sheep affected with the disease. In man it causes an influenza-like illness often complicated by meningeal symptoms, before slow recovery, sometimes with prolonged debility. In Grouse the disease is often fatal and may have contributed to the major reduction in their numbers during the last decades.

When I first visited Aberfeldy in 1960 to work in the practice of Dr Jack Swanson, the Moness moors, above the town, were stiff with Grouse. I have memories of them lining the road shouting 'Go Back' at my car as I drove towards Amulree. On subsequent Scottish holidays I used to see Grouse commonly but these sightings grew less frequent. In a fortnight in the Hebrides in 1994 I only saw one Grouse; in two weeks of June 1995 I travelled widely throughout Scotland listing 108 species …but no grouse. As a result, when walking in Scotland one is noticeably less aware of the heart-stopping experience of Grouse exploding from the heather under one's feet.

Nowadays I seem to see the threatened Black Grouse more often than its red cousin. A mark of their scarcity has been the high price of young birds in recent seasons. However this scarcity does not seem to be universal, for some gamekeepers report that their moors have done well. Bags of Grouse which used to number 2½ million birds before World War I averaged between 10 and 25% of that figure in the 1980s and are probably smaller still by now.

Henry Douglas-Home, brother of the former Prime Minister, told a lovely story about a tame cock Grouse at Cawdor in Aberdeenshire.[53] During the shooting season in the early part of the twentieth century this entertained breakfast guests by walking up and down the dining-room table helping himself occasionally from a plate and calling 'Go Back! Go Back!' at the guns, about to set off for a shoot. One year a visiting Englishman was so enchanted with this bird that he managed to obtain it from his host. The Grouse was carefully packed and sent by train five hundred miles south to Henley-on-Thames. Two weeks later the bird was missing and its new owner decided that a cat must have eaten it. He wrote to Cawdor to break the sad news only to hear that the bird had beaten his letter north by a day.

There can be no doubt that this small, very Scottish, game-bird has been of great importance to Scotland and to Highland Perthshire in particular; what a loss it has been to the economy of Scotland since it has become such a rarity. It is to be hoped that it stages a come-back as dramatic as the Grouse from Cawdor. But even though there are few Grouse to be seen on our moors, at the beginning of the twenty-first century the Red Grouse must be one of the best known birds of Britain thanks to its regular appearance as a television star advertising a well-known brand of whisky.

Unlike the early twenty-first century the twentieth was the heyday of rail travel. In the 1930s the glorious twelfth, when everyone who was anyone left London for the Grouse moors, posed a transport problem. The railways responded by putting on special trains, with seven a day from St Pancras and a further three night trains from Euston. Marvellous pictures from the thirties show the great London Termini littered with Labradors and bristling with burberrys as the city took to the North.[125] One can imagine how branch lines, such as that to Aberfeldy, hummed with activity as the sportsmen detrained at tiny stations like Grandtully. All this brought wealth to the Highlands; huge hotels burgeoned and the great houses of rich industrialists appeared almost overnight.

Because the Red Grouse is a highly prized table bird there was a race to get the first birds to the tables of fashionable London restaurants, and in 1922 a letter to *The Shooting Times* reported: 'For the first time actually on the Twelfth itself, grouse was served at luncheon at the Savoy Hotel on Saturday

72

last. Some of the earliest birds shot on a well-known moor near Ripon were carried away by motor car and transferred to an aeroplane, and thus reached London in the forenoon'.[94]

With the loss of the Red Grouse as a source of major revenue many estates have changed to rearing Pheasants, which in many places are big business. These, unlike the Grouse, are not wild birds but are reared artificially for release before October 1st when their season opens. They are often so tame that they practically give themselves up and the carnage on the roads is appalling. Keepers dread good acorn years; pheasants love acorns, especially when they have been crushed by the wheels of motorcars; that is why there are so many pheasant fatalities on our roads.

The reduction of numbers of some species of birds during the twentieth century became alarming. Rachel Carson brought this to world attention with her seminal book *Silent Spring*[36] pointing out that DDT and other toxic chemicals, such as organochlorine seed dressings, passed up the food chain to concentrate in Peregrines and other raptors. Though this was less marked in Scotland than in England many Scottish raptors moved south in winter, leading to a serious decline in northern populations of hawks and falcons. Ironically this occurred after the respite from strict keepering, during two World Wars, had allowed an increase in raptor populations. Legislation to control toxic insecticides has put a brake on the decline since the mid 1970s.

Other species were to be affected by changes in farming practice throughout Britain. One factor was the loss of hedgerows, grubbed out to make extensive fields more suitable to modern harvesting. Hedgerows provided nesting sites for birds and corridors for migrants. Perhaps the most significant change was from traditional haymaking to silage production. This disturbed ground-nesting birds, particularly the Corncrake whose numbers and range have reduced dramatically (though there is recent evidence of a slow recovery in the Hebrides and Northern Isles).

In the twentieth century there was an increase in both numbers and affluence of the population, leading to more and more people living in what were formerly rural areas. This has reduced suitable habitats for birds. At the same time there has been increased mobility in an age when the motorcar has changed from being a luxury, through being a necessity, almost to being a disaster. Increased mobility has led to more people using remote areas, mountains, beaches and waterways for recreation, which disturbs wildlife and impairs breeding performance. On top of this, pollution from greenhouses gases pollutes the atmosphere bringing acid rain and threats of climate change. Coastlines change with rising sea levels and our seas are threatened by large discharges of crude oil and by the discarding of refuse at sea. A walk along some Scottish west coast beaches is distressing for the amount of plastic detritus. Sights such as that of a Gannet strangled by the plastic collar-wrapper of a quartet of beer cans become all too common.

In Scotland, we are cushioned to some extent by the vastness of our wilderness, but one only has to see what has happened to huge areas of rural England to see that the same thing could happen here. Despite this picture of gloom there is hope. People are becoming aware of the need to clean up our environment and in some cases the news is good. Some reintroduction programmes with lost Scottish species have been very successful. The Osprey, lost to Scotland in 1916, is now once more a common sight in summer. The White Tailed Eagle spreads its plank-like wingspan over some of the Hebrides and the Red Kite is to be seen in Aberdeenshire and, occasionally, in Perthshire.

Birds and Food

David Craig[44] quoted an islander: 'In Raasay we ate Cormorant, if the dog brought one in. Lovely broth with a Cormorant in it—it was not fishy at all, more like a chicken or a Grouse... Father used to row out to a wee island and take seagull's eggs—they were lovely.'

Guga is still a popular, if acquired, taste. There is always an over-subscribed waiting list for Guga and it is despatched by post to Lewismen in distant parts of the globe. Derek Cooper quotes a friend who has eaten Guga and testifies to its tensile strength and toughness: 'more a tribute to tradition than a gourmet feast. It tastes a bit like sea-saturated duck'. In Barra it was called Mingulay duck.[43]

There are still recipes for the Gannet, as in this modification of a St Kildan recipe for Braised Solan Goose given me by Ann Wyllie of Montrose:

Pluck, prepare and hang the bird in the usual way. Place the bird in a pan of cold water along with carrots, herbs such as lemon balm, thyme, bay leaf and parsley. Add salt and freshly ground pepper and simmer gently for two hours. Test with a fork (hard boiling will toughen the meat). Allow to cool in the liquor. Serve the meat cold with vegetables; a sauce may be made by reduction of the vegetables and liquid from the cooking pot 'chaudfroid' (A jellied sauce rather like aspic.) Another recipe for Gannet recommends cooking them as for Wild Goose.

Dr Janet Henderson of Grantown-on-Spey wrote to me that her cook remembered roasting Capercaillie with an onion in its crop—but she hung it for a week first. There is another school of thought, she added, which prefers burying to hanging. Some stuff their Cappers with steak, while yet others say the bird is so unpalatable that recipes suggest hanging the bird for weeks with onions and then discarding the bird in favour of the onions!

74

The 1912 edition of *Mrs Beeton's Book of Household Management*[16] shows that many birds still found their way to the kitchen. In her introduction she says 'There is no bird, nor any bird's egg, that is known to be poisonous, though they may, and often do, become unwholesome by reason of the food that the birds eat, which at all times greatly changes the quality of the flesh, even in birds of the same breed'.

Some of Mrs Beeton's recipes sound almost like nursery rhymes, for example 'Blackbird Pie': 'After stuffing the birds with forcemeat they are halved and placed in a pie-dish on top of sliced rump steak and interspersed with hardboiled eggs. The dish is then half filled with good stock and baked for an hour and a half.' (Mrs Beeton commented 'cost uncertain, blackbirds being seldom sold'). Thrush must be buttered and covered in paper (not bacon which would impair the delicate flavour of the birds) and roasted side by side on a skewer and served on croutes with a garnish of watercress. Corncrake, she said, should be trussed with the head under the wing and the thighs close to the sides and roasted.

Several writers, having experimented with birds which were popular food items of the past, commented on them: as for the young Fulmar— 'experimentally, we ate it, fried in its own grease. A chicken cooked in engine oil might have been similar'.[12] And W.H. Hudson[91] found Shelduck tough, dry and fishy-tasting. 'We loved to see the Sheldrakes flying about on the coast, but how we hated to see them brought in to be cooked for dinner.' Hudson also tells a tale of two sisters whose brother shot a Heron and proclaimed it to be a great luxury. Days and weeks went by and the Heron was suspended in a vacant room. When the brother judged the Heron to have reached perfection the sisters were instructed to pluck and clean it. A trout about a foot long was found decomposing inside the bird's gullet. The horrible smell of the bird cooking pervaded the whole house but the brother assured his sisters it would be a delicacy. The time came to carve the bird and he took a large mouthful. A change came over his face, he turned pale and, with his mouth still full, he rose and fled from the room.[91]

Scottish birds are not all so unpalatable. F. Marian McNeill eulogises soup made of Grouse, Pheasant, Blackcock, Ptarmigan, Partridge and other game as better in Scotland than elsewhere, but notes that old birds are nearly hopeless except as soup.[127]

Birds and fashion

By the 1950s more ladies were in the butts potting away with their menfolk. There were not many of them but their influence turned many rather basic bachelor shelters into comfortable and gracious homes. The 'twelfth' became increasingly fashionable with city tailors and dress designers catering for the need of smart, practical clothes for the moors. In the 1930s golf jackets and plus-fours (*de rigueur* for the butts) cost six guineas and Ladies sports coats and matching skirts were ten guineas ...with a 10% discount in August! Everyone was in on the act and advertisements informed the sportsman of all he needed from his boots to the game despatch boxes he would use to send his trophies home. Of course the motor salemen were to the fore; the indispensable transport between the wars was 'a Ford V-8 30 h.p. Utility Car ideal for the Country House.' It cost a mere £260! One advertisement discreetly pointed out that marksmanship was improved by a regular intake of Eno's Fruit Salt. Shooting magazines in the early 1900s carried advertisements for accessories such as silver hip flasks (the pint size then cost £5.42p in current coinage) and shooting sticks were a guinea. A solid gold case containing ivory counters for allotting positions on a drive cost little more. Jewellers flourished, with diamond-spangled Grouse depicted on brooches, bangles, pins and cuff-links. A Woodcock brooch made of fine quality diamonds with a ruby eye could be had for a mere £23.10 shillings.[125]

At this time the millinery trade in plumage was astronomical. In the first decade of the twentieth century Britain alone imported 6,000 tons, or 20 million pounds worth of feathers. Between 1906 and 1908 65,000 Terns of various species were sold in London purely for human decoration. Even fishermen were a threat to birds, and in Scotland the Dotterel and many other species were sought after for tying fishing flies. In 1917 regulations were introduced leading to the banning of importation and use of plumage in 1921.

PART TWO: THE BIRD FAMILIES
Introduction

In this part of the book the object is to create a picture of the commoner Scottish birds by examining their history, nomenclature, literary references and mythology.

The species are arranged as they are found in most field guides. Each is introduced by a note on the Order to which it belongs with an indication of numbers within that Order both worldwide and in Scotland.

The Standard name for each of 195 species is followed by its scientific, or Linnaean, name with its meaning.[96]

Under the rubric SCOTS NAMES are listed names for the species used in Scotland now or in the past.[37, 79, 108] Where names are associated with regions these are indicated using abbreviated forms of the former Scottish counties (for list of abbreviations see p.xi). Where such names are in general Scottish use they are not followed by county names. The names of species draw on several different languages of Scotland including Norn, Gaelic, Lallans and English. Norn, derived from Norse, was the language of Orkney and Shetland, which was spoken there rather than Gaelic until the nineteenth century. Lallans, the language of the Lowlands, is a complex language derived from many others including English, Gaelic and some continental languages. It was the literary language of Scotland from about the fifteenth century. Occasional references are made to some other European languages where they have influenced common Scottish bird names. One other manner of speech, sometimes referred to, is noa. Formerly, especially among fisherfolk, some topics were thought to be associated with ideas of such profound significance that even to mention a name risked invoking disaster. Thus, instead of referring to the Devil, a noa substitute might be 'The Dark One'.

The rubric GAELIC NAMES precedes Gaelic names.[35, 56, 61, 121] Gaelic is so rich in synonyms, to say nothing of alternative spellings, that for some birds there are many such names. For the sake of brevity they are here limited to a maximum of three. Gaelic names are italicized and are followed by approximate translations in regular typeface. Translations are often difficult because a single word may have many meanings depending on context, thus a given bird name may have several possible translations.

A brief history of the species follows the explanation of names. Early history is available mostly from England, where more alkaline soils have preserved fragile traces of Pleistocene avifauna better. However the presence of highly mobile bird species in the south indicates the likelihood of them also being present in Scotland during relatively warm interglacials.[19, 59, 82, 86, 108, 162, 178, 201]

Q: Indicates one or more quotations for most species. These are drawn from Scottish literature, or from writing about Scotland by authorities of their day, with a handful of references of classical or general interest

T: Finally the influence of the species on tradition, mythology, superstition, folk and religious belief is discussed with examples from various writers, including Celtic and Scandinavian sources, which have been important in the development of Scottish culture.[10, 35, 48, 61, 111, 177, 190]

ORDER: GAVIFORMES
Family: *Gaviidae*, the Divers
(Latin *Gavia:* a gull or sea mew.)
No. in world, 5; no. in Scotland, 4.

Red-throated Diver
Gavia stellata
(*stellata:* Latin, sparkling or glittering.)

SCOTS NAMES: Arran Ake [Dumb], Burrain [Ayr], Kakera, Loom [Shet], Lumme, Rain Goose [NS], Speckled Diver, Sprat Loon.

GAELIC NAMES: *Learga-chaol*, also *Learga-fairge* or *-mhor*. *Learga* refers to the shore or surface of the sea. *Chaol* means narrow, *fairge* also means sea and *mhor* is great. The Gaelic names refer to breeding sites in small lochs.

The name Red-throated Diver derives from Red-throat Ducker or Loon of Edwards in 1737;[58] the present name dates from Pennant in 1776.[148] Loon, from the Old Norse *lomr*, now literally means fool, which probably derives from the bird's loud wailing cry, so characteristic of Divers. Burrain is a Gaelic word meaning roarer and Kakera is onomatopoeic.

Like all Divers this is a very primitive bird, which may have been more numerous in the Pleistocene when Tundra was more widespread. Fisher[59] mentions records from the Pleistocene of 160,000 years ago and evidence of the Red-throated Diver has been found in Norfolk as long as 500,000 years ago. Distinction between the Red and Black-throated Divers was not made until Pennant separated them in 1776 after he had seen them in Assynt in 1772 on his tour of Scotland.[147] Though decreasing during the nineteenth century the species is now more numerous (especially in Northern and Western Scottish islands) and believed to be increasing. In winter resident birds are joined by migrants from Greenland and Arctic Scandinavia.

The most northerly of divers, Red-throats breed on small hill lochs in the Scottish Highlands and Islands from Arran to Shetland travelling long distances to feed at sea. In their spectacular courtship display they race across the water, their bodies half submerged with head and neck pointed forward, looking so like serpents that this is called the snake ceremony. Courtship includes bill-dipping and splash-diving. During these displays pairs duet with a wailing chorus. The flight call has been represented as 'Kwuk-kwuk-kwuk'.

Q: In MacGillivray's mid-nineteenth century *History of British Birds* it is noted that in winter 'numerous individuals of this species are met with on most parts of our coasts, but more especially in bays and estuaries ...In the end of spring the greater number probably betaking themselves to the arctic regions, although very many remain to breed by the inland lakes of the Highlands, Hebrides, Orkney and Shetland.'[118]

Seton Gordon describes watching a pair swimming in their sleep in a South Uist loch.[71]

Describing the birds on Skye, Richard Perry wrote: 'Solitary Red-throated Divers, with beautiful mole-grey mantles and dazzlingly white bellies were to be seen off the promontories. They nested on the opposite mainland, a thousand feet up on the naked Gneiss hills, on lily-carpeted lochans among the bogs...'[149]

T: Divers play a large part in mythology from earliest times and are supposed to have helped in the creation of the world by diving beneath the waters to bring up mud.

In Northern Scotland the Red-throated Diver is said to predict rain with its cry. 'The rain goose, bigger than a duck, makes a doleful noise before a great rain.'[126]

It was believed that divers incubated their eggs under the wing where they had a special pouch for the purpose, much as the Emperor Penguin has. This belief persisted into the nineteenth century, probably because early bird artists, such as Audubon, working from specimens damaged by shooting, tried to arrange their subjects in life-like postures and in so doing produced anatomical distortion.

Black-throated Diver
Gavia arctica
(*arctica*: pertaining to the North)

SCOTS NAMES: Lumme, Lesser Imber, Northern Doucker, Speckled Loon.

GAELIC NAMES: *Learg dubh, Broilleach-bothan*. See Red-throated Diver; *dubh* = black, *broilleach* is breast and *bothan* like a sheiling or hut.

The Black-throated Diver is rare in Britain and has attracted few local names, many of which also apply to the Great Northern Diver.

The Black-throated and Great Northern Divers are not as ancient as the Red Throated and probably date from late Pleistocene. Black-throated Diver populations declined during the nineteenth and early twentieth century. There are now some 150 breeding pairs, mostly in Scottish islands where the population is thought to be stable or in gradual decline due to egg predation and water level fluctuations.

Q: Seton Gordon stated: 'The Black-throated Diver never comes to land and lays her eggs as near as possible to the water's edge, so that she may dive, seal-like, into the friendly depths on the approach of danger.'[69]

Atkinson describes how these divers sometimes submerge until only head and neck were showing like a periscope.[12]

T: The legs and feet of divers are set very far back and Scandinavian Peasants believe that this came about because the bird was originally formed without feet and that Nature, realising its mistake, flung a pair of legs after it. In Benbecula and North Uist it is said that in dry weather the Black-throated Diver calls '*Deoch! Deoch! Deoch! thair loch a trasgadh*': 'Drink! Drink! Drink! The loch is drying up'.

Black-throated Divers nest close to water and sometimes lose their brood if water levels dry up; when that happens they sing:

> *Mo chreach! Mo chreach!*
> *M'eoin is m'uibhean.*
> My sorrow! my sorrow!
> My chicks and eggs.[35]

Great Northern Diver
Gavia immer

(*Immer:* Scandinavian name for ember goose; also possibly from Icelandic *himbrimi*, the surf-roarer)

SCOTS NAMES: Allan or Arran Hawk [Ayr, Arg], Ammer Goose [Aber, Loth], Bishop, Bunivochil [Heb], Carara Loon, Cobble, Ember [Ork], Ember Goose or Gos, Great Doucker, Gunner, Holland Hawk, Imber Diver, Immer, Immer Goose [Ork, Shet], Leam, Loom, Loon, Ring-necked Loon or Diver [Loth], Naak or Nauk.

GAELIC NAMES: *Muir-bhuachaill* or *Bun-bhuachaill.* Great, or dumpy, herdsman, shepherd of the sea.

81

'Arran Hawk' is not a geographical name, as one might suppose, but comes from the Gaelic word *aranaig* which imitates the bird's call. Bishop, from the Gaelic word *easbuig*, came about as a noa word because names of this species were tabooed as its eery cry associated the bird with many superstitious supernatural qualities. The Hebridean name of Bunivochil is a corruption of Gaelic *buna-bhuachaill*. Carara and Holland Hawk are also derived from *aranaig*. Ember, from the Norwegian word *imbre*, arose because, traditionally the bird arrived off the Norwegian Coast during the ember days before Christmas. The reference to Christmas may have been another attempt to modify the evil reputation of the bird. Naak and Nauk refer to the call.

The Great Northern Diver is an Arctic species, from where it extends its winter range to include Scotland and Scandinavia. It is a doubtful breeding species though there may be occasional nesting pairs in small Scottish islands (such as Soay off the Southern coast of Skye).[64] In winter numbers in British coastal waters may reach over 4,000. A related species, the White-billed Diver, *Gavia adamsii*, is occasionally seen in northern Scottish waters.

Q: Writing of the Great Northern Diver (in 1698) Martin Martin said: 'The minister of North-Uist told me that he killed one of them, which weighed sixteen pounds and an ounce. There was about an inch deep of fat upon the skin of it, which natives apply to the hip bone, and by experience find it a successful remedy for removing the sciatica.'[126]

In the *Old Statistical Account*[145] a Shetland minister commented: 'This bird is remarkable for its strong structure of body; for though considerably less in size than the common grey goose, it weighs a great deal more. It is never seen on the land; and though it has pretty large wings, it is never seen to fly... Nor does nature seem to have intended that it ever should fly; for in whatever manner it is attacked, pursued, or suddenly surprised, it always has recourse to diving for its safety.'[145] 'The Great Northern Diver is becoming quite scarce, whereas it used to be common.'[119]

T: Highland tradition tells of a great sea-monster, the *uilebheist*. A similar creature, the *boobrie*, haunted lochs in Argyllshire where a witness described it as resembling an enormous Great Northern Diver with white patches on the neck and breast: 'the neck was long and the beak hooked like an Eagle's. The feet were webbed with tremendous claws. The footprints of the *boobrie* covered a space equal to that contained within the span of a pair of large antlers, and its voice was like the roar of an angry bull'.[177]

It was believed by the people of the Western Isles that this Diver grew through several stages before it reached maturity. For the first seven years of its life it was a Dabchick. It then changed into a Green Cormorant or Shag, then it became a Cormorant with white spots on its belly and it was not until it was twenty-one that it became a Bun a' Bhuchaille or Great Northern Diver.[69]

ORDER: PODICIPEDIFORMES
THE GREBES

Family: *Podicipitidae*, the Grebes

(From *Podiceps Podex*: Latin, vent, *Pes*: foot, hence vent-footed.)
No. in world, 21; no. in Scotland, 4.

Great Crested Grebe
Podiceps cristatus

(*cristatus:* Latin, crested)

SCOTS NAMES: Arsefoot, Crested Douker [Loth], Tippet Grebe. Douker is a local variant of diver.

GAELIC NAMES: *Gobhlachan laparan*: *Gobhlachan* means horned, *laparan* probably comes from *làpch* a swamp.

The paucity of Scottish names probably reflects the bird's recent arrival in northern Scotland. Arsefoot refers to the posterior position of the bird's legs and Tippet refers to the nineteenth century use of the bird's plumage for millinery (see p.64). The generic name Grebe is said to derive from Breton *Grib*, a comb.[61]

Remains of the Great Crested Grebe are absent from Ice Age deposits but appear in Bronze and Iron Age sites in Eastern England. Numbers remained low through the Middle Ages and started to increase during the eighteenth and nineteenth centuries. Pennant[147] saw several Great Crested Grebes in the fens as he travelled to Scotland in 1771, but would have been unlikely to see the species in Scotland where it was not recorded breeding before 1877,[13] when a pair bred on the Loch of the Lowes in Perthshire (and where they still do). Since then the species has gradually colonised Central Scotland; there were about 7,000 in 1979 and the number has increased since.

Most Great Crested Grebes breed in northern Eurasia and move south to the Mediterranean, to Asia Minor and northern India in winter.

The population has increased with the flooding of gravel pits and extension of reservoirs so that most stretches of open water south of the Great Glen now have their Great Crested Grebes.

Q: 'They have a wonderful courtship-ceremony: both birds hold weeds in their bills, meet each other breast to breast with their necks raised and shake their heads at each other with their chestnut-and-black ear-tufts spread'.[93]

Writing in the nineteenth century, MacGillivray observes: 'In winter it occurs along our sea coasts especially in estuaries, but seldom in large numbers... Although indigenous it is much more uncommon in summer than in winter.'[118] A little later in the century another writer finds that its numbers are increasing: 'Notwithstanding the persecution to which this remarkably beautiful species was formerly subjected, to satisfy the fancy of ladies for its breast feathers for their personal adornment... of late years it has appeared and breeds in several localities where it was previously almost unknown.'[107]

Slavonian Grebe
Podiceps auritus

(*auritus*: Latin, having large or outstanding ears.)

SCOTS NAMES: Horned Grebe, Dobchick, Sclavonian Grebe

GAELIC NAMES: *Spàgritòn* (also Little Grebe). *Spàgair*: one who walks awkwardly and *ton*: anus or breech.

Horned grebe or Dobchick dates from Pennant[148] but was later superseded by Sclavonian (an obsolete form of Slavonian) Grebe by Yarrell.[201] The name first appeared in Montagu's *Ornithological Dictionary* of 1802[135] with reference to it being found in Sclavonia (a region bounded by the rivers Danube, Sava and Drava).

There is little evidence of this Grebe before the Bronze Age. The bird was first recorded in Britain in 1796. Scotland holds the entire British breeding population of Slavonian Grebes. It is a migrant, breeding in the Arctic, but nesting was first recorded in Inverness in 1908, and the main area of expansion has been based around there. Nesting has been recorded in Sutherland and Caithness since 1929. In 1973 a pair bred at the Loch of the Lowes in Perthshire.[192]

Slavonian Grebes breed from Iceland, and from Scandinavia to northern Scotland, migrating as far south as the Black and Caspian Seas. Occasional wintering birds may be seen in sheltered inland waters but are easily missed as the winter plumage is dull at distance. They are less shy than other Grebes and may be seen in remote Scottish lochs where they breed. The distinct breeding plumage and a courtship behaviour similar to that of the Great Crested Grebe make them easier to identify in summer than in winter. The young may be carried on the backs of the swimming adults.

Q: 'This bird,' according to Lord Lilford at the end of the nineteenth century, 'although by no means an uncommon autumnal or winter visitor... has not yet been found breeding in any part of the United Kingdom.'[107] Saunders, writing at about the same time, adds 'In Scotland it is generally distributed on both coasts, and in the Hebrides, Orkneys and Shetlands it is even common.'[162]

A single Slavonian Grebe, the first seen in Perthshire by the author, was spotted in mid-December 2000.

Black-necked Grebe
Podiceps nigricollis
(*nigricollis*: Latin, *niger* black, *collum* neck.)

SCOTS NAMES: Black Grebe, Eared Grebe, Lesser Crested Grebe, Dusky Grebe or Black and White Dobchick.

GAELIC NAMES: None.

Called the Eared Grebe by Pennant since 1768[148] the name was changed to Black-necked Grebe in 1912, adjusting it to the scientific name *nigricollis*.

Like the Slavonian Grebe the Black-necked was a relatively late invader of Britain. Pennant identifies the species as inhabitants of the Fens in 1771, describing it as the 'black and dusky Grebe' referring to its summer and winter plumage. It is a rare British breeder, almost confined to oligotrophic lochs in north-west Scotland. It colonised Scotland in 1930 and occasionally breeds as far south as Midlothian. There was an estimated Scottish population of about 150 pairs in the late 1980s. In winter it may be found on similar waters, but without cover, or on the sea close to shore, but it seeks large expanses of water with good reed cover when breeding. Behaviour is like the Slavonian Grebe but shyer, especially when breeding, rarely moving away from cover until dusk. It may be seen taking insects off the water surface with quick right and left head movements.

Q: Keith Brockie, in his lovely book *The Silvery Tay*,[23] portrays a Black-necked Grebe sketched among other birds at Morton Lochs near Tayport in August 1987.

Little Grebe or Dabchick
Tachybaptus ruficollis

(*Tachybaptus*: Greek, *tachus* swift, *bapto* dip, hence 'quick dipping'. *Ruficollis*: Latin, *rufus* red, *collum* neck.)

SCOTS NAMES: Assefoot or Arsefoot, Bonnetie [For], Didapper, Diver [Renf], Dobchick, Dobbler, Doucker [Perth], Little Footy Arse [Ork], Loon, Mither o' the Mawkins [Stir], Penny Bird, Small or Little Doucker [Loth] or Ducker, Tom Pudding.

GAELIC NAMES: *Spàgaire tonn*, *Gobhachan* or *Fàd-monaidh*. (See Slavonian Grebe.) Little scold or peaty one of the moors.

Many of the vernacular names reflect the Little Grebe's habit of diving when threatened. Some names, like Loon or Arsefoot (see Gaelic name) it shares with other Grebes, and Bonnetie suggests association with the millinery trade. Mawkins or Malkins were lewd women, a name also applied to hares. Hares were known as bawds in Lowland Scotland and were reputed to be disguised witches. Why the Dabchick should have mothered them is obscure but perhaps relates to their sudden disappearance when pursued.[61] Tom Pudding refers to the bird's rounded shape.

Iron Age evidence of Little Grebes is to be found in England. With increasing cold between the fourteenth and nineteenth centuries its numbers declined but rose again with the warmer period after that. It is susceptible to cold in hard winters and this probably accounts for its rarity in early Scottish records, however it is now abundant in the Central Lowlands though scarce in the north-west Highlands and Islands.

A shy and skulking species, it dives quickly and suddenly, often with a distinct 'plop', and may remain underwater for up to 25 seconds. Sometimes, when alarmed, it will dive and then cautiously rise to 'periscope' depth with only its head above the surface observing its surroundings. Often more heard than seen: the common call is a high-pitched whinny like a horse heard from a distance.

Q: Writing early in the nineteenth century Charles St John described the

Little Grebe's migration to Scotland: 'Another singular bird visits this country regularly in the spring, the lesser grebe (in England commonly called the dabchick). It is difficult to understand how this bird makes out its journey from the region, wherever it may be, where they pass the winter. No bird is less adapted for a long flight, yet they suddenly appear in some rushy loch.'[161]

Half a century later MacGillivray commented: 'In summer, this species is not uncommon even in the most northern parts of Scotland, as well as in the Outer Hebrides, where, however, I think it is not found in winter. Although generally dispersed, it is not plentiful in the middle and southern parts of Scotland.'[118]

ORDER: PROCELLARIIFORMES
THE TUBENOSES

Family: *Procellaridae*, the Shearwaters and Petrels

(Latin: *procella* a storm.)
No. in world 72; no. in Scotland 4 (+ some vagrants).

Manx Shearwater
Puffinus puffinus

(*Puffinus* is a contrived Latin word from Middle English *pophyn*, derived from 'puffing out'. Puffins and many other seabirds used for food have round, puffed-out bellies.)

SCOTS NAMES: Baakie Craa [Shet], Booty [Shet], Common Shearwater [N. Atl], Facach, Leerie, Lyre or Lyrie [Ork], Night Bird, Puffin, Rockall Jack, Scrabe or Scraber [Heb], Scraib, Scrapire, Skapur [Far], Skidder.

GAELIC NAMES: *Sgrail, Fachach.* See Puffin. (No distinction is made between several common food species.) In Gaelic the young Shearwater, commonly used as food, is called '*Gille bog*': a soft, fat fellow (young birds were often given in large numbers in lieu of rent[61]).

Many Shearwater names reflect their flight, which shears or cleaves the waves; for example the Shetland name 'Booty' probably derives from the

Norse word *byta*, to divide (which also gives rise to the meaning of booty as a share). In the Faeroes it is Skapur (probably from *Skrabe* which is Norwegian for scraper), which, in turn, led to several Scottish names such as Skidden, Skinner and Scraber. Baakie, in Baakie Cra or Crow, is a Norn name (from Old Norse *svartbakr* for black back—see Greater Black Backed Gull). Lira was possibly an Old Norse name, since Lyre and Lyrie occur among Scottish and Orcadian names for Shearwaters.

Fossil evidence confirms the presence of the Manx Shearwater in Britain since the early Holocene. The species has few enemies other than man but, because of the burrow-nesting habit of this and other Shearwaters, its eggs and young are easily collected. Traces of Manx Shearwater have been found in Pictish middens of the eighth or ninth century. Until 1800, when it was destroyed by rats, the stronghold of the species was the Calf of Man where the colony was the largest ever known. The birds did not breed in Man again until 1967, but are now established there again. There were also small colonies in the Faeroes and the Hebrides (especially Rum).

Manx Shearwaters are almost entirely pelagic except when breeding. In autumn they migrate to the South Atlantic, wintering on the South American coast. Returning in February they take a westerly route via eastern Canada before returning to the breeding grounds.

Q: In the *Old Statistical Account* for Kirkwall the writer commented: 'The lyre, which is a bird somewhat larger than a pigeon, and though extraordinary fat, and moreover very fishy tasted, is thought by some to be extremely delicious.'[145]

And in the *New Statistical Account* for the Parish of Kilmuir in Skye: 'They lay in burrows, which are dug horizontally in the ground... in winding little passages from 10 to 15 feet in length. The male, for the most part, undertakes the task of forming this little circuitous tunnel, and for that purpose he throws himself on his back, in which position he picks and digs with his hard sharp bill, and casts out the loose earth or mould with his broad webbed-feet.'[142]

'In late summer and autumn Manx Shearwaters are beginning to disperse from their breeding slopes on Rum and are often encountered, skimming gracefully over the waves with rigid straight wings.'[48]

T: Fraser Darling tells the story of a mainland shepherd who took a job in Eigg unaware of the nesting Shearwaters. He had not been in his house a week when the birds began shrieking all night, and after this nothing would induce him to remain.[49]

Fulmar
Fulmarus glacialis

(*Fulmarus* is an old Norse word from *ful* meaning foul and *mar*, a gull.
Glacialis refers to Iceland where the species was first recorded.)

SCOTS NAMES: Mallie [Shet], Malmock, Mallduck [Ork, Shet], Mallemock,
Mallemuck, Mallimoke [Ork, Shet], Molly-mawk, Mallimack or Mall Duck
[Ork].

GAELIC NAMES: *Fulmair*, *Mulcaire* or *Eun-crom*; i.e. Fulmar, one who
dives, or *Eun* a fowl, *crom* curved.

Many of these names are derived from the Dutch *mal*: foolish, *mok*: gull, a
description introduced by Dutch sailors. Its 'foolishness' is probably ascribed
to it because the bird sits so tightly on its nest that it can be caught by
hand. Woe betide the man who tries, for the Fulmar will spit copious quantities of foul-smelling oil over him. This has given rise to the name Fulmar,
which literally means 'foul gull' and probably derives from *Foumart*, a pole-
cat, because of the bird's unpleasant smell.

Fulmars may have been comparatively rare in Northern waters until the end
of the eighteenth century when whaling became commonplace. Originally the
Fulmar was unique to St Kilda. Thomas Edward, writing in the latter part
of the nineteenth century, noted that the 'Fulmar Petrel was an occasional
winter visitor to the Banffshire coast' but he had only had one specimen.[174]
   In 1878 twelve pairs of prospecting birds colonised Shetland; the species
reached Orkney in 1900 and the mainland of Scotland in 1902. Since then
there has been a geometric population increase, from 50,000 in 1904 to 270,000
in 1959. This rise mirrored the production of fish offal which rose from

400 cwt. in 1904 to 1,700 cwt. in 1959. Like all the *Procellaridae* Fulmars feed greedily on oily substances and the early whaling practice of flensing carcasses along the ship's side provided banquets for them and their population increased very fast. Today fish offal produced by fish factory ships also contributes to their success.

Young Fulmar spend several years wandering widely at sea before breeding and there are few oceans where they are not seen. Breeding sites now include Britain, Iceland, Greenland and islands in the north Pacific. Following breeding there is a widespread dispersal in August or September throughout the northern hemisphere. Fulmars start congregating at nesting sites in early summer. When not brooding its young the Fulmar spends hours wheeling with rigid wings and fanned tail round the cliff on which it has built its scanty nest.

Q: Writing in the middle of the twentieth century, Rintoul and Baxter commented: 'The spread of the Fulmar as a breeding bird in Scotland has been so rapid as to merit the epithet phenomenal. Until 1878 its only known breeding colony in Scotland was on St Kilda; in that year it was recorded breeding on Foula and since then has spread until at the present day it breeds in great numbers on many of the cliffs round our coasts and on the islands.'[13]

A romantic description of the bird appears in Seton Gordon's *A Highland Year*: 'How silently do the Fulmar petrels glide, for a moment they are seen, sailing on wings which seem held always so stiffly, so rigidly, and then, almost before the eye has realised their presence, they are gone, steering an unerring course through mist-held aerial seas.'[69]

T: A St Kildan belief states that a Fulmar seeking land indicates bad weather. In Iceland it is believed the name derives from *Fole mar*, sea horse, from its sound when breathing heavily like a snorting horse or because it resembles a horse's gallop when taking off from water.

Family: *Hydrobatidae*, the Storm Petrels

(Greek, *hudro-* water; *bates* a dweller; or possibly *baino* to go or tread).
No. in world 20; no. in Scotland 2 (+ vagrants).

Storm Petrel
Hydrobates pelagicus

(*pelagicus*: Latin, from *pelagus* the open sea.)

SCOTS NAMES: Alamonti [Ork], Allamotti or Alamouti [Shet], Assilag
[Heb], Gourder or Gourdal, Goylir, Little Petrel, Mitey, Mitty, Mootie
[Ork], Mother Carey's Chicken, Oily-mootie [Foula], Storm Finch [Ork], Sea
Swallow or Swallow [Shet], Spence, Spencie or Spency [Heb], Stormy Petrel,
Waterwitch or Witch.

GAELIC NAMES: *Assilag, Luaireag, Paraig.* Storm petrel, of St Peter.

The name Petrel derives from Italian *Petrello*, little Peter, because, like St
Peter, during storms these birds appear to walk upon the water as they
fly through the wave troughs patting the water with their feet. Alamonti
(in various spellings), Mitey and Mitty also come from Italian *ala*, a wing
and *monte*, to mount, so meaning a bird for ever on the wing. Gourder or
Gourdal derive from the Gaelic word *guadaire*, a whirler, from the flight
behaviour of Storm Petrels over their nest burrows. Assilag is from the
Gaelic word *easchal*, a storm, as are the Witch names. Goylir is also Gaelic,
used in Lewis of a bird the size of a Swallow, said never to come ashore,
except in the month of January.[56] The Hirundine-like flight at sea and white
rump give rise to names involving Swallow or Martin, and the common

Procellariform habit of ejecting stomach contents at aggressors adds 'oil' as in Oily-mootie. This name recalls the island custom of threading a wick through the carcase of a Storm Petrel, from cloaca to bill, and lighting it as a lamp. Spence, sometimes with the Norn suffix -ie (as in Bonxie), is of unknown origin.

There is little known about the past history of the Storm Petrel before the end of the nineteenth century, though Martin Martin[126] mentioned them breeding in St Kilda. During the twentieth century there was a decrease in the Scottish population of Storm Petrels, but because of their nocturnal visits to nesting sites on remote islands they are difficult to count. They breed in large communities on islands in the North Atlantic and Mediterranean between April and October and migrate south as far as South Africa between October and April. Storm Petrels are pelagic except when breeding. Dusk and dark gloomy days give the best chance of seeing them.

Q: Martin Martin, writing about the life of seventeenth century St Kilda, gives a precise description of the Storm Petrel: 'The assilag is as large as a lint-white; black bill, wide nostrils at the upper part, crooked at the point like the fulmar's bill'.[126] Osgood Mackenzie describes expeditions in the 1920s to *Eilean Fuara*, where his terrier discovered Stormies nesting in the cracks in the peat. *Fuara* became famous afterwards among ornithologists until herring fishermen took to hanging their nets there to dry, driving the Petrels away.[119]

Storm Petrels sometimes are blown far inland, as Bishop Stanley reported: 'In 1832 upwards of twenty instances occurred, and many of them in the midst of crowded towns; thus after a series of tempestuous weather, one was captured, which had been seen flying up and down the streets of a populous town, about seven or eight feet above the ground, apparently much exhausted.'[178]

Fraser Darling mentions otters catching them on Eilean a' Chleirich, biting off the head, and the tail with the legs attached, then eating the body but leaving the wings.[49]

T: Sailors detest Storm Petrels as harbingers of bad weather; they were believed to be invisible during calm weather but appeared at the threat of storm. They caused more fear than the storms they supposedly predicted.

Petrels are said to embody the souls of wicked captains who have ill-treated their crews and, as punishment, are condemned to fly forever over the deep. Others say they are the souls of drowned men imploring prayers from the living, or they are sent from Hell to hover over the corpses of those lost at sea. They are known in many languages as Mother Carey's Chickens, but her identity is unclear. Yarell[201] says that the name was bestowed by Captain

Carteret's sailors from some unknown hag of that name who may have been a witch (hence Waterwitch as a name for the Storm Petrel). Others suggest the name may have originally been Mother Mary or have derived from *Mater Cara*, Dear Mother, the Virgin Mary, protector of these birds and from whom they are sent as warnings of storms.[111] Nailing a horseshoe to the mast deflected the Storm Petrels' evil powers. The combined influence of iron and horses protected against evil.[10] The phrase 'Mother Carey plucking her chickens', in common usage among Scots, refers to snow falling.

Leach's Petrel
Oceanodroma leucorhoa

(*Oceanodroma:* Greek, *okeanos* the ocean and *dromos* running; *leukos* white, *orrhus* the rump.)

SCOTS NAME: Forkie (little distinction is made between British and Leach's Storm Petrel's vernacular names.)

GAELIC NAME: *Gobhlan Mara*. Forked-tailed Storm Petrel; literally, forked one of the sea.

At present Leach's Storm Petrels breed on St Kilda, the Flannan Islands, North Rona and Sula Sgeir and a few areas in Shetland.[86]

Q: Writing about a visit to North Rona, Fraser Darling describes hearing the sound of Leach's fork-tailed Petrel from midnight on.[49] Robert Atkinson found that little featherweight Storm Petrels, 'neat and smoothly glossy with black bills tiny and hooked, little spindle legs' made the fork-tails seem almost clumsy.[12]

Michael Robson records Harvie-Brown's visit to Rona in 1885: 'They set to work heaving out the stones from the walls and digging away at the earth so as to uncover the birds in their burrows. After an hour and a half they had discovered several forktailed and two stormy petrels.'[158]

ORDER: PELECANIFORMES
PELICANS AND ALLIES

Family: *Sulidae*, the Gannets and Boobies

(*Sula*: an Icelandic name for a booby or foolish person.)
No. in world, 9; no. in Scotland, 1.

Gannet
Sula bassana

(*Bassana*: from the Bass Rock in the Firth of Forth.)

SCOTS NAMES: Bass Goose, Basser [For], Booby, Channel Goose, Gant [Aber, Fif], Mackerel or Herring Gant, Solan Goose, Soland [Low], Spectacled Goose.

Guga or Goug: the young gannet prized as a food delicacy in St Kilda and the Hebrides.

GAELIC NAMES: *Sùlaire, Caraid-nan-Gàidheal, Eun bàn an sgadain*. Gannet, Spouse or lover of the Gael, White bird of the herring.

The Gannet has played a large part in man's affairs as a food source, so that its names are old and of confused etymology. The word gannet derives from the same roots as goose (Latin *ganta*) and was interchangeable until the late fifteenth century. The old Norse word *Sula* would also have been used. Eventually 'Gannet' became the accepted English term while names deriving from *Sula* became absorbed into Gaelic. The archaic Gaelic word *sulan* literally means a cleft stick and refers to the crossed black wingtips of a sitting adult bird, which would have been easily seen by hunters at the gannetries. The word *sulan* derives in turn from another Norse word *svala*, which later gave rise to another bird name: swallow (see p.220). Other names refer to the sites of huge colonies such as the Bass Rock.

Remains of Gannets have been identified from stone age sea-caves from a period which ended about 2000 BC, and from mesolithic shell mounds in Orkney. Since the Iron Age the Gannet has been a human food source because it is easily caught (hence the name 'booby' meaning foolish) and highly nutritious. It was mentioned in Anglo-Saxon poetry[18] in which the sea is referred to as 'the Gannet's bath'. Gannet remains have been found in Pictish middens of the eighth to ninth centuries. St Kilda has been known as a gannetry since the eighth century.

Gannets are now protected (apart from Sula Sgeir, North of Lewis, where Guga are still legally hunted from September to January by men from Ness).

From breeding sites on rocks such as Ailsa Craig, the Bass and Sula Sgeir dark-plumaged youngsters accompany their parents for the first six months of life while learning to fish. They then disperse and, for six years, wander south to the coast of Africa. Aging, they slowly return via the Mediterranean to their breeding grounds.

The spectacular sight of Gannets fishing, when they circle at height, before diving, bomb-like, to crash into the sea, is breathtaking.

The cacophony at Gannetries is overwhelming but birds know their mates' voices. Gannets returning to the nest fly to the bottom of the cliff, ascending on the updraft, calling as they climb. The mate on the nest ignores the mass of calling birds until it hears the unmistakable (to it) call of its mate, when it replies immediately.

Q: The Gannet was mentioned in Bower's *Scotichronicon* (written in the 1460s)[82] as breeding at the Bass Rock, and it featured along with many other birds in a satirical poem on James II of Scotland, *The Buke of the Howlat.*[90]

Ray wrote of Gannets at the Bass Rock in 1661: 'The young ones are esteemed a choice dish in Scotland, and sold very dear 9 for 1s. 8d plucked. We ate of them at Dunbar.'[155] Curiously Ray did not realise that the Solan Geese he saw at the Bass Rock were the same species as the Gannets in Cornwall, where Gannets were caught 'by tying a pilchard to a board... so that the bird comes down with so great a swiftness that he breaks his neck against the board.'[112] A similar method was used in some Hebridean Islands. Robert Gordon of Stralloch in *The Story of the Bass* (1654) gives a full and beautiful description of the Solan Goose, perpetuating the idea that the birds incubate their eggs under foot: 'This island has a quite wonderful bird usually called the Bass Goose... The people of Edinburgh sell their feathers (which are nice for making beds) dearly enough to their neighbours.'[74]

Gordon appreciated the force that the Gannet was subjected to in diving for fish and explained: 'The bone which we commonly call the bril in other birds can be separated from the breast-bone, but in these Geese it cannot; indeed, so firm is it that no force can divide it... in order that when they chase the Herrings, and plunge into the sea, they should not break their necks by their extreme violence.' (The bril was the *furculum* or wishbone)

T: It used to be believed among the Scottish peasantry that Gannets grew by the bill from the rocks of St Kilda, Ailsa Craig and the Bass.

Family: *Phalacrocoracidae*, the Cormorants

(Greek, *phalacos:* bald-headed, *corax;* raven.)
No. in world, 32; no. in Scotland, 2.

Cormorant
Phalacrocorax carbo

(*carbo:* Latin, coal i.e. black.)

SCOTS NAMES: Black Douker, Brongie (young birds) [Shet], Coal Goose, Corvorant, Cowe'en Elders [Kirk], Gor Maw, Hiblin or Huplin [Ork], Lerblade or Lerblading [Ork], Loren, Lorin or Loering [Shet], Mochrum Elders [Wig], Norie, Palmer [Ork], Scart, Scarf or Scarth [Ork], Sea Crow, White-headed Cormorant, White-spot Cormorant.

GAELIC NAMES: *Sgarbh, Geòcaire, Ballaire-bóthain.* Cormorant (but also used of Shag and Bittern); *Geòcaire* means glutton, Cormorant of the bothy.

The name Cormorant derives from old french *corp*, a raven, and *marenc*, of the sea (and earlier from Latin *Corvus marinus*: Sea Raven), which also has led to Gormer and Gor Maw (Maw is a northern name for a gull). Cormorant derives from the early name *Corvus viorans* (voracious Raven) Many of the Cormorant's modern vernacular names describe its black appearance (as in 'coal') also, ironically but aptly, because of its preaching stance with outstretched wings like parsons or church elders. (Loch Mochrum, where there is a famous cormorantry in continuous use since 1663, hence Mochrum Elders, is near Wigtown). Hiblin or Huplin, Lorin or Loering are all corruptions of old Norse words *hypplingr* or *laringr* meaning 'with a white hip', describing the white flank patch of the breeding plumage. Such words linger in Orkney and Shetland from Norn. Scarf and Scart derive from the Norse word *skarfr* imitating the Cormorant's calls. Norie or Norrie usually refers to Puffins but is sometimes used of Cormorants.

An ancestral Cormorant, named *Elopteryx,* dates from the Cretaceous period of 140 million years ago. There is evidence of the modern Cormorant from the Middle Pleistocene of about 3 million years ago. Remains of Cormorants have been identified from Stone Age sea-caves of about 2000 BC and much later eighth to ninth century traces have been identified in Pictish middens in Orkney.

British-bred Cormorants are partially migratory; some 10% of birds ringed in Scotland have been recaptured as far away as Norway and Spain.

Q: According to MacGillivray, writing in the mid-nineteenth century: 'The Great Cormorant occurs in considerable numbers, here and there, on all our rocky coasts, frequenting bold headlands, high cliffs, and rugged insular crags.'[118] Saunders (1899) adds: 'From Flamborough northward to Caithness it is more abundant than the Shag; though in Shetlands, Orkneys and the Hebrides it is usually in the minority.'[162]

T: The very name of the bird exemplifies greed.[61]

Shag
Phalacrocorax aristotelis

(*aristotelis* refers to Aristotle, after whom it was named by Linnaeus.)

SCOTS NAMES: Crested Cormorant, Green Cormorant, Green Scout, Scarf [Shet], Skart or Skrath [Ork], Tappie Whaesie [Ork], Tufted Skart.

GAELIC NAMES: *Sgarbh-an-sgumain, Cailleach-bheag-an-dhubh.* Cormorant with a forelock, Little black nun.

The word shag means a ragged mass of hair, as in shaggy, and refers to the recurved tuft on the breeding bird's forehead in spring. The Orcadian name Tappie Whaesie is similar; 'tap' is a Scots form of top (as in 'tappit' or crested hen). Whaesie is a diminutive for the dialect word wase, from German, used for a wisp of straw forming a pad on the head to ease the pressure of a burden. Neolithic skulls at the Tomb of the Eagles in Orkney show the pressure effects of carrying burdens with a thong across the head. So this old Orcadian name, derived from Norn, may be a linguistic link with the people of Skara Brae.

The Shag has left far fewer archaeological traces than the Cormorant. However remains of Shags have been identified, with those of Cormorant and Gannet, from Stone Age sea-caves from a period which ended about 2000 BC and, more recently, among Pictish middens in Orkney. The Shag escaped persecution but its numbers declined during the nineteenth century. Since 1930 numbers have increased, especially in northern and western Scotland where Shags now outnumber cormorants.

Shags are largely resident but some birds disperse in winter throughout the North Sea and south as far as the Mediterranean.

Q: Margaret Fay Shaw explains a proverb from St Kilda, 'Let every man take his own shags from the cliff': 'A St Kildan was assisted down a cliff to gather Shags. When asked by the man holding his rope at the clifftop if he had enough he replied "*Biodh a ch-uile duine toirt sgairbh a creig dha fhéin*" [Let every man take his own shags from the cliff]. The man at the top replied "Let every man be at the top of his own rope" and flung the rope away'.[172]

Robert Atkinson (1949) is ambivalent about shags though he appreciates their beautiful jade eyes and glossy and iridescent feathers. But he came across them nesting among piled-up boulders in a stench of decomposed fish when their noisome dens were shown by the whitewash of young and old.[12]

Seton Gordon tells of a great frost in the Outer Hebrides which froze Shags to the rocks so that they starved to death.[69]

ORDER: CICONIIFORMES
HERONS, STORKS AND IBISES

Family: *Ardeidae*, the Herons, Bitterns and Egrets

(*Ardea*: Latin, a heron.)
No. in world 60; no. in Scotland 2 (and occasional vagrants).

Bittern
Botaurus stellaris

(From Latin, *bos* meaning oxen and *taurus* a bull; *stellaris* set with stars or
starry. Hence, 'starry bird which roars like a bull'.)

SCOTS NAMES: Bleater or Blitter, Bog Bird, Bog Blutter, Bog Bumper,
Bog Drum, Box [Rox], Bumble, Bumpy Cors or Coss Heather Bluiter or
Blutter, Miredrum.

GAELIC NAMES: *Bonna-mine* or *Buiriche*, *Corra-ghrian*. Bittern, Heron of
the sun, the lowing one.

The Bittern is rarely heard nowadays and even more rarely seen. Many of its
vernacular names refer to its booming call. Surprisingly, even though a rare
vagrant in Scotland, it has many vernacular names.

The Bittern was present in Neolithic Britain but, with land drainage, has
slowly retreated since. In the fourteenth century Bitterns were common, and
often mentioned in household inventories, when they were popular table
birds because they were less fishy than herons. In 1384 the price of a bird was
fixed at eighteenpence. Habitat loss became critical in the nineteenth century
and by 1830 it was no longer a Scottish breeding species.[100] It still occurs as a
vagrant but there are only three records in the Outer Hebrides between 1890
and 1917.[47] More recently a Bittern has been a regular visitor to Duddingston
Loch in Edinburgh.[100]

Q:　　　　　'Ye Bitterns, till the quagmire reels
　　　　　Rair for his sake.'
(From Robert Burns' *Elegy on Captain Matthew Henderson*.)[29]
　　In Roxborough, according to the *Old Statistical Account*, 'the bittern was
formerly numerous, but is now seldom to be seen.' And in Ayrshire 'A bird,
which the people here call a hether blutter, (it makes a loud roaring noise)

built its nest on the island in the loch, but as some superstitious people suggested that its loud and uncommon cries forboded no good, was soon either destroyed or banished.[145]

MacGillivray (1837) notes: 'Formerly plentiful in England, is now of rare occurrence in any part of Britain, and especially in Scotland, where I have seen many specimens, and even obtained one for dissection.'[118]

T: An old belief holds that if a Bittern flies overhead at night one should make a will.

Grey Heron
Ardea cinerea
(*cinereus*: Latin, ash-coloured.)

SCOTS NAMES: Craggy, Craigit or Craigie Heron [Banf to Loth], Craigit-necked Heron [NE], Cran or Crane, Diddleton Frank, Hegrie, Hegril's Skip or Skip Herie [Shet], Herald [For], Herle or Erle, Hern, Heronshew or Heronis saw, Huron, Jemmy Lang legs (or neck), Jenny or Jinny Heron [SW], Lang-necked Haaran [Berw], Lang Sandy, Long Necky [Dumf], Tammie Herl [Perth].

GAELIC NAMES: *Corra-ghritheach, Corra-ghrain, Corra-riabach. Corra* means heron or crane and is said to have derived from the old root 'Kar' to scream, *ghritheach* means learned or wise; it is also onomatopoeic but alternatively it may refer to feathering of the Heron's thigh. *Ghrain* means disgusting or deformed and *riabach*, grizzled.

The Old English name of *Hragra* gave rise to many of the bird's vernacular names via *hayroun* of about 1300. Later names included Hernsaw and Heronshaw, possibly influenced by the French *hairon* or *heronceau*, a young Heron. Bewick[19] gives another spelling of the Heron's name as Heronsewgh or Heronshaw. The harsh cry of the heron has been imitated by the name Frank and possibly Jack, names for the male, and Joan, or sometimes Moll, the female heron. Its long neck features in names such as Craigit (Gaelic *craig* means neck or throat), Longie and Longnix. Gaelic names reflect the bird's character, colour and posture.

Remote ancestors of today's herons date back to the Eocene of 50 million years ago. Traces of Herons, as known today, may date back as far as 400,000 years, when much of the landscape was marsh. Later Heron traces have been found among Bronze Age deposits, and a tenth century list of Latin and Saxon animal names[1] includes the '*Ardea* or *Hragra*'. During the Middle Ages Herons were reckoned to be of considerable value on a country property, as food and for falconry, and as such were protected. A 1384 statute controlled their price at 16*d* each, a considerable sum at that time. Stringent statutes of 1427, 1493 and 1504 protected heronries, and adult birds could be taken only with a hawk or a longbow; the more accurate crossbow was specifically proscribed. A similar act in Scotland of 1567 made slaughter of herons with 'a culverin, crossbow or handbow' unlawful.[82]

Recently, Herons have become more numerous, although suffering in severe winters after which breeding is often more successful. Herons eat almost anything they find, though they are principally piscivorous and will take fish of three or four pounds. This leads to a tremendous feat when the bird may struggle to swallow its meal. In Scotland it has been known to feed on gralloch after a stag is gutted. In a severe frost in Holland, where the species is very common, Herons were seen knocking on doors to beg food from housewives.

Q: A puddock sat by the lochan's brim,
        An' he thocht there was never a puddock like him...
        A heron was hungry and needin' to sup,
        Sae he nabbit the puddock and gollup't him up;
        Syne runkled his feathers: 'A peer thing', quo' he,
        'But—puddocks is nae fat they eesed tae be.'

               (From J.M.Caie's 'The Puddock'.)[34]

A delightful poem for children by J.K.Annand needs a little translation:

        A humphy-backit heron
        Nearly as big as me
        Stands by the waterside
        Fishin for his tea.
        His skinnie-ma-linkie lang legs
        Juist like reeds
        Cheats aa the puddocks   *all the frogs*

Soomin 'mang the weeds.   *swimming among*
Here's ane comin,
Grup it by the leg!
It sticks in his thrapple   *throat*
Then slides down his craig.   *neck*
Neist comes a rottan,   *next, rat*
A rottan soomin past.
Oot gangs the lang neb   *nose*
And has the rottan fast.
He jabs it, he stabs it,
Sune it's in his wame,   *stomach*
Flip-flap in the air
Heron flees hame.[4]

T: Pliny wrote of herons 'During the night they place sentinels on guard, each of which holds a little stone in its claw; if the bird should happen to fall asleep, the claw becomes relaxed, and the stone falls to the ground, and so convicts it of neglect.'[63] This strange belief, perpetuated by many including Gerald of Wales, was held right up until the sixteenth century.[65]

ORDER: ANSERIFORMES
WATERFOWL

Family: *Anatidae*, the Swans, Geese and Ducks

(*Anas*: Latin, a duck)
No. in world, 148; no. in Scotland, 28.

Mute Swan
Cygnus olor

(*Cygnus*: Latin, a swan, *olor* swan-shaped.)

SCOTS NAMES: Cob or Tom (m), Pen or Jenny (f), Cygnet (imm).

GAELIC NAME: *Eala*, Mute Swan

Cob meant big or stout but could also mean head, eminent, large or powerful, hence male as in Cob Swan. Pen derives from Latin *penna* a feather: most early writers used a Goose or Swan quill as a pen. Until 1785 this species was called the Tame Swan but the name was altered by Pennant to Mute Swan 'as this species emits no sound'. In contrast to the noisy Whooper Swan this is relatively true but the Mute Swan actually has a wide vocabulary including grunts, honks and hisses. 'Mute' is doubly odd when the name swan derives from Sanskrit word *svanas* and the Latin *sonus*, both of which mean 'sound'. Words such as assonance and sonnet arise from the same root.

Mute Swans have a short history in Britain with their earliest evidence in the Bronze Age. They were introduced into Scotland about the first century AD. A tenth century list of Latin and Anglo-Saxon animal names[1] includes the '*Cignus*, *ylfete* and *Olor* or, swan'. In the fourteenth century sacred oaths were sworn on swans; for example in 1306 Edward I vowed upon the swan that he would take vengeance upon Robert the Bruce.

Though it has been suggested that Mute Swans derive from introduced domesticated stock, there is evidence that the species is indigenous. Domestication started at the end of the twelfth century. Until the eighteenth century Swans were the property of the Crown in England but not in Scotland. Their population rose, doubling to peak in 1961 after which there was a sudden drop, partly because of disturbance due to increased recreational use of waterways, to collision with overhead wires and to cold winters. Later mortality was attributed to poisoning from lead fishing weights, but after prohibition of these fishing weights numbers improved.

Breeding over much of Western Europe, the Mute Swan disperses south and west as northern waterways freeze. This boosts numbers in the Hebrides. In July moulting birds gather on sheltered water, for example in South Uist where one may see hundreds, particularly on Loch Bee.

Swans feed on waterweed; though they will occasionally kill young birds or amphibians they do not eat them. As the name suggests the species is largely silent apart from hisses and grunts. The non-vocal noise of the Mute Swan's wingbeats is one of the finest in nature, suggesting immense power and majesty. Mute Swans are renowned for their marital faithfulness; the pair-bond is long-term and monogamous. However study of English Mute Swans has revealed a low 'divorce' rate of between 3 and 9%.

Q: 'At the present day [1953] the Mute Swan breeds commonly in almost every part of Scotland and in some places is abundant'.[13]

T: Few birds have given rise to so much legend as the Swan. In classical mythology Jupiter fell in love with Leda when she was bathing, and visited her in the guise of a swan. The Leda legend has given rise to much literature and painting; for example Jupiter's seduction of Leda was painted by both Michelangelo and Leonardo da Vinci. Pliny and Aristotle refer to the belief that the swan sings before its death. Many poets used the image of a swan song, Coleridge adding humourously:

> Swans sing before they die, twere no bad thing
> Did certain persons die before they sing.[40]

Swan-worship was commonplace in Europe with stories of maidens being turned into swans. Swan-maidens were fairies of northern folklore, who could become swans by means of donning a magic garment called a swan shift. If the shift were stolen the fairies had to remain as swans until rescued by a knight. This legend has many versions, not least that of Tchaikovsky's Swan Lake.

In his *History of Witchcraft in Scotland* Charles Kirkpatrick Sharpe records the disappearance of the Swans from the loch on the north side of Linlithgow after the English had defeated the Scots and occupied Scotland. The birds did not return until King Charles I was restored.[171]

In Scotland Swans were regarded with awe; it was unlucky to kill one, even accidentally, because they were believed to embody human souls. Even as late as the 1930s Scottish fishermen refused to strike a match on a box of 'Swan Vestas' because injuring the Swan might incur bad luck.

Bewick's Swan
Cygnus colombianus bewickii

(*Colombianus* after the Columbia River, cf. Whistling Swan, *C. c. columbianus*; *bewickii* from Thomas Bewick.)

SCOTS NAME: Tame Swan.

GAELIC NAME: Eala-bheag, Little Swan.

The standard name was proposed by Yarrell in 1830 to commemorate the Novocastrian Thomas Bewick [1753-1828], who revolutionised bird illustration with his skilful woodcuts.

The Whooper and Bewick's Swans both have longer British histories than the Mute Swan and their remains have been found as far back as the middle Pleistocene. However since no distinction was made between these two species there are no records relating to Bewick's Swan before 1824. In the nineteenth and early twentieth centuries Bewick's Swans were relatively common as winter visitors in the Western Isles of Scotland, particularly the Uists. Numbers in mainland Scotland have increased recently especially at Caerlaverock in the Solway Firth. Bewick's Swans arrive in Britain from breeding grounds in Siberia from October to January. This journey lasts several weeks, with frequent stops at places where they can rest and feed.

They are seen mostly on coastal areas of low-lying wet pasture or flooded grassland with adjacent winter cereal. They are the noisiest Swans, with a high pitched, almost yelping, disyllabic call and a goose-like honking when flying. On land or water they have a soft crooning contact call. They do not produce the remarkable pinion noise of flying Mute Swans.

Q: The writer of a recent handbook notes: 'Formerly plentiful in the Long Island in winter until the 1920s this swan is now almost unknown... This decline... is thought to have been due to to a change in wintering habits following drainage of the Zuider Zee in Holland, which became the favourite wintering site'.[47]

105

Whooper Swan
Cygnus cygnus

SCOTS NAMES: Elk, Hooper, Wild Swan, Whistling Swan.

GAELIC NAME: *Eala bhàn*, Wild or White Swan.

The Old Norse name of *Elkt*, meaning swan, gave rise to some of the names of the Whooper Swan. Originally, and purists say correctly, the name was Hooper after the hooping cry. Some writers described this sound as whistling, giving an alternative name.

Whooper Swans were present in Britain in the Middle Pleistocene and were hunted for food by Stone Age man. Traces of the species have been found in Pictish middens in Orkney dating from as early as the eighth century. The species probably bred in Britain during the cold period of the Little Ice Age (1400-1880). Though there have been occasional reports of breeding in the Outer Hebrides[47] and also in Perthshire[182] the species appears not to have bred in substantial numbers in Scotland since the late eighteenth century when there are records in Orkney. At the end of the nineteenth century numbers of Whooper Swans were greater than those of Bewick's but this has now been reversed. A recent cause of decline has been change in the feeding habits of Whooper Swans which have turned to newly sown winter wheat, which still has toxic dressing.

Whooper Swans breed in the taiga from Siberia to Iceland, and individuals from there winter in Scotland. Some 6,000 Whooper Swans arrive after an unbroken journey of 800 miles. In one year of exceptional weather conditions, migrating Whooper Swans were tracked on radar flying at over 8,000 metres with a groundspeed of 86 mph. They made the journey from Iceland to Scotland in record time. This is astonishing for, at 8,000 metres, the temperature is down to -50°C and oxygen tension extremely low. Birds may be carried to high altitude by thermals but appear to fly high deliberately to avoid turbulence at lower levels.

Q: The minister for Kilmuir in Skye wrote in the 1790s that they 'come hither in the beginning of winter, and live on a lake in this neighbourhood, till the hatching season comes on. Hundreds of them, at a time, may be seen moving in all the majesty, that any of the feathered tribe can be possessed of, on the surface of the lake'.[145]

T: The swan was a favourite bird of good omen. To hear it on a Tuesday morning when fasting was much to be desired. Seven or a multiple of seven swans on the wing ensured prosperity for as many years.

Swans are said to be ill-used religious ladies under enchantment, driven from home and forced to wander.[35]

Greylag Goose
Anser anser

(*Anser*: Latin, a goose.)

SCOTS NAMES: Grey Goose, Lag, Quink Goose, Stubble Goose [Loth], Wild Goose.

GAELIC NAME: *Gèadh-glas*, Grey goose.

The oldest name, Grey Goose, derives from Old English, and from the Germanic *Graugans* and Norse *Gragas*. The name Greylag was introduced later, probably by Ray in 1713,[155] from the old word *lag* meaning goose, itself derived from the farmyard habit of calling geese by shouting 'lag-lag-lag', which is reminiscent of the farmyard goose's call. This word is very old and may be related to the Gaelic word *lacha* for duck. Another suggestion is that it is a corruption of the Anglo-Saxon word *leag* or *lea* meaning a field, distinguishing it from the Brent Goose which is the *rut* or root goose. Another explanation suggests that the word is a contraction of laggard, and denotes the grey goose that stays behind when others go.[196] Quink is onomatopoeic and other names describe its grazing habit on open territory.

This, the forefather of domestic geese, was breeding in Britain from the early to middle Pleistocene when it was extensively hunted by Neolithic man. Human domestication of the goose began during the Iron Age when much of Britain was marshland.

The feral population is increasing while truly wild Greylags are decreasing. The wild population breeds in the north-west of Scotland, especially in the Western Isles. In winter resident birds in south-eastern Scotland are joined by migrants from Iceland, when numbers may reach as many as

100,000, many concentrated on farmland to the dismay of local farmers. Goslings feed on insects using the protein for rapid growth, but adult birds are almost entirely vegetarian, feeding on grass, farm crops, *zostera* and water weed.

In flight the far-carrying 'gag-gag-gag' may be heard long before the high-flying V-shaped skein of geese is visible.

Q: David Craig recently described changeable skeins of Geese buffetted sideways and almost unravelling in gales from the ocean, recovering themselves and struggling on southwards to a chosen winter pasture.[44]

T: The story of the goose that laid golden eggs derives from an ancient Greek legend of a countryman who killed the goose to find its stock of gold and was left with nothing.

In Scotland Geese flying north mean good weather and their pattern in flight is significant. When God wrote the law on the Tablets of Stone Geese flew over Mount Sinai damaging the lettering, and since then are believed in Scotland to form the missing letters in their flight pattern and they have been condemned to sacrifice their pinions for men to write with.

(See also Gabble Ratchet, pp.12, 176, 177, 210.)

Pink-footed Goose
Anser brachyrhynchus
(*brachyrhyncus*: Greek, *brachy* short, *rhyncus* beak.)

GAELIC NAME: *Gèadh*, Goose.

This Goose has few names, presumably because it was not recognised as a separate species until recently. The Pink-footed Goose was not distinguished as a species separate from the Bean Goose until 1833.

Winter populations may be as high, or higher than those for greylags. They concentrate on barley stubble around southern and central Scotland, especially the Solway Firth. Numbers are increasing in these areas though there was a slight reduction in 1992 due to poor breeding success. This goose breeds in Greenland, Iceland and in Svalbard; Icelandic breeders migrate to Scotland. From late September huge flocks graze coastal farmland or salt marshes, roosting on estuarine mudflats. Like most geese the Pink-foot is vegetarian, eating grasses and, though it grazes on farmland, rarely grain. It is highly vocal, its calls resembling those of the Greylag but of higher pitch.

Q: Eric Parker tells of an Aberdeenshire farmer who had 20 acres of clover seeds. To keep Pink-foots off his crop he lit a chain of hurricane lamps. One night a gale blew out the lamps… in the morning there was not a blade of clover to be seen, as 2,000 Pink-foots flew slowly out to sea.[146]

White-fronted Goose
Anser albifrons

(*albifrons*: Latin, *albus* white, *frons* forehead)

SCOTS NAMES: Laughing Goose, White-faced Goose.

GAELIC NAME: *Gèadh-bhlàr*, Goose of the moor.

Gerald of Wales, in the twelfth century,[65] was the first to write about this species. Its recognised name was introduced by Pennant in 1768 in preference to the name Laughing Goose, from its loud harsh cry.

Present in Britain from the middle Pleistocene as a possible breeder during colder periods, otherwise a migrant from warmer areas. European White-fronted Geese breed in taiga and tundra of Greenland and Siberia. The Siberian breeders winter in the Netherlands and in southern England. The Greenland race favour south-east Ireland, northern Scotland and Islay, and number some 17,000, probably the entire world population. Seton Gordon noted them in South Uist as late as mid-May.[71]

It occupies similar habitats to Greylag but prefers uncultivated fields, salt-marshes and wet grasslands. In Islay concentrations of geese have impoverished farmers, and shooting licences have been granted there posing a threat to this species. White-fronts are noisy with typical cackling and a musical, laughing call.

Q: Seton Gordon described White-fronted Geese on a hill lochan in Wester Ross: 'At length as the dusk was deepening, the Geese rose in a body from the lochan, and with hoarse cries made their way into the sunset.'[72]

Canada Goose
Branta canadensis

(*Branta*: Anglo-Saxon, burnt, *canadensis*: Latin, from Canada.)

SCOTS NAME: Cravat Goose [SS].

GAELIC NAME: *Gèadh dubh*, Black goose.

Cravat describes the chin and throat pattern of this goose's plumage.

This goose was probably first introduced into England by Charles II in 1665, either for sporting or ornamental purposes. In Scotland it was introduced in the 1750s where it increased slowly until 1940, after which it suddenly declined, perhaps because of shooting during wartime food rationing.

It is now a widespread resident. The birds graze farmland and ornamental city parks where their copious droppings cause pollution. It feeds by day on grass, waterweeds and young cereal crops. The numbers of Canada Geese present problems for farmers; it is said that three Canada Geese represent the grazing of two sheep.

Q: Saunders noted in 1899 that 'The Canada Goose has been domesticated in this country for more than two centuries, and stragglers are occasionally shot out of the hundreds of unpinioned birds now in existence; but there is no evidence that wild American birds visit us'.[162]

Brent Goose
Branta bernicla

(*Branta*: Anglo-Saxon, red or burnt—the latter in this context; *bernicla*: Latin, a barnacle, from the ancient belief that some geese hatched from barnacles.)

SCOTS NAMES: Black-headed Barnacle, Brand Goose, Clack Goose or Clakes, Clatter Goose [Loth], Crocker, Horra or Horie Goose [Shet], Quink or Quink Goose [Ork], Rat, Road, Rood, Rute, Rutt or Rott Goose, Rout or Routhurrock [Ork], Ring-necked Barnacle, Ware Goose.

GAELIC NAMES: *Gèadha-got, Cathan*. Brent Goose, *Cathan* is common to both Brent and Barnacle Geese.

The confusion between Brent and Barnacle Geese is apparent in their vernacular names, many of which are common to both species. Crocker and Horra derive from the bird's call. Hurrock is a derivation of this with the addition of the diminutive suffix -ock. Rat, Road etc also are echoic, deriving from Norse *ratgas* meaning snoring goose. Routhurrock has come about from a misprint in Leslie of 1578[105] where the two names Rout and Hurrock were accidentally elided. Quink is a sixteenth century Orcadian name, probably from Old Norse. Ware is seaweed, and other names refer to the black or burnt colour or to a superficial likeness to the Barnacle Goose.

Brent Geese are later inhabitants of Britain than Barnacle Geese but there are a few records in the late Pleistocene and Holocene. This may be because Brent Geese feed on the intertidal zone, where they were less prone to hunting by early man. Distinction between Brent and Barnacle geese was not made until

110

Willughby and Ray[155] who, with the Frenchman M. Brisson, separated the species. Brent Geese were formerly more abundant than they are today, with large numbers visiting Sutherland and Ross and Cromarty in the 1860s when, in some areas, Brent were said to outnumber other wildfowl by a hundred to one. Nowadays they are rarely seen outwith the south-east of Scotland.

Brent Geese breed in the Arctic. They winter in Britain from as early as September in huge flocks on tidal mud flats, often with Wigeon. They graze intently, leaning forward as they feed on eelgrass. They have a soft, croaking, monosyllabic 'rott', which echoes widely when many birds protest together at being disturbed.

Q: The *Old Statistical Account* for Kirkwall mentions the horie geese 'which take their departure from Orkney in the spring for the north to obey the dictates of nature'.[145] And MacGillivray adds: 'This species is very abundant on many parts of our coasts, from the end of October to the middle of April.'[118]

Barnacle Goose
Branta leucopsis

(*leucopsis*: Greek, *leucos* white, *opsis* appearance)

SCOTS NAMES: Bernicle, Clack, Claik, Clait, Clakis or Clayk, Horra Goose [Ork], Rood Goose, Rothermuck, Routhecock or Routhurrock [Ork], Tree Goose.

GAELIC NAME: *Cathan*, Barnacle or Brent Goose

The name Barnacle is old and arose from *bernicle* at the end of the sixteenth century; that in turn derived from Middle English *barnakylle*, a word thought to stem from the archaic Celtic word *bern* meaning a cleft.[112] Many vernacular names reflect the confusion existing between the two species of black geese (see Brent Goose). Claik and Clakis are onomatopoeic and 'Tree' reflects the ancient legend that Barnacle Geese grew on trees.

Barnacle Geese are present in deposits from the late Pleistocene when they probably bred in Britain. Barnacle Geese now breed in Greenland and Spitzbergen. The Greenland population winter in western Scotland from Caithness to Wigtownshire, especially in Islay. Spitzbergen geese winter on the Solway Firth where numbers have risen sharply since the 1950s. In Islay they caused economic damage and shooting has reduced them substantially.

Q: In the 1950s Baxter and Rintoul remarked that Barnacle Geese were abundant on the west coast from Solway to the Outer Isles between the 1890s and about 1920, but that since then numbers had declined.[13]

T: Gerald of Wales describes the fabulous origin of these geese: 'There are many birds here that are called barnacles, which nature, acting against her own laws, produces in a wonderful way. They are like marsh geese, but smaller. At first they appear as excrescences on fir logs carried down upon the waters. Then they hang by their beaks from what seems like seaweed clinging to the log, while their bodies, to allow for their more unimpeded development, are enclosed in shells. And so in the course of time, having put on a stout covering of feathers, they slip into the water, or take themselves in flight to the freedom of the air. They take their food and nourishment from the juice of wood and water during their mysterious and remarkable genera-tion.'[65] Gerald adds that since they are not born of flesh it was permissible to eat them in times of fasting (this was readily accepted by churchman seek-ing excuse for improving their Lenten diet). Perhaps this contributed to the persistence of the belief that these geese were derived from fish. This belief persisted into modern times.[69]

Shelduck
Tadorna tadorna
(*Tadorna*: a Shelduck.)

SCOTS NAMES: Annet, Burrow Duck, Links Goose [Ork], Ringer Goose [Ork], Ruddy Goose, Scale Duck or Drake [Ork], Sheldrake, Sheld Fowl [Ork], Skell or Skeel Duck or Drake or Skeeling Goose [Ork, Shet], Skel-lgoose, Sly Goose [Ork], Stock Annet or Stoukannet.

GAELIC NAME: *Cràdh-gheadh*. *Cràdh* = pain or anguish, gheadh = goose; but in another spelling *Cra griadh* means blood or red goose.

Links means a bar of sand as found on a seashore (hence golf-*links*). Skel is a northern corruption of shell. Annet is an obsolete name for the Kit-tiwake or Common Gull and Stock comes from a Norn word (see Mallard). Shell, shelled or sheld mean pied. An explanation of Sly Goose, given by Turner in 1544, is that the Shelduck by reason of its instinctive cunning is the *chenalöpex*, or Fox-goose, of the ancients, and this has given rise to the Orcadian name.[195]

There is a single occurrence of Shelduck in the last glaciation of the Pleis-tocene, otherwise little is known about its history in Britain. It probably improved in numbers after the introduction of the rabbit provided burrows for nesting. During the nineteenth century shooting reduced numbers, which have since improved. Breeding pairs in Britain now probably reach 12,000, and this number is inflated in winter to 65,000 by migration of about half the Western Europe population. Largely coastal and estuarine, Shelduck are gregarious and frequent sandy and muddy shores, feeding by sweeping shallow water for marine invertebrates.

Q: Stanley, in 1857, describes how the birds were caught by hunters. 'The Sheldrakes, which build in rabbit-burrows, are caught by snares placed before the hole, into which the birds are traced by the marks of their feet on the sand.'[178]

Mallard
Anas platyrhynchos

(*Anas*: Latin, duck; *platyrhynchos*: *platus* Latin, flat or wide, *rhyncos* Greek, beak.)

SCOTS NAMES: Common Duck, Grey Duck [Dumf], Mallie, Mire Duck [For], Moss Duck [Aber, Renf], Muir Duck [Stir], Stock Duck [Ork, Shet], Stock Dyook, Wild Duck.

GAELIC NAME: *Lach riabhach*, Wild Duck (*lach* = duck; used alone it means Wild Duck or Mallard) *Riabhach* = brindled or grizzled.

Originally the word malard or maulard came to us with the Normans and, being specifically male, applied only to the drake. Traditionally the female was called a wild duck and only the drake was a Mallard until Pennant[148] adopted the name Mallard for both sexes. Several names describe habitat or feeding and Stock Duck comes from a Norn word, which still exists in the Icelandic name *Stokkönd* for a Mallard.

This ancestor of the domestic duck is the most frequently occurring duck among remains from the Ice Age, with evidence from the early Pleistocene.

113

As with the Greylag Goose it became domesticated during the Iron Age, after which, with drainage of marshland, numbers are likely to have fallen.

Wild duck have been caught for generations in traps designed in Holland where they were called *Ende-kooi*, duck-cages, from which the English word decoy is derived. The familiar Mallard is probably the most observed of all Britain's birds, since it readily comes to be fed at ponds and rivers. Mallards are very violent in their mating habits, sometimes even drowning their mates. As a boy I used to wonder where the drakes went in the summer. In fact all male dabbling ducks lose their brilliant breeding plumage to assume a more camouflaged appearance during their period of flightlessness. At this time they look very like their dowdy mates in protection against predation.

Q: In 1953, Baxter and Rintoul wrote: 'Although the drainage of many of its former nesting places has made the breeding Mallard less abundant than of yore, it still breeds commonly on the Scottish mainland, nesting in every county... the Mallard is also a common breeding species in the Islands'.[13]

T: According to Pliny 'the blood of Mallards is good for any such indirect means wrought by poison or witchcraft; and therefore their blood is ordinarily kept dry in a thick mass, and as need requireth is dissolved and given in wine; but some think that the blood of the female Duck is better than that of the Drake'.[63]

The Mallard is associated with foretelling the future. The merrythought or wishbone was considered an indicator of future weather and was examined carefully for portents: dark wishbones foretell a harsh winter. A remnant of this belief exists today in the pulling of the wishbone, when wishes come true for whoever holds most of the bone.

When anti-Christians were pursuing Christ a good crofter hid Christ under a pile of corn. Fowls attacked the heap of grain, the ducks trampled and ate the corn but the hens scattered it with their feet. Ever since the hen has been 'sever-toed' and confined to land, to bathe in dust and hate thunder. But the duck, because she helped to conceal Christ, was given three joys, of land, of air and of water, and would rejoice in thunder, hence the Gaelic saying 'Thou art like a duck expectant of thunder.'[35]

Teal

Anas crecca

(*crecca:* Greek, *Kreko*, make a harsh sound.)

SCOTS NAMES: Atteal [Ork], Jay Teal [Kirk] Speckled Teal, Tael Duik.

GAELIC NAMES: *Crann-lach*, *Lach-bheag* or *Lach-eigir*. *Crann-lach* is the Teal and also the Red-breasted Merganser; Little Duck or Elf Duck.

Apart from the Norn word *Atteal*, in Orkney, this species has been called *teles* from as early as the fourteenth century and later teeles, or teyles; the present accepted spelling dates from Ray.[155] Jay Teal refers to the brightness of the male's plumage.

Teal were present from the middle Pleistocene but were uncommon as a prey of early man because of their shyness and agility. Teal are among the most widespread of Palearctic duck with a population estimated at 250,000 in Western Europe. In Scotland it is thinly distributed as a breeding species with the winter population boosted by many thousands of continental birds. In summer Teal are birds of the north, where they breed on oligotrophic Scottish lochs. The Duck is usually silent but in winter the Drake has a short sonar-like double note audible at distance.

Q: According to Saunders (1889) 'Except in the Outer Hebrides, where it is rare even in winter, it is a widely distributed species in Scotland.'[162]

T: In *Carmina Gadelica* the *Lacha shith* is described, the teal whose coming warns of storm. When it is seen approaching the shore people hurry to secure their boats.[35]

Garganey
Anas querquedula

(*querquedula*: Latin, complaining (referring to the call))

SCOTS NAMES: Crackling Teal, Garganey Teal, Pied Wigeon, Pied Wiggon, Summer Duck.

GAELIC NAME: *Lach-crann.* ?Plough or Tree duck.

The Garganey has an insect-like call giving rise to references to crickets. As a small summer visiting duck, little larger than a Teal and smaller than a Wigeon, it borrows names from both and is frequently referred to as a Summer Teal. Garganey derives from a local name in Northern Italy, *gar-ganello*[66] and based on the onomatopoeic root *garg-* as in *gargarismoto*, gargle, from the bird's raucous call.

Though found among remains dating from the Iron Age there are no written records before 1667 when Merrett misprinted it as 'Crickaleel'.[131] It has never been a frequent species and was probably very scarce in the last few decades. There have been a few records of Scottish breeding since 1928.

Q: 'The Garganey Teal...' wrote MacGillivray in 1853, 'had not, I believe, been observed in Scotland until March 1841, when four individuals said to have been shot near Stirling, were exposed for sale in the Edinburgh market... It is said also to have been seen in small numbers in the Montrose Basin.'[118]

Gadwall
Anas strepera
(*strepera*: Latin, *strepo* rattle, describing the call.)

SCOTS NAMES: Gadual, Gadwell, Gray, Grey Duck, Rodge.

GAELIC NAME: *Lach-ghlas*, Grey Duck.

The noisy drake, at distance looking rather dowdy, close up has a beautifully marked breast covered in subtle vermiculation. Its name is onomatopoeic and it has been suggested that the origin lies in the Latin *quedul*, to quack, also found in the scientific name for the Garganey. Merrett[131] gave the spelling as 'gaddel' which, it is suggested, may be an error for gabble. Gadual may be derived from *gad*, an osier or withy, or from the Old English *gad*, a stick, which may explain the name of the species. Rodge, a common diminutive of Roger, may derive from the slang use of that name for a Goose.

A bird of temperate climates, the Gadwall was absent during much of the Ice Age and it seems to have been absent from Britain during the Little Ice Age from the fourteenth to the nineteenth centuries. Though Pennant[147] mentions the Gadwall in Scotland it is a recent addition to the Scottish list. It has bred on Loch Leven since 1909 and has spread into Fife, Perthshire and Angus. It also breeds in North Uist and Orkney.

A dabbling duck, the Gadwall is sociable, often seen in small parties with other ducks feeding on water weeds. Its song is a piping whistle punctuated by rasping burping sounds, usually heard together.

Q: Saunders (1899) comments that it was abundant on Tiree[162] and Cunningham (1990) mentions 'three sightings of Gadwall in Lewis, none in Harris though the species is not uncommon in the southern isles'.[47]

Wigeon
Anas penelope

(*penelope*: after Odysseus' wife, see below.)

SCOTS NAMES: Bald Pate, Half Duck, Pandle-whew, Red-headed Wigeon, Smee, Smeeth or Smeath, Whewer, Whim, Whistler.

GAELIC NAMES: *Lochlannach*, *Glas-lach* (also Gadwall). Wigeon, Grey duck.

Wigeon derives from Old French *vigeon*, which is onomatopoeic, as are winder (a variant of whimper) whew, whewer, whim etc. Other names refer to the cream crest of the drake, as in Bald Pate, or to the bird's feeding preference.

Traces of Wigeon have been found dating from the middle Pleistocene. They first bred in Sutherland in 1834, later colonising most of eastern Highland Scotland with additional breeding sites in the Hebrides, Argyllshire and the Borders. Huge winter influxes take the British population to nearly half a million birds, approximately half the population of western Europe. Wigeon graze in huge flocks in fields or beside muddy estuaries and inland near lochs. The Drake has a melodious, whistling 'whew' call, sounding as if the bird is amazed. This may be heard wherever there are Wigeon, and is one of the most evocative sounds of winter wetlands.

Q: According to MacGillivray, in the mid-nineteenth century, 'In the north of Scotland Wigeon are uncommon; on its north-west coast scarcely ever seen; in the Outer Hebrides, I believe, never; but in Orkney they are very numerous, and may be seen on all the lochs; and as we proceed southward we find them gradually becoming more plentiful'.[118]

Dr. C.L. Williams noted seeing them at Stormont Loch near Blairgowrie in April 1914.[198]

T: As a child, Penelope's father exposed her to the elements because the oracles told him that she would be the most dissolute of her sex and disgrace his family. She was rescued by seabirds called penelopes.

The McAndies, who used to live on Berneray in the Sound of Harris, were a dissatisfied clan who admired the freedom of the Wigeon. A local druid offered to change them into these ducks and half the clan accepted. Now half of the McAndies work the land while the remainder fly free and whistle their satisfaction at life.[10] This is probably a variant of the McCandlay story associated with the Long Tailed Duck (see p.123).

117

Pintail
Anas acuta

(*acutus*: Latin, sharp (referring to the tail).)

SCOTS NAMES: Cracker, Sprig Tail, Thin Neck, Winter Duck

GAELIC NAME: *Lach-stiùreach*, Rudder Duck (also used for Long-tailed Duck).

Most names refer to the characteristically long tail and slender neck. Cracker may refer to the call of the courting male but, in modern usage, the word is often used to describe any spectacular bird. The recognised name was coined by Pennant in 1768.[148] Though less common in Britain than many other duck the Pintail are probably the most abundant duck species in the world.

Pintail are comparatively rare among Pleistocene remains, perhaps, like Teal, because they were difficult prey for early man. This highly migratory species breeds throughout the northern Holarctic, but there are probably fewer than 50 British breeding pairs, mostly in Caithness and Orkney, though winter populations may reach 30,000. Pintail are highly sociable and may be seen on any open water in winter, but are shy and suspicious, taking off at distance from any disturbance. They feed by dabbling and up-ending in shallow water, where its long neck allows the bird to reach food left by other dabbling duck.

Q: Four nests were discovered on Loch Leven in 1898.[162]

Shoveler
Anas clypeata

(*clypeus*: Latin, shield-shaped as the vault of heaven (referring to the bill).)

SCOTS NAMES: Spoon-bill or Spoon-beak.

GAELIC NAME: *Gob-leathan*, Broad bill.

Until Ray separated the names of shoveller and spoonbill there was confusion between them, since both names refer to spade-like bills.[155]

The Shoveler is a species of temperate zones and so in the past was a bird of warmer periods with few records before the Iron Age. In Scotland Shoveler first bred in 1843. Before 1850 they were rare, but since then there has been extensive colonisation south of the Great Glen, with additional breeding colonies in Orkney and the Uists.

Found on most open fresh waters, maximum numbers of Shoveler may be seen in November when northern birds arrive before Scottish breeding birds move south. They are sociable and often seen in pairs or small parties, feeding by combing the surface of shallow water for food particles with their huge filtering bills. Shoveler are mainly silent, but in spring males have a nasal song, heard from February to April, and represented as 'tolk tolk'; this sounds, from a distance, like an old-fashioned typewriter with irregularly pressed keys.

Q: 'In Scotland,' according to Saunders in 1899, 'it nests in Kirkudbrightshire, Roxburgh, and some other southern counties, but its principal breeding-haunts are between the Forth and Tay.'[162]

Also writing in the late nineteenth century, Eric Parker observes: the 'bill is a wonderful instrument, lined at the sides with sensitive plates, which enable the bird to test the quality of the food it seeks on the surface of the water.'[146]

Pochard
Aythya ferina

(*Aythya*: *Aithuia*, Greek, gull or diving bird; *ferina*, Latin, flesh of wild animal or game.)

SCOTS NAMES: Atteal or Attile Duck [Ork], Curre, Diver or Douker [Rox], Dun Bird [Dum], Poker Duck, Red-headed Poker, Red-eyed Poker, Red-Headed Curre, Red-Headed Wigeon [NS].

GAELIC NAME: *Lach-mhàsach*, Dun Duck, Pochard.

This duck has a variety of vernacular names; many refer to colour, particularly to its red head. Pochard itself derives from poker, describing the feeding habits of many ducks including Wigeon. Confusion between the names of Pochard and Wigeon abound, though the latter is a dabbling rather than a diving duck. Curre imitates the growling call of the bird.

Pochard breed in temperate zones and there is little evidence of them during the cold historical periods. With warming at the end of the nineteenth century numbers increased from its first record in 1844. Pochard colonised Scotland as breeding birds in 1871[100] and now breed sporadically in south-eastern counties and in Orkney. The British breeding population is now estimated at under 400 pairs and there is concern over the future of this slow-breeding duck. Winter numbers in Britain are boosted by 40-50,000 birds from Russia.

Pochard feed by diving and up-ending and spend much of the day asleep in close-packed rafts on open water. They feed on leaves, roots of aquatic plants and some invertebrates.

A quiet species, Pochard make a nasal wheeze similar to air passing in and out of bellows. The duck has an explosive growl like noseblowing.

Q: The Pochard duck is described well in nautical language as 'Dark brown fore and aft, and a rather lighter brown amidships'.

Tufted Duck
Aythya fuligula
(*fuligo*: Latin, soot.)

SCOTS NAMES: Blue Neb, Douker [Islay].

GAELIC NAMES: *Lach-sgumanach*, *Curracag*. Tufted or Crested Duck; *Curracag* is a woman's headress (see Lapwing).

Coined by Gesner,[66] the name Tufted Duck became official after its adoption by Pennant.[148] The name refers to the small pigtail-like crest most obvious in the male; Blue Neb refers to the bill colour of the drake.

Although this species stands cold better than Pochard it was rare in the Pleistocene, increasing in the warmer interglacial periods. The first record of breeding in Britain was in 1849. In Scotland the species has expanded rapidly since 1872[100] when it was first recorded as breeding, since when numbers have increased dramatically so that it is now the commonest of the diving ducks. This increase is partly due to warmer weather over the last century, but also to the increase in man-made waters such as reservoirs or gravel pits.

Tufted Duck, though omnivorous, eat molluscs and so have a predilection for alkaline waters supporting freshwater shellfish. They may be seen on any open fresh water including many urban lakes, so that the Tufted Duck has become almost as widely known as the Mallard. The song is a quiet vibrant giggling.

Q: Collett describes it aptly in 1906: 'A small black duck, with a white patch on each side, shaped much like a Dutch wooden shoe, with the toe pointing towards the tail.'[41]

Scaup
Aythya marila
(*marila*: Greek, embers of charcoal or coal dust.)

SCOTS NAMES: Grey Backed Curre, Holland Duck [For], Norwegian Duck [Banf], Spoonbill Duck [Loth].

GAELIC NAME: *Lach-mhara*, Sea Duck.

This diving sea duck rarely breeds in Britain, so many Scottish east coast names reflect its migration from Scandinavia or Holland. Scaup feed largely on mussels and other molluscs, which lie on beds or scalps (called scaups in Scotland).

There is no definite evidence of this North American species in Britain before the end of the eighth century. The first breeding record in Britain was in 1897, though a female with young were observed in Sutherland in 1834. Since 1899[100] a few pairs have bred irregularly in Northern Scotland, indicating that it is at the margin of its breeding range. Despite this, Scaup are seen in the Outer Hebrides on salt or fresh water in most months.

Q: MacGillivray (1853) writes: 'The Scaup Pochard arrives on our coasts in the end of October, and continues to increase until the middle of winter. In the estuaries, and along the flat shores, it is met with plentifully, often in very large flocks.'[118]

Goldeneye
Bucephala clangula

(*Bucephala*: Greek, *bous* bull, *cephale* head; hence bullhead; *clangula*: from Greek *clagge*, the scream of birds, also the whistle of the wind when they take off.)

SCOTS NAMES: Buffle-headed Garrot, Brown-headed Duck or Brownhead (f. and imm.), Freshwater Wigeon, Curre, Diver, Doucker, Gingling Curre, Golden-eyed Garrot, Gowdy Duck [Ork], Kwink [Ork], Olive-tufted Duck, Pied Curre, Pied Wigeon, Popping Wigeon, Rattlewings.

GAELIC NAME: *Lach a'chinn uaine*, Duck of the green head.

As with many ducks there is a confusing mixture of names, such as garrot, curre and wigeon, used indiscriminately for ducks as a whole. 'Buffle-headed' refers to the relatively large head, as in a buffalo, compared with the overall size of the duck (this is also apparent in the scientific name). Females and immatures, often referred to as 'brown-heads', lack the striking plumage of the male, which at distance appears to be black and white, accounting for 'pied' in several names. Gingling, a form of jingling, presumably relates to calls made by immature Goldeneye, as, presumably, does the Orkney name of Kwink. Other names derive from whistling sounds, said to resemble a small tinkling bell, made by Goldeneye's wings especially when taking off at speed from water, hence Rattlewings, popping, whistling etc. The accepted name, Goldeneye, dates from Ray, who remarked that 'the irides of the eyes are a lovely yellow or golden colour';[155] but one is lucky to get close enough to this shy species to see the eye.

This cold-weather sea duck breeds in Arctic forest zones. Although it was present in Britain during the Pleistocene there was little evidence of it, though it may have bred in Scotland. Following cooler weather in the 1970s[100] and the introduction of suitable nest boxes, a few species have bred in coniferous forests near lochs in Inverness-shire since 1970. In recent years Goldeneye have bred on Lochs Tummel and Faskally in Perthshire. They are sociable birds forming large closely packed rafts, especially in the Firth of Forth. Towards winter's end there is an elaborate courtship display with much head bobbing and extension, so that the head lies on the bird's back as if it were looking at the sky. Goldeneye are often silent, their most characteristic sound being the whistling of their wingbeats.

Q: The Goldeneye is listed as present in Angus and Dumbarton in the *Old Statistical Account*,[145] and more plentifully in the *New Statistical Account*,[142] but without specific comment. 'As a rule,' says Saunders (1899) 'comparatively scarce in the Outer Hebrides, though common in the Orkneys and Shetlands'.[162]

Long-tailed Duck
Clangula hyemalis

(*Clangula*: from Greek *clagge*, the scream of birds; also the whistle of their wings when they take off; *hyemalis*: Latin, of winter.)

SCOTS NAMES: Baloo or Caloo, Calaw [Ork and Shet], Coal and Candlelight [Ork], Col-candle Wick [Fif], Col-cannel-week, Coldie [For], Cracker, Darcall, Long-tailed Hareld, McCandley's Bird [Harris], Northern Hareld [Aber], Sea Pheasant, Sharp-tailed Duck, South-southerlie, Swallow-tailed Sheldrake.

GAELIC NAMES: *Lach-bhinn* or *Eun buchainn*, Long tailed Duck, Warbling or melodious bird.

This sea duck appears off British coasts in winter; it has a characteristic call, which accounts for many of its names. Coal and Candlelight combine both the sound and the colouration of the bird. Other onomatopoeic names include Caloo, Darcall and Coldie. Calaw may derive from callow (from Old

English *calu* and German *kahl* meaning bald or unfledged). Hareld, given by Chambers English Dictionary as 'a long-tailed northern sea-duck', derived from a misspelling by Ray[155] of the Icelandic word *haferla* (from *haf-*, sea and *–erla*, wagtail.)

The Long-tailed Duck is the only member of its genus. Though present in the British Pleistocene there is little evidence of it until the 1890s when it is thought to have bred in Shetland. It breeds in the Arctic, where its total population is estimated at over 10 million. It winters around Scotland, and may be seen in the Outer Hebrides as late as May. The drake is very vocal with a characterisic musical call represented as 'ow owoooolee'—the 'coal and candlelight' call which gives it one of its Scottish names.

Q: According to Alexander Carmichael writing in *Carmina Gadelica*, 'The Long-tailed Duck is singularly graceful and melodious. In colour it is the water wagtail, in form the pheasant, and in song the nightingale, of the sea.'[35]

In the late twentieth century Martin Cook noted: 'The flock of Long-tailed Ducks roosting in Burghead Bay is still of international importance, thousands of birds entering the bay each evening.'[42]

T: Cunningham writes of it: 'Known as McCandlay's bird in Berneray where McCandlay was a common surname and the duck's call was likened to the name.'[48]

Eider
Somateria mollissima
(*Somateria*: Greek, *soma* body; *mollissimus*: Latin, very soft.)

SCOTS NAMES: Colk, Coo-doos, Crattick, Dunter Duck, Dunter or Dunter Goose [Ork & Shet], Dusky Duck, Edder, Great Black and White Duck, St Cuthbert's Duck.

GAELIC NAME: *Lach-Lochlainneach*, Wigeon-like duck.

123

Eider comes from the Icelandic name for the species *ödr*. Many of the names for this bird relate to the use of its down, as seen in its French name, *Eider à duvet*. Colk probably derives from the sixteenth century archaic Gaelic word *colcaidh*, a featherbed. Coo-doos is an onomatopoeic name exactly imitating the soft courtship calls of the drakes and likening their affectionate murmurings to those of doves. It is called St Cuthbert's duck because it breeds in the Farne Islands, where St Cuthbert lived part of his life in a cell, and it figures in legends surrounding the Saint. Dunter derives from Norn, and means 'one who bobs up and down', accurately describing Eiders at sea. Swainson[190] suggests that the name derives from Old Swedish *dun* meaning down and *taer* meaning to gnaw, hence down-plucker.

There are traces of Eider in Sutherland from early in the last glaciation. Until 1870 it was only in west coast islands but by 1890 it had spread to Orkney and Shetland where it was cropped for its eggs. Since then it has spread widely and may be seen on most British coasts, though breeding is limited to north of Northumberland. Farming of Eiders, once widely practised, still continues in Iceland and Norway, but the down has been largely superseded by synthetic, less allergic material. During World War II Eider numbers declined when it was shot for food, but it has since recovered to be the most abundant sea duck in the world. Since 1850, with protection following the use of its down for quilts, its numbers have increased and the western European population now numbers some 2 million.

Eider frequent shallow inshore waters, where they form large flocks throughout year. The amorous 'ah-*oo*-oo', stressing the second syllable, of courting males may be heard on Scottish coasts from late winter onwards.

Q: In 1549 Sir Donald Monro describes 'Colk' at Sula Sgeir: 'In this ile ther haunts ane kynd of foule callit the colk, little less nor a guise, quha comes in the *ver* to the land to lay hir eggis, and to clecke hir birds quhill she bring them to perfytness, and at that time her fleiche of fedderis falleth of her all haílly, and she sayles to the mayne sea againe, and comes never to land quhyll the zier end againe, and then she comes with her new fleiche of fedderis. This fleiche that she leaves zeirly upon her nest hes nae pens in the fedderis, nor nae kynd of hard thinge in them that may be felt or graipit, bot utter fyne downes'.[133]

T: In Orkney the Eider is synonymous with laziness, probably because the Drake plays no part in raising the young.

Common Scoter
Melanitta nigra

(*Melanitta*: Greek, *melas* black, *niteo* shining; *niger*: Latin, black.)

SCOTS NAME: Black Diver

GAELIC NAMES: *Lacha-bheag-dhubh*, Little black Duck.

Until Yarrell introduced the name Common Scoter[201] this bird was commonly called Black Scoter. The name Scoter may derive from Old Norse *sceotan*, meaning to move rapidly, as in scoot.

Pleistocene fossil remains of Common Scoter have been found but there is no evidence of them breeding in Britain before 1855, and since then there have been only scattered reports of about 100 breeding pairs in north-western Scotland[100] but numbers appear to be falling. The few breeding pairs favour acid moorland lochs in Sutherland, Caithness and Inverness-shire. Non-breeding winter Common Scoter occur at sea on all British coasts and occasionally are seen inland on migration, when flocks may fly considerable distances over land.

Q: Seton Gordon describes them: 'In their jet-black plumage with yellow bill the Common Scoter drakes are handsome beside their mates, dressed in sober-coloured brown'.[69]

T: A Norwegian writing in 1755 observes: 'The flesh of the Scoter is so rank and fishy that it is allowed as food for Catholics on fast days and in Lent'.[152]

Velvet Scoter
Melanitta fusca

(*fusca*: Latin, brown; but the word covers a range of colours from grey, through brown to black.)

SCOTS NAMES: Black Diver, Double Scoter, Great Black Duck, Velvet Duck, White-winged Black Duck.

GAELIC NAME: *Lacha-dhubh*, Black duck.

The name Velvet Scoter is purely descriptive, based on the soft texture of the plumage, and distinguishes the species from the Common Scoter.

There is no confirmed record of breeding in Britain, though this has been suspected in Shetland as recently as 1945. Up to 8,000 Velvet Scoters arrived from the north-east to winter, especially in the Moray Firth, during the early 1980s, but there has been a marked drop in numbers of both Common and Velvet Scoters in the last few years.

Q: A recent bird report on the Outer Hebrides states: 'Scarce passage or winter visitor, probably uncommon winter visitor until the 1880s, most recent records come from the Sound of Taransay, Harris.'[153]

SAWBILLS

Goosander
Mergus merganser

(*Mergus*: Latin, diver; *merganser*: *mergus* and *anser*, goose.)

SCOTS NAMES: Harle (female and immature), Herald Duck, Rantock [Ork], Sawbill [Stir], Sawneb [Aber], Sawyer, Sparkling or Sparling Fowl, Spear Duck, Spear Wigeon.

GAELIC NAME: *Lach-fhiacailleach*, Duck which shows its teeth.

The Goosander and Red-breasted Merganser have many names common to them both.

The derivation of Goosander is obscure. It was spelt 'gossander' before Ray adopted the present name.[155] The name Harle, originally French, seems to have become confused with Orcadian names such as Herald and Earl Duck. Other names apply to the bill either as a saw or a spear. Some names refer to the bird's plumage which in the male slightly resembles that of the Shelduck. The Orkney name Rantock is presumably basically Norn but Lockwood[108] questions its etymology. Bewick[19] gives Dundiver or Sparling Fowl as the Red-breasted Merganser, possibly confusing the female

Goosander with the female Red-breasted Merganser as is all too easy to do.

There are late Pleistocene records of Goosanders, but by the mid-nineteenth century the species seems to have been exterminated, probably because of damage to fisheries. Breeding was first recorded in Scotland in 1871[100] and, following an influx in 1875, numbers increased, only for the bird to be persecuted because of its threat to fishing. In the winter of 1992-3 wildfowl counts for Goosander reached nearly 3,000; a marked increase since the mid-1960s, but the species is now declining again.

Recent work[124] on movements of Goosander on the Dee watershed in Scotland showed that the species favoured hill lochs in winter and early spring, moving to the upper reaches of the river to breed in spring and summer before the females and young moved to the deeper lower reaches in late summer and autumn. Feeding almost entirely on fish, especially trout and small salmon, fishing Goosander may swim with the head underwater watching for prey. Both sexes have a low quack and the displaying male has several purring and croaking calls, which, when uttered repeatedly, sound bell-like.

Q: The predation of salmon by Goosanders is considerable. Two goosanders shot on the River Bran, Ross and Cromarty, contained 30 and 32 tags respectively, from salmon which were part of a consignment of 250 marked smolts released only three days before. Murton also gives evidence that fish stocks improve in direct relation to the numbers of Goosanders shot on a river.[139]

Keith Brockie protests that sawbills are still much persecuted for the heinous crime of taking salmon parr, though there is little scientific data either to prove or disprove whether this damages fish stocks. When salmon lay up to 15,000 eggs, only a few are needed to perpetuate the species.[23] However the quantity of fish species taken varies with locality and ease of access. Fishfarms should question the need to kill sawbills. Though the birds show a preference for salmonid species they also take predators of salmon.

Red-breasted Merganser
Mergus serrator

(*serrator*: Latin, toothed like a saw—referring to the bill.)

SCOTS NAMES: Dundiver, Earl Duck, Grey Diver (f) [Islay], Harle [Ork], Herald [Shet], Herald Duck [Shet, For], Sawbill [Aber, Stir], Sawneb [Aber].

GAELIC NAME: *Síolta-dhearg*, Red Wild Duck

See Goosander. This bird, called Red-breasted Goosander by Edwards,[57] was renamed in its present form by Pennant.[148]

The Red-breasted Merganser occurred in Britain during the Pleistocene when it was a common prey of Mesolithic man. It has a longer-recorded history than the Goosander, being first mentioned in the ornithological glossary of Ælfric the Grammarian of 998.[1] Like the Goosander the Merganser suffered because of its threat to fish-rearing, but managed to spread, gradually extending its breeding range from Scotland where it started breeding in 1885.

Red-breasted Mergansers are more commonly birds of salt water in contrast to Goosanders, which prefer fresh water, however they sometimes breed on lochs and may be seen on fresh water during migration.

Red-breasted Mergansers feed on fish, especially sand-eels, eels, lampreys and crustacea, but they also take small trout and salmon. There is no evidence that predation on young salmon has any significant effect on subsequent runs, but where fish are concentrated on farms economic loss may be serious.

Q: Saunders (1899) observes: 'In Scotland it is resident and breeds in considerable numbers on the fresh-water lochs as well as on the coasts of the northern and western mainland especially in Ross and Sutherland; while it is abundant in the Hebrides and Orkneys.'[162]

Smew
Mergus albellus
(*albellus*: Latin, little white.)

SCOTS NAMES: Magpie Diver, Pied Diver, Red-headed Smew (f), Sawbill, Smee, Smee Duck, White-headed Goosander or Merganser, White Nun.

GAELIC NAME: *Síolta bhreac*, chequered or piebald wild Duck.

The word smew is probably a variant of small and dates from Charleton, who recorded 'the Diving Widgeon or Smew' in 1668.[38] Ray[155] preferred the name White Nun, which so well describes the 'habit' of the drake. Smew became standardised by Pennant.[148] Many names derive from small or smee, and the latter is sometimes used to imitate whistling bird calls, as in Smient (see Wigeon).

Despite being the rarest of the sawbills today, the Smew was plentiful in the Pleistocene, when its remains were commoner than those of the two larger sawbills.

Breeding in arctic Scandinavia and Russia along wooded stream banks, the Smew is now an infrequent winter visitor to the fresh waters of Western Europe. Like other mergansers Smew submerge their heads when hunting for fish and crustacea. They are silent except in display when the drake has a rattling sound like the winding of a small clock.

Q: Keith Brockie painted a Smew on 23 March 1987 at Loch Faskally, Pitlochry, and noted that it had been there since at least 11 January.[23]

Ruddy Duck
Oxyura jamaicensis

(*Oxyura*: Greek, *oxus* sharp, *oura* tail; *jamaicensis*: Latin, from Jamaica.

SCOTS NAMES: none.

GAELIC NAMES: none

This controversial species was introduced into Britain from America in the 1950s. Young birds escaped from Slimbridge Wildfowl Trust and, over the next thirty years, spread throughout England. Ruddy Duck colonised Scotland in 1974,[100] since when they have become widespread from Orkney to the Borders. They are now frequently seen in Perthshire. The species threatens to spread to Spain where it may interbreed with the endangered White-headed Duck. The debate on culling Ruddy Ducks to protect the White-headed Duck continues.

Q: Ruddy Duck are reported as a vagrants even in the outer Hebrides.[47, 153]

ORDER: FALCONIFORMES
BIRDS OF PREY

Family: *Pandionidae*, the Osprey

(Greek: All god-like. Pandion was a legendary King of Athens. The Osprey
is thus either regal or as a Deity.)
No. in world, 1; no. in Scotland, 1.

Osprey
Pandion haliaetus

(*haliaetus*: Greek, *halis* sea, *aietos* eagle.)

SCOTS NAMES: Bald Buzzard, Buzzard, Eagle Fisher, Fish or Fishing
Hawk, Sea Eagle, Water Eagle.

GAELIC NAMES: *Iolair-an-t-iasgair*, *Iolair-uisge* or *Ailean Iasgair*. Fishing
Eagle, Water Eagle or Alan the Fisherman.

Pliny[63] wrote of the Lammergeier, describing it as an ossifrage or bone-
breaker. A shortened form of the same word appeared in Old French as
osfraie and at some time substitution of *p* for *f* led to the word osprey. Until
Pennant[148] corrected the confusion the Osprey was muddled with the White-
tailed Eagle, and this confusion still exists in some Scottish names.

The Osprey is poorly represented among fossil remains in Britain. After the
Ice Age it was widespread in Britain but was destroyed as vermin. It was
widely persecuted throughout Scotland by gamekeepers and egg collectors
and was virtually eradicated as a British species when its Scottish nesting sites
were deserted in 1916. Protection has allowed the Osprey to recover; Scottish
birds nested again in 1954. By 1987 Ospreys had increased to more than 50

130

pairs and now are so common in Scotland between April and September that they are seen several times a week over my garden in Strathtay.

Ospreys have a worldwide distribution and most Scottish Ospreys winter in Subsaharan Africa. Scottish breeding sites include Loch Garten and the Loch of Lowes, but migrating Ospreys may turn up on any open water with suitable fish prey. Ospreys have evolved a unique evolutionary speciality among raptors, for while many pick fish from the surface, only the Osprey has the ability to dive for its prey. They often immerse themselves completely, talons first, to take quite large fish. (There are records of Ospreys catching fish so large that they were unable either to rise or let their prey escape, leading to the bird's death.) The birds carry the fish to a favourite feeding site, which may be at considerable distance from fishing haunts.

The call is a repeated high-pitched, buzzard-like mew.

Q: 'The Osprey or water eagle,' wrote Patrick Graham in 1812, 'which feeds principally on fish, built lately in the lofty trees of Inchmahome, and probably still builds occasionally there: she is said to build regularly in a small island towards the North end of Lochlomond. She is often seen watching her prey, upon a small rock which rises a little above the surface, about the middle of Upper Lochard.'[75]

T: In the twelfth century there were some odd ideas about Ospreys:

> …One of their feet is armed with talons, open and ready to snatch; but the other is closed and peaceful and suitable only for swimming… There is a remarkable thing about these birds and I have often witnessed it for myself. They hover quietly on their wings high up in the air over the waves of the sea. In this way they can more easily see down into the depths below. Then, seeing with their sharp eyes through such a great distance of air and troubled water little fishes hiding below the waves, they dive down with amazing speed. While they enter and leave the water they control themselves by their swimming foot; but with their grasping foot they catch and carry off their prey.[65]

These ideas about an Osprey's feet were widely believed well into the sixteenth century.

White-tailed Eagle
Haliaeetus albicilla

(*Haliaeetus*: Greek, *halis* the sea; *aietos* an eagle, *albicilla* white tail.)

SCOTS NAMES: Eirn, Erne, Yirn [Ork & Shet], Cinereous Eagle, Sea Eagle.

131

GAELIC NAMES: *Iolair-bhreac* or *–ban*, *Iolair-chladaich* or *–mhara*. Spotted Eagle, White Eagle, Eagle of the shore, or the sea.

These names come from the middle English *ern*, an eagle, and ultimately derive from ancient Indo-European languages, persisting in celtic as *eryr* (Welsh) and *iolair* (Gaelic). The Old Norse name was *örn* and Orcadian names, which apply specifically to the White-tailed Eagle, probably derive from this via Norn. The earlier name of Cinereous Eagle was coined by Pennant[148] but was not used after 1835.

White-tailed Eagles were well established in the Bronze Age throughout the whole Palearctic. In Orkney they had some special function in the funerary rites of the Bronze Age inhabitants of about 3000 BC (See *Tomb of the Eagles* p.5). As farming increased the species was regarded as harmful and was increasingly persecuted, until by 1794 it had ceased to breed in England. In Scotland it hung on; the last breeding pair was in Skye in 1916. A reintroduction programme started in 1968, first in Fair Isle and later, and more successfully, in 1975, with birds from Norway being released in Rum. Slowly, and not without opposition, the species has become established in the West of Scotland. They now breed in Mull.

Most of the diet is made up of fish and carrion but it will take live prey, especially seabirds, from the size of a goose downwards. It has a bad reputation for taking lambs, but these are more often carrion than live. Despite protection it is still subject to persecution, however numbers are slowly rising in Britain.

Q: The Eagle, as Captain Burt wrote in 1730, 'is frequently seen among the mountains and felt by the inhabitants in the loss of their lambs, kids, and even calves and colts...

In the west and north-west of Scotland there is repairing of a fowl called the erne [Scottish Eagle] of a marvelous nature... This eagle has been known to carry off fowls, lambs, pigs and as Sir Robert Sibbald says even young children. Premiums for producing two eagle's feet gradually diminished from a guinea to half a crown as the birds became less frequent.'

Burt also described how baits of dead sheep were set out attracting first Kites, Ravens, Carrion Crows, Magpies and finally the Eagle, which was shot.[33]

The *New Statistical Account* of 1843-5 related that, in the Parish of Tweedsmuir, Peebles-shire, 'So great were its ravages among sheep, that every effort was made to extirpate it, and for many years past there has been reason to think that these efforts were successful. But in the course of the season just closed, it reappeared in the same as well as in other parts of the parish, and committed several depredations.'[142]

Seton Gordon later bemoaned their loss: 'there is not one pair of these birds nesting in Britain at the present day [1929]. The Sea-eagle has shared the fate of the Osprey and other of our rare birds.'[73]

T: Eagles are notoriously long-lived birds: for example in 1896 it was reported that a White-tailed Eagle, a Scottish one, had lived in captivity for forty years.[109]

Golden Eagle
Aquila chrysaetos

(*Aquila*: Latin, eagle; *chrysaetos* Greek, golden.)

SCOTS NAMES: Aanie-onyoo [Ork], Aigle or Airn, Black Eagle, Erne, Mountain Eagle, Ringtailed Eagle.

GAELIC NAMES: *Iolair-dhubh* or *Iolair-bhuid*, Black eagle or Golden Eagle.

This bird has been the Golden Eagle ever since Aldrovandi's meticulous description of it in 1599[2] when he chose the Greek word *chrysaetos* (gold) as its designation. The original word for Eagle in Britain was Ern, which was modified after the Norman invasion to become Eagle after the Old French word *egle*. Aanie-onyoo is probably Norn in origin or may be onomatopoeic related to the Eagle's Buzzard-like call. It is sometimes called a Ringtailed Eagle because of the dark grey tail being banded in black.

The Golden Eagle was present in Britain from the end of the Ice Age but has never been widespread. It was found in mountains till the eighteenth century after which it was shot as vermin by those preserving Grouse moors. It was also alleged to take live lambs, but about 70% of lamb carcasses found in eyries were carrion. The fortunes of the Golden Eagle were tied to game preservation and the myxomatosis panzootic, which decimated the

133

rabbit population and removed a principal prey species. Toxic chemicals, especially dieldrin used in sheep dip, influenced eggshell thickness and caused breakage during the early 1960s, but following prohibition of dieldrin this has improved. There has been a slight increase in numbers in Scotland to about 600 pairs, about a quarter of the entire European population.

Q: Seton Gordon recalls the classic story of an aircraft travelling at approximately ninety miles an hour, which was overtaken by a Golden Eagle flying on the same course.[69]

'A quarter of a century ago I spent an Easter holiday in Arran, hill-walking with my father. Goatfell, a perfect cone of a peak, rises Fujiyama-like out of a broad bay. Its lowest slopes are wooded with rhododendron, oak, and pine, from which red squirrels swear at walkers. Higher, the moors are quartered by hen harriers and fierce merlins harry the meadow pipits. The summit is a scramble amid cyclopaeian walls of fissured basalt sparkling with quartz, and far below, the sun-speckled sea reflects the changing cloudscape. But the glory of this summit lies in crossing to its western face, where the deep cleft of Glen Rosa gapes before a skyline as crenellated as any in Scotland.

The sun broke through as I paused at that view. And then I saw him. Perched on an overhang not twenty feet below with the vernal sun lighting his full glory he contemplated his kingdom. A pebble moved; he glanced up and for a moment eagle and boy looked each other in the eye. With unhurried disdain at a trespasser in his mountains he eased forward till gravity caught him and he fell wing-crooked into space. The great bird plunged till, finding a thermal, the perfect pinions opened and he wheeled so that the sun reflected on his majestic copper-red back. For a mile he soared without a wingbeat, first down past Cir Mhor's jagged crest, then, as a cross-breeze caught him, up and up over the shoulder of Beinn a' Chliabhain till he crested A'chir to leave a boy, breathless with wonder, staring after the wildest being in the air and pinching himself in disbelief.'[92]

T: Pliny described Ætites or 'eagle-stones' which were found in eyries. Even as late as the eighteenth century these were believed to be of use in obstetrics:

'The Stone Ætites held to the Privities, is of extraordinary Virtue, and instantly draws away both Child and Afterburden, but great Care must be taken to remove it presently, or it will draw forth the Womb and all'.[63]

In Irish-celtic mythology Adam and Eve still exist as eagles living in Galway. Eagles are believed capable of flying 1,000 miles in a day, which like their longevity takes a bit of swallowing! An old celtic rhyme about the longevity of eagles ran:

> Thrice the age of a dog is that of a horse,
> Thrice the age of a horse is that of a man,

Thrice the age of a man is that of a deer,
Thrice the age of a deer is that of an eagle.

Red Kite

Milvus milvus

(*Milvus*: Latin, bird of prey)

SCOTS NAMES: Crotchet-tailed Puttock, Glead, Gled or Greedy Gled, Puttock, Salmon-tailed Gled.

GAELIC NAMES: *Clamhan-gobhlach, Casgarrach, Croman-lochaidh. Clamhan* is possibly from *chlamhair*, a greedy rapacious person, *gobhlach* means forked. *Casgarrach* is a sanguinary person; all mean Kite.

The oldest name for the Red Kite is Glede or Glead, derived from Old English, and also found in Norse as in *gleda*, meaning to glide. Names implying gliding are particularly apt for, as Pennant observed: 'Sometimes it will remain quite motionless for a considerable space; at others it glides through the sky, without the least apparent action of its wings.'[148] Another obvious feature of the Red Kite is its markedly forked tail which gives rise to several of its vernacular names, including 'Puddock', because the divided tail recalls the legs of a frog (but see under Buzzard, p.140).

The Red Kite story is fascinating: poorly represented in Ice Age remains, it became widespread by the early Holocene. It prospered as a scavenger of urban waste at a time when rubbish disposal was minimal. In the fifteenth century the species was commonplace in London and was renowned for its tameness and audacity. Pennant[148] recorded Kites breeding in Grays Inn in London. Kites took food from children's hands and stole laundry to adorn their nests. Until the end of the eighteenth century they were a common sight, but with the introduction of managed game birds for sport the Red Kite was persecuted and by 1870 had been exterminated in England. In Scotland Red Kites ceased to breed in 1884, though it may have done so again during the 1914–18 war due to reduced gamekeepering. Thomas Edward[174] recorded a single specimen being shot near Banff in the latter half of the nineteenth century.

Following a re-introduction programme in Northern Scotland in 1991, and later in the Central region, the Red Kite is now recovering. I saw my first Scottish Red Kite in 1998 in Perthshire.

Kites are, for the most part, scavengers feeding on carrion, but they also take small birds, mammals, frogs, snakes and invertebrates, particularly worms. Kites have a mewing call like a Buzzard but are rather more silent.

135

Q: Osgood Mackenzie said that in the early 1800s Forked-tailed Kites swarmed, until his father poisoned the carcase of a horse with strychnine. 'The last kite had disappeared before my time'.[119] 'Having once been described as the commonest hawk around Spynie, none was seen after 1848... In 1989 the RSPB and NCC began a programme of reintroduction of the Red Kite to the Highlands.'[100]

T: A former superstition held that when Kites fly high fine weather is coming. The name Royal Kite originated from the idea that only the King's falcons could take the Kite because its powers of flight were greater than those of falcons belonging to lesser men.

The Kite appears in *Carmina Gadelica*:

> The nest of the kite
> Is high on the mountain slope,
> My little one shall sleep and he shall have the bird.
>
> From a lullaby sung to a child. [35]

Kites are reputed to steal small garments such as handkerchiefs and brassieres from washing lines to line their nests. Hence 'When the Kite builds, look to lesser linen'. (Shakespeare, *Winter's Tale*.[170])

Hen Harrier
Circus cyaneus

(*Kirkos*: Greek, a hawk that flies in circles; *cyaneus*: Greek, dark blue, dusky, gloomy.)

SCOTS NAMES: Blue Gled, Blue Hawk [Loth], Blue Kite, Blue Sleeves, Brown Gled or Brown Kite (f), Catabelly [Ork], Dove Hawk, Dove-coloured Falcon, Faller, Flapper [Caith], Goshaak [Ork], Katabella [Ork], Miller, Mittane or Mitten, Moor Hawk, Ringtail (f) [Loth], White aboon Gled [Stir].

GAELIC NAMES: *Clamhan-nan-cearc, Clamhanluch, Bréid-air-tòin*. Hawk of the hen or mouse.

The Gaelic name *Bréid-air-tòin*, loosely translated as 'sail on tail', is apt.

The name Hen Harrier derives from Hen Harrower, mentioned by Turner.[195] Ray[155] describes the bird 'as a sort of puttock called a Hen-harrier from chasing, preying upon poultry'. Coloration gives rise to many names including blue, white and, perhaps, Miller (who was dusty with flour) in the male and brown in the female. 'Ringtail' for the female (because of the pale rump) dates from 1538 when the female was thought to be a different species. Flapper and Faller relate to the typical flight of harriers as a whole. Goshaak, though resembling Goshawk, is probably from gorse hawk. Catabelly is unexplained and may well be of Norn origin.

There is no trace of the Hen Harrier in prehistoric deposits but it is recorded in the early sixteenth century as predating on domestic poultry. Despite being treated as vermin it was widespread over Britain until the late eighteenth century when changes in agricultural practice reduced the suitable habitats. Later increased game preservation led to its near extinction over most of Britain and it was banished from the Scottish Highlands to the islands in the nineteenth century. It recovered slightly, as did many birds of prey, during the relatively keeperless Second World War and with the rise in rodent population consequent upon the conifer plantations. Hen Harriers feed on rodents and young birds, earning them a bad reputation among gamekeepers on grouse moors; however recent evidence suggests that the two species can coexist on well-managed moors.

Q: The Minister for Campsie in Stirlingshire recorded in 1796: 'But of all the birds of prey amongst us, the Hen-harrier or White Aboon-glade, as he is called, is the most destructive to game, both partridges and muirfowl. They breed on the ground amongst rushes in the muirs, and fly low along the surface of the earth in search of prey...'[145] 'Though of so small and light a frame, the hen-harrier strikes down a mallard without difficulty; and the marsh and swamp are his favourite hunting-grounds.'[161] And Seton Gordon observed a female Hen Harrier flying with leisurely gliding flight across the machair. 'Her flight became more rapid as she urged herself forward with powerful clean-cut wing-thrusts, and just ahead of her I saw a Red-necked Phalarope endeavouring to escape.'[69]

T: In the Hebrides if a person had an exceptionally fortunate day he was said to have seen the *clamhanluch*.

Goshawk
Accipiter gentilis
(*Accipiter*: Latin, hawk; *gentilis*: Latin, noble.)

SCOTS NAMES: Goosehawk, Great Hawk; Tiercel or Tercel (m)

GAELIC NAMES: *Seabhag-riabach, Seabhac-mhór, Glas-sheabhag*. Grey Hawk or Great Hawk.

The name derives from Old English *goshavoc*, which literally means goose hawk, though it is unlikely that the Goshawk ever took Geese.

Goshawk remains date from the end of the Pleistocene. As a woodland raptor it may well have flourished in early Holocene forests but would have diminished as they were cleared. As it became prized for falconry in the Middle Ages, it would have been protected. To the falconer this was the practical food-gathering hawk, especially for game such as rabbits and Partridges. Later, nineteenth century forest clearance and the increase in gamekeepering led to its extermination as a wild species in Britain. In Scotland the Goshawk was exterminated in 1883, but was re-established by the 1960s and a few birds are seen in Perthshire and the Borders, where they may be breeding. They are loathed by gamekeepers who speak of them as 'killing machines'.

Q: Baxter and Rintoul, writing in the 1950s, remark that Goshawks, almost always immature, occur from time to time in Scotland.[13]

T: The Goshawk, or 'Falcon gentle', was suitable for a prince or a young man.

Sparrowhawk
Accipiter nisus
(*Accipiter*: Latin, a hawk; *nisus*: Greek, Nisus, the King of Megara.)

SCOTS NAMES: Blue Hawk [Stir, Loth], Blue Merlin [Perth], Gleg Hawk [Renf], Hack, Hedge Hawk, Maalin [Shet], Musket, Spar Hawk, Spare Hawk or Spur Hawk.

GAELIC NAMES: *Speirag, Ruadhan-aille*. Both mean Sparrowhawk (*Speirag* also means slender limbed girl and hence any slender creature of feminine gender).

It seems likely that the name Sparrowhawk arose from the Old English term *spearhafoc*. Many of the Sparrowhawk's vernacular names derive from sparrow but also from other prey such as pigeons. Gleg, an obsolete Renfrew word, means sharp-eyed, but may also derive from *gled*, to glide (see Red Kite). Blue hawk is applied to many raptors and is unhelpful. On the other hand Hedge Hawk accurately describes the low level, hedge-hopping attack of the hawk. Musket is interesting: this was originally a falconer's name for the male Sparrowhawk, possibly derived from the same word used for a crossbow bolt. Later the early firearm was also named a musket. It may be that as weapons developed they took over some falconry functions, so suggesting names to the manufacturers. Several firearms, such as sakers, falcons and falconets, were named after birds of prey. However musket may also have derived from the Old French word *mousquet* or *mouchet*, from *mouche* a fly, referring to the small size of the male Sparrowhawk.

Sparrowhawks are present in fossil remains from the early Holocene when it was probably common. There were as many as half a million in medieval Britain. Subsequently, especially at the end of the nineteenth century, numbers fell dramatically due to game preservation. After World War II there began a catastrophic reduction in numbers due to concentration of toxic chemicals ascending the food chain; this was less marked in Scotland than in England. Control of toxins has arrested the decline, and since the mid-1970s the species has again increased. In Scotland Sparrowhawks are widely distributed in wooded areas, chiefly in the lowlands, but are scarce in the relatively treeless Outer Hebrides and Northern Isles. In winter numbers are boosted by immigrants from Europe.

Q: At Campsie in Stirlingshire during the 1790s, the Sparrowhawk was so common in the upper parts of the strath that the children of the villagers amused themselves by taming them.[145] 'This bold, dashing hawk—sharp-faced, needle-beaked, yellow-taloned, with eyes like jewels—is an easy subject for the watcher.'[180]

T: Holinshed says that the Sparrowhawk is an enemy to young children… but he doesn't say why.[61]

Buzzard
Buteo buteo

(*Buteo*: Latin, a hawk.)

SCOTS NAMES: Bald Kite, Bissart, Bizzart or Bussard, Buzzard Hawk [For], Glaid or Gled [NS], Goshawk, Puddock, Puttock.

GAELIC NAMES: *Clamhan, Bleidir, Finneun*, Buzzard (Possibly from *chlamhair*, a greedy rapacious person), beggar, fair or light bird.

As with other raptors many vernacular names are common to several species, so 'Hawk' or 'Goshawk' are confusing. Puttock, a name also applied to the Kite, is from *poot* or *poult* and *ock* is a corruption of hawk, hence 'chicken-hawk'. Buzzard derives from Old French *busard* and was first recorded in 1300. Originally the word came from the onomatopoeic syllable *But*, which, when pronounced in French, represents the mewing cry. This is also present in the Latin name.

Buzzard remains are found as far back as the early Pleistocene of some 1-1.5 million years ago, though their bones are difficult to distinguish from those of Rough-legged Buzzards. The species remained common up to the fifteenth century when it was listed as vermin because it took domestic poultry and rabbits, the latter being then protected as game. The Buzzard was lucky to survive persecution that became intense with the increase in kept game. By the middle of the nineteenth century it had disappeared from southern and central England. Thomas Edward[174] noted that the Common Buzzard was much less common than the Rough-legged in Banffshire in the late nineteenth century.

The respite of the two World Wars led to improvement but then, in the 1950s, the Buzzard decline began again, hastened by toxic chemicals during the 1960s. Reduced sheep farming with consequent reduction in carrion also contributed to the decline. Now once again Buzzards are increasing; it is a rare day when there are not several of them wheeling and mewing above my Perthshire garden.

Q: 'Buzzards were almost lost when myxomatosis temporarily destroyed the rabbit. Rabbits have survived and are now [1977] building up immunity to the disease but in the meantime the Buzzard has drastically altered its diet, scavenging off all forms of carrion and channelling its hunting instincts into the capture of frogs, rodents and even beetles.'[53]

T: To be 'Neither hawk nor Buzzard' was to be of doubtful social position, too good for the kitchen yet not good enough for the family, much as private tutors and governesses were. The Buzzard was an inferior hawk and so the name was applied as a term of abuse for any stupid or worthless person.[112]

Family: *Falconidae,* the Falcons

No. in world, 59; no. in Scotland, 3.

(Falcon derives from *falc*, meaning a sickle, curved or clawed.[61])

Kestrel

Falco tinnunculus

(*Falco*: Latin, falcon; *tinnunculus*: Latin, Kestrel possibly from its ringing call.)

SCOTS NAMES: Keelie or Keelie Hawk [Loth], Maalin [Shet], Mouse falcon, Mouse Hawk or Moosie Hawk [Ork], Red Hawk [Stir], Sparrow Stanchel or Stenchil, Staniel, Stannel, Stanyel, Stannel Hawk, Stonegale, Stonegall, Steingale, Willie whip the wind, Wind Cuffer [Ork].

GAELIC NAMES: *Speireag-ruadh* or *Clamhan ruadh*, *Deargan*. Red Sparrow-hawk, Red Hawk, Red Stain.

This common, attractive bird with its characteristic hovering, bright colour and sharp cry has attracted more British vernacular names than most other species. The original name comes from the Old French *cresselle* from which Cress or Cristel Hawk lead on to Kestrel. The oldest English name appears to be Stanyel dating from about 1475. This may have come from the German word *Steingall* but it is also suggested that it may derive from the Old English word stangale, meaning stone-yeller, because noisy Kestrels perch on stones and build nests on rocky ledges. Whatever the origin, many names used in Scotland from the sixteenth to the eighteenth centuries stem from this root. As in other raptors there is confusion between species as in Maalin (Merlin) and Sparrow hawk. The principal prey creeps into Kestrel nomenclature as in Mouse or Moosie Hawk, and its cry is echoed in the Edinburgh name 'Keelie'. However it is the bird's incredible hovering that has really attracted man's attention and hence a richness of vernacular names. So Fanner, Vanner or Hover appear in names used elsewhere in Britain, as do the references to Wind.

With a wide distribution throughout Eurasia and Africa the Kestrel has been found among fossil remains dating from the Pleistocene. It then probably declined with the general afforestation of Britain since it is largely dependent on voles, which live in open grassland. It suffered badly at the hands of gamekeepers during the late eighteenth and nineteenth centuries. Rallying during the wars, the Kestrel population fell again as a result of toxins in the food chain. Just as it began to recover it lost most of its nest sites with the plague of Dutch Elm Disease. Then, of all unlikely assistants, man created

141

miles of unmolested grassland lining the motorways, leading to an explosion of the vole population and in turn benefitting the Kestrel, the modern bird of the motorway. In Scotland it is widespread, but scarce in the Hebrides and absent as a breeding species from Shetland. Most Kestrels are sedentary but some European birds migrate south, even as far as tropical Africa, feeding on small rodents and beetles.

Q: As Baxter and Rintoul observe (1953): 'The Kestrel is resident in Southern Scotland up to the line of the Grampians; north of this it is a summer visitor.'[13]

T: A hawk of base kind, suitable for a knave or servant, hence a worthless fellow.

Merlin
Falco columbarius

(*columbarius*: Latin, of dove or pigeon, referring to its prey.)

SCOTS NAMES: Hawk Kestrel [Shet], Hobby [Shet], Jack (m), Maalin [Shetland], Marlzeon or Merlzeo, Redhawk, Rock Hawk, Small Blue Hawk [Stir], Sparrow Hawk, Stone Falcon.

GAELIC NAMES: *Méirneal, Seabhag-gorm-an-fraoich*. Merlin, Blue Hawk of the heather.

The Merlin resembles a Peregrine but is much smaller, hence similarities of names with other falcons. The name Merlin almost certainly comes from the Old French *emerillon* and was brought to us by the Normans; and it has been suggested that this in turn may have derived from the Latin *Merulla*, a blackbird. Marlzeo (see p.25) was used generally in Scotland from the fifteenth to the seventeenth centuries and Redhawk was a sixteenth-century name. Male Merlins are called Jacks and the bird's habit of plucking its prey on a stone may account for Stone Falcon or Rock Hawk. The female is reddish and the male greyish, giving rise to Red or Blue Hawk.

This bird of upland heathland is present among fossils from the end of the Pleistocene. Following afforestation at the end of the Ice Age it is likely to have suffered with other species which had adapted to hunting open country. Later, with forest clearance, its numbers improved, only to suffer from game preservation over the last two centuries. The species is now rare except in the Scottish islands, with a population estimated at some 600 pairs. Many Merlins are resident but British numbers are boosted in winter by birds from Scandinavia.

Q: MacGillivray, writing in the 1850s, remarked: 'This beautiful little Falcon is by no means uncommon in many parts of Scotland.'[118]

T: A falcon suitable for a lady. There seems to be no connection with the Merlin of Arthurian mythology.

Peregrine
Falco peregrinus
(*Falco*: Latin, falcon; *peregrinus*: Latin, wanderer.)

SCOTS NAMES: Blue Hawk, Cock o' the doos, Faakin Hawk [Stir], Game Hawk, Tiercel (m).

GAELIC NAMES: *Seabhag-ghorm, Seabhag-an-seilige.* Blue Hawk, Hawk of the hunted.

Peregrine falcons for falconry were not taken from the nest but while migrating, giving rise to 'peregrine' meaning outlandish or making a pilgrimage. It is also suggested that the bird was so named because of its habit of moving with migrating birds to find prey. Many names describe its colour, but these are not specific to the Peregrine. 'Doo' and 'game' describe its prey, though it is by no means limited to such birds for food. Faakin is a corruption of Falcon and Tiercel reminds us that the male is about a 'tierce', or third, smaller than the female.

Traces of the Peregrine have been found among remains dating from the end of the Ice Age. During the sixth century the Peregrine became the most valued species of hawk. This ensured its protection until the seventeenth century. Thereafter it was slaughtered in the name of game preservation. Unlike its effect on other raptors the Second World War did not boost numbers of Peregrine, because they were seen as a threat to the carrier-pigeon communication essential to cross-channel espionage, and some 600 Peregrine were shot around the south coast of Britain where the species was almost eliminated. Today, bounties offered by Pigeon-fanciers in Belgium still pose a threat to the species. The Peregrine's habit of taking pigeons has been used to clear birds from airfields where they pose a strike threat to aircraft. During the 1960s there was a marked decrease in numbers due to poisoning with organochlorine seed dressings, which passed up the food chain to concentrate in raptors. In Scotland the species is widespread wherever there are mountains and seacliffs, and it recovered quickly after the banning of organochlorine seed dressings in 1967.

Q: 'The terrific force with which a resolute hawk comes down on a Grouse must be seen to be believed. The Grouse is knocked head over heels amid a cloud of flying feathers and the bird bounces up again when it hits the ground... Peregrines kill their quarry quickly by biting through the neck and then begin to eat the head.'[109]

T: A falcon suitable for an Earl.

A Gaelic charm recorded in *Carmina Gadelica* appeals to St Bride for protection of livestock:[35]

> From the blue peregrine hawk of Creag Duilion,
> From the brindled eagle of Ben-ard,
> From the swift hawk of Tordun,
> From the surly raven of Bard's Creag.

Lannair from lann, a spear or lance, is the name of the Peregrine.[35]

ORDER: GALLIFORMES
GALLINACEOUS BIRDS

Family: *Tetraonidae,* the Grouse

No. in world, 17; no. in Scotland, 4.

Red Grouse
Lagopus lagopus scoticus

(*Lagopus*: Greek, *lagos* a hare, *pous* foot—refers to the Grouse's hairy foot.)

SCOTS NAMES: Gor (-cock or -hen), Gorock or Groose, Muir-hen [Per], -fowl -cock or -pout [Ork].

GAELIC NAMES: *Cearc-fhraoich, Coileach-fraoich, Eun-ruadh.* Hen or Cock of the heather, Red bird.

The term Red Grouse was coined by Pennant[148] and became the standard name after Yarrell in 1843.[201] Most of its vernacular names include habitat terms such as Moor (in various spellings) Heath and Moss. Muircock is probably the oldest and dates from the fifteenth century. Gor echoes the harsh repeated 'go-back, go-back' cry of disturbed grouse.

There is evidence of Grouse during the Pleistocene of about 500,000 years ago. The birds developed as cold-weather inhabitants of heathland. Following the Ice Age Grouse spread over northern upland unforested areas. It was important as a food source quite early but it was not until the fifteenth century that laws were passed to protect it. During the eighteenth century farming practice competed with the bird's increasing popularity as sport. From the second half of the nineteenth century elaborate game preservation and elimination of predators caused huge increases of Grouse, which, by the early part of the twentieth century, reached summer populations of 5 million, of which 60% were shot during the season. Numbers have since fallen and probably now reach less than one million. This is less likely to have been caused by reduction in persecution of predators, since the crucial factors in determining Grouse population are the environment and the fluctuation of disease. Grouse disease has been responsible for many problems on the lucrative sporting estates of the North (see p.71).

The alarm call of the Red Grouse is, as mentioned above, often described as sounding like a shouted 'Go, go, go, go back, go back'. In Scotland this is sometimes written '*Co, co, co, co, mo-chlaidh, mo-chlaidh*' meaning 'Who? who? who? who? my sword, my sword!'

Q: The Bonie Moor-hen

The heather was blooming, the meadows were mawn,
Our lads gaed a-hunting ae the day at the dawn,
O'er moors and o'er mosses and mony a glen,
At length they discover'd a bonie moor-hen.

                    Robert Burns.[32]

'In October there is not a more beautiful bird in our island; and in January a cock grouse is one of the most superb fellows in the world, as he struts about fearlessly with his mate, his bright red comb erected above his eyes and his rich dark-brown plumage shining in the sun.'[161]

T: The nest of the red hen
              Is in the green red-tipped heather,
              My little one shall sleep and he shall have the bird.

                    From a lullaby sung to a child.[35]

Ptarmigan
Lagopus mutus

(*mutus*: Latin, silent, quiet.)

SCOTS NAMES: Cairn Bird, Grey Ptarmigan, Rock Grouse, Rock Ptarmigan, Snow Chick, Snow Grouse, Tarmachan, Tarmagan, Termigant, Tormican or Tormichen, White Game, White Grouse, White Partridge.

GAELIC NAMES: *Tarmachan breac na beinne, Eun bàn an t-neachda, Gealag-bheinne.*

The spotted Ptarmigan of the mountains, White bird of the snow, White one of the mountain. According to Carmichael *Tarman* or *tarmigan* is the 'Murmur Bird' from *tarm* to murmur.[35] However it is generally thought to be derived from the Gaelic *Tarmachan*, a croaker; this name echoes the noise heard on Scottish mountains where a flock may sound like a plague of frogs. Variations of this name have been used in Scotland since late sixteenth century.

The 'pt' prefix seems to be an affectation introduced by Sibbald[173] in false analogy with the Greek (as in *pteron* a wing). Pennant[148] adopted Sibbald's 'Ptarmigan', which has since become standard. The Ptarmigan's dimorphic plumage gives rise to 'white' and 'grey' in its names and its mountain-top habitat to 'Cairn' and 'Rock'.

The Ptarmigan has fossil remains dating from the middle Pleistocene of about half a million years ago. During the warmer Holocene it was probably less successful, retreating northwards and higher into the mountains. Though protected as a game bird since the sixteenth century it has gradually retreated. As the species is sedentary, rarely seen below 2,000 feet, once a colony has disappeared it is almost impossible for it to re-establish itself unaided and it gradually disappeared from many of the Scottish islands during the nineteenth century. It was recolonised in Arran in 1977 (where Pennant[147] had stated that they were to be found). Populations fluctuate cyclically with periods of abundance every ten years or so. Skiing in the Highlands has led to reduction of numbers of Ptarmigan due to mortality from colliding with ski-lifts, disturbance of birds by skiers and Crows attracted by food waste left by them.

Q: Dwelly, author of the dictionary, describes it thus: '*Tarmachan breac na beinne*. This is a rare species of moorfowl, seen on the tops of the highest Highland hills. The size of the ptarmigan is nearly that of the grouse, and its colour light grey, but in winter it is perfectly white. It is a very shy and timid bird; but when the sportsman comes upon it by surprise, it is daunted even to stupidity, and has not the courage even to fly from danger.'[56]

The accusation of stupidity is echoed by Graham, writing in 1812: 'The ptarmigan is found in the higher regions. Whether from stupidity of nature, or from being seldom disturbed by the intrusions of man, the ptarmigan fears not his approach, but sits still till you are almost close upon him.'[75]

T: Legend tells of two nuns who rescued a woman and child from a shipwreck in the Western Isles. The woman was an Irish Princess and her son when grown up succeeded to the throne in Ireland. The nuns composed poetry about the mysterious lady:

> Who is she the melodious lady-lord?
> Not the lark,
> Not the merle
> Not the mavis
> Not the murmuring ptarmigan
> Of the hill is she.[35]

The nest of the ptarmigan
Is in the rough mountain,
My little one shall sleep and he shall have the bird.

From a lullaby sung to a child.[35]

Black Grouse
Tetrao (formerly Lyurus) tetrix

(*Tetrao*, see Capercaillie; *Lyurus*: Greek, *Lyra* a lyre, *ouros* a tail; *tetricus*:
Latin, forbidding or harsh, referring to its voice (see below).)

SCOTS NAMES: Black Game, Heath Bird, Heath Fowl, Killockdoe.
(m) only: Black Cock, Heath or Heather Cock.
(f) only: Birch Hen, Brown hen, Grey Hen or Gret Hen, Grigear, Hasel Hen,
Heath Hen.

GAELIC NAMES: *Coileach-dubh*, *Liathchearc*, *Eun-liath*. Blackcock, Grey
Hen, Grey Bird.

Ray[135] used the names Black Grouse, Heathcock and Black Game between
1674 and 1678 and Yarrell later standardised the name.[201] The male is a handsome creature almost all black with white tail, a red wattle over each eye
and a lyre-shaped tail. The female is dowdy, accounting for the differences
in gender names; Gret Hen was in general use in Scotland in the fifteenth
century. Other names refer to habitat and the bizarre Killockdoe probably
derives from Killick or Killock, an anchor, and Doe a dove, an evocative
name in view of the shape of the tail and the amorous cooing of the courting
male, which is anything but 'harsh'.

The Black Grouse is more of a woodland species than other related birds
and its early records are found only in milder periods of the Pleistocene, but
it flourished in the warmer Holocene. It was fairly widespread throughout

Britain until the end of the last century when shooting reduced its numbers considerably. Between the wars there was a sharp decline so that shooting returns were only 20% of former bags. Much of this decline is attributed to changed agricultural policy, especially the increase of conifer plantations and overgrazing by sheep. It has now virtually disappeared apart from northern and central Scotland and appears to be in slow long-term decline. The courtship rituals of the Black Grouse are among the most spectacular of all Scottish birds. The 'lek' is a sort of displaying area, where each cock holds a tiny territory, defending it against other cocks. Each cock tries to woo a female by drooping his wings and spreading his tail as she passes through his territory. The females choose the dominant cocks, ensuring selection of the best genes.[194]

Q: Osgood Mackenzie, in 1921, lamented the bird's passing: 'The Black Grouse is a bird of the past... Even on my own small property I used to kill from 20 to 30 brace in a season. In 1915 only one pair remained.'[119]

T: Black Grouse crowing at dawn are reputed to dispel evil spirits of the night, but it is ominous to hear the greyhen after dusk. Apart from the evil it bodes, the sound is extremely eerie.[35]

> The nest of the heath-hen
> Is in the marshland mound,
> My little one shall sleep and he shall have the bird.
>
> From *Carmina Gadelica*: a lullaby sung to a child.[35]

Capercaillie
Tetrao urogallus

(*Tetrao*: Latin and Greek, black grouse; *urogallus*: Greek and Latin, *oura* tail, *gallus* cock.)

SCOTS NAMES: Auer-calze or Avercalzie, Caercailzie, Caper, Capercalie or Capercally, Capercalye, Cobber-kelly, Cock of the Mountain, Great Grouse, Horse of the Woods, Wood Grouse.

GAELIC NAME: *Capall coille*, Horse of the woods (Some Gaelic scholars hold that the name should really be *Gabhar-coille*, the goat of the wood, because of the cock bird's goat-like beard and sexual aggressiveness.)

The name Capercaillie has come about because the male's frenzied nuptial song is said to sound like a horse. Apart from obvious habitat names most of the Scots names come from Gaelic, including Auer-calze which is a misspelling

149

dating from 1526. Cock of the Wood was a translation of the Irish *Coileach feá*, used by Ray.[155] Burt used the term Cobber-kelly.[33]

Capercaillie were present in southern England from the end of the Pleistocene and are likely to have increased during the warmer forested early Holocene. They gradually declined and Pennant, in 1768, recorded the species as rare, 'formerly common throughout the Highlands found only north of Inverness'.[148] But by 1785 it was disappearing from Scotland. In 1838 Capercaillie from Sweden were re-introduced in Perthshire (see p.59) from where they slowly extended to peak in the 1950s since when, despite topping up from Sweden, they have again declined.

Q: 'Two nests, each with seven eggs, females differing, near Glenalmond 11 May 1913. In each case on ground, at foot of a tree, circular, large, deep, one quite unprotected above, of dried pine needles, lined grass with a few feathers.'[198]

David Millar[132] opens a long a poem about the River Tay with a reference to the Capercaillie:

> The capercailzie wake the woods—
> The deer starts from its lair...

'On rare occasions a displaying cock capercaillie becomes aggressive towards human beings... Because of its powerful beak... a bird like this could take a piece out of you.'[180]

T: The record bag of Capercaillie was 69, shot by seven guns on 4 November 1910 at Dunkeld in Perthshire.

Family: *Phasianidae*, the Pheasants and Partridges

No. in world, 185; no. in Scotland, 3.

Red-legged Partridge
Alectoris rufa

(*Alectoris*: Greek, cock; *rufus*: Latin, red.)

SCOTS NAMES: French Partridge, Frenchman, Green Partridge, Guernsey Partridge, Red Leg, Red Partridge.

GAELIC NAME: *Cearc-thomain dhearg-chasach*. Hen of the hillock with red legs.

The successful introduction of this species to Britain from France in 1770 inevitably led to it being called the French Partridge, though Ray[155] had already named it 'Red-legged' in 1678. 'Green' distinguishes it from the Common or Grey Partridge but, at least to this colour-blind observer, there is nothing green about this bird.

It was first brought to Britain from France by Charles II who attempted, unsuccessfully, to establish it in Windsor Great Park. More successfully, thousands of eggs from France were incubated under domestic fowls in Suffolk in 1770. From here the species has extended until the 1950s when its population was similar to that of the Common or Grey Partridge. Since 1961 its population has increased while that of the Grey has fallen. This has mirrored changed agricultural policy. The Red-legged Partridge was introduced into Scotland in the 1970s and is now reasonably common in Perthshire.[100]

Q: And she loved little things,
Parrots
And red-legged partridges
And the golden fishes of the Duc de Guise
And the pigeon with the blue ruff
She had from Monsieur d'Elboef
Alas! Poor Queen. [Mary Queen of Scots][6]

T: 'A partridge in a pear tree' from the 'First Day of Christmas' originally was a forfeit game but is now firmly established among Christmas Carols. It was derived from France so it is possible that the bird in question was a 'frenchman' or Red-legged Partridge; this bird perches in trees much more frequently than the Grey, or English Partridge. There is also the pun on the French for partridge, *perdrix*, which sounds like 'peartree'.

Grey Partridge
Perdix perdix
(*Perdix*: Latin and Greek, partridge.)

SCOTS NAMES: Aiten, Paitrick [Ayr], Pairtrick [Loth], Pertrick [Aber], Perdrix.

GAELIC NAMES: *Cearc-thomain, Pioghaid thruisg, Cearc-chrudach.* Hen of the hillock; *Pioghaid* means a useless, talkative young woman, *thruisg* or *truisig* apparently means flock, *chrudach* means a horseshoe, referring to the male's breast pattern.

The original name of pertriche dates from the Norman and Old French *per-triz*. From this base Partridge and many local variants have arisen. The name of Common Partridge was introduced by Ray in 1678[155] but has been shortened to Partridge as the only truly British species. Aiten is an eighteenth-century name of obscure Scottish origin.

This is a native bird of Britain, which also occurs widely throughout Europe and Eurasia. It has been found among late Pleistocene remains, fluctuating as increased afforestation diminished its grassland habitat. The population increased from the eighteenth to the beginning of the twentieth century. More recently the population has slumped due to changed agricultural practice, with the removal of hedgerows and use of chemical sprays. In Scotland the decline of Grey Partridges has been less marked: however they are down by 70% since 1970 and are limited to the southern and eastern counties. This most delicious of all the game birds is sadly now becoming rare.

Q: The minister for Clunie in Perthshire recorded that they were common in 1797: 'The partridge nestles in almost every clover field, where sometimes the poor dam, while she sits on 18 or perhaps 24 eggs, has her head cut off by the scythe.'[145]

But things had changed by Osgood Mackenzie's time (1921): 'From Cape Wrath to the Clyde the Partridges are extinct, or very nearly so.'[119]

Forbes adds: 'It is predominantly a bird of the low grounds, where the "portly" sportsman can, with some assistance, slay it.'[61]

T: Perdix of Greek mythology was the nephew of Daedalus who, in a fit of jealousy, tried to push him from a high tower. Perdix turned himself into a partridge and flew to safety but never returned to his rightful shape. Thereafter he avoided heights and stayed very close to the ground where he continually reminded hearers of his uncle's perfidy by telling his story over and over again in his hoarse voice.

In 1678 the bird was regarded as a delicacy: 'Palate men and such as have skill in eating do chiefly commend the Partridge's wing preferring it much before the leg as indeed it is much better hence that English proverbial rhythm:

> If the partridge had the woodcock's thigh
> Twould be the best bird that ere did fly

This saying was in vogue among epicures in the reign of Charles II.'[155]

Pheasant
Phasanius colchicus

(*Phasanius*: Latin, a Pheasant; *colchicus* from Colchis, an ancient mythical country between the Caspian and Black Seas. The country was drained by the River Phasis—now the Rhioni which enters the Black Sea south of Poti—and was associated with sorcery.)

SCOTS NAMES: Comet, Ephesian, Fasian or Feesant [Per, Fif, Loth], Phesand.

GAELIC NAME: *Easag*, Pheasant, also a Squirrel.

For a common bird, much sought after by sportsmen and poachers, it is remarkable that Pheasants have so few names. Comet is a poacher's name, apt for a creature with a long tail, which rises explosively and steeply.

The Pheasant has probably had more influence on the landscape of Britain than any other creature except the horse. It has also influenced the ecology of many of its natural predators through man's determined effort to eliminate them.

Pheasants originated in southern Eurasia from the Black Sea to China. The Romans brought the first birds to Britain but the main invasion came with the Normans in 1066 and they gradually dispersed through England. In the sixteenth century Pheasants were introduced into Scotland and the stage was set for the growth of organised shooting as a rural sport. In the twentieth century there has been a waning of major estates due to changed economy and the structure of society. This has had some effect upon Pheasants but, as Grouse diminish, many estates are turning to Pheasant-rearing to supply sporting revenues. It is estimated that some eight million wild birds exist, with an annual release of another 15 million. Most of this huge population will be shot in the season, but thanks to the Pheasant's large clutches of eggs it manages to maintain its numbers.

Q: Alexandra Stewart records an ingenious way of catching the birds: 'The blacksmith at Keltneyburn picked up a slightly disreputable supply of pheasants during his regular trips up the Glen Lyon to see to the horses at Meggernie castle. He left grain soaked with whisky on the way up and collected the fuddled birds on the way back.'[189]

T: According to Pliny, Pheasants will die of lice unless they bestrew themselves with dust.[63]

ORDER: GRUIFORMES
CRANES, BUSTARDS AND RAILS

Family: *Rallidae,* the Rails and Coots
No. in world, 124; no. in Scotland, 5.

Water Rail
Rallus aquaticus
(*Rallus*: Latin, rail; *aquaticus*: Latin, of the water.)

SCOTS NAMES: Bilcock, Brook Ouzel, Brook Runner, Brown Hen, Darcock, Grey Hen, Grey Moorhen, Oarcock, Runner, Scarragrise (scared-in-the-grass), Skiddy Cock, Skel, Skelby, Skitty Cock, Velvet Runner, War Cock.

GAELIC NAMES: *Snagan-allt, Gearradh-dubh-nan-allt, Snagan-dubh.* Creeper of the burn or black creeper; *Gearradh* is used of many species but also means to taunt, so this bird, which teases observers by its loud calls from hiding, becomes the 'Taunter of the burn'.

The Bilcock or Water Rail was recorded by Ray in 1678;[155] the former from the Middle English word 'bulten', to bolt, recalling the Water Rail's habit of dodging between cover; Dar(t)cock has a similar meaning as have Runner, Skitty (from skit, to slide), Rat hen and Scarragrise. Brook Ouzel is something of a misnomer, as the Rail is quite unlike other 'ouzels' except perhaps in overall dark coloration when, as usually, briefly glimpsed. Brook Runner is much more appropriate.

The Water Rail, present in remains dating from the middle Pleistocene, probably fluctuated with climatic change thereafter. Water Rails are rarely seen because of their skulking nature but are not all that rare; summer breeding birds were estimated in the 1980s at between 2,000 and 4,000 pairs and the winter numbers are increased by southern migration. The species is absent from much of Scotland during the breeding season when Rails require dense aquatic vegetation. Water Rails are very noisy in spring, making pig-like calls, called 'sharming'; this may often be the only clue to their presence.

Q: At the end of the nineteenth century it was observed that: 'In Scotland it is found chiefly during the cold season... it even passes the winter in the Shetlands.'[162]

T: 'Herding a water rail' is a Lowland saying indicating an impossible task.

155

Corncrake
Crex crex

(*Crex*: Latin and Greek, bird with a sharp notched bill.)

SCOTS NAMES: Corncraik, Corn Scrack [Aber], Daker, King of the Quail, Land Rail, Quailzie, Weet-my-fit.

GAELIC NAMES: *Traona, Garra-gart, Racan-arbhai.* Landrail, Mowing grass (cf. Quail) *Garra* (?) from *garrag* a yell, Croaking one of the cornsheaf.

Originally named 'Corne Crake' in Scotland and known there from 1455, the name was introduced into English ornithological literature by Bewick in 1797.[19] Most of this secretive bird's names derive from a combination of its favoured habitat and its strange voice. Daker has been derived from the Norse *Ager-hoene* (Cock of the field) but it also simulates the bird's call.

The history of the Corncrake illustrates the effect of change in farming which has almost driven this bird to extinction. Present in the early Holocene as a bird of open grassland, it is likely to have increased its range as woodland was cleared. When horses became important and as the need for hay increased the Corncrake flourished. But by the end of the nineteenth century Corncrakes were disappearing in England though they remained abundant in Scotland until the 1930s. As mechanised grass-cutting superseded the scythe the Corncrake retreated northwards and westwards. The tendency towards earlier grass cutting for silage led to disturbance of young birds and hastened this retreat. New methods of harvesting silage grass involve cutting outwards from the centre of a field, which affords escaping birds cover towards the periphery of the field. Nevertheless by the end of the 1970s only a dozen birds were to be heard south of the Scottish border and the main population of some 700 birds were in the Scottish islands.

Q: Mourn, clam'ring craiks at close o' day;
'Mang fields o' flowering clover gay;
And when ye wing your annual way
Frae our cauld shore,
Tell thae far warlds wha lies in clay,
Wham we deplore.

Robert Burns, 'Elegy on Captain Matthew Henderson'.[29]

At Glenalmond Dr Williams[198] recorded the date he first heard Corncrakes: 14 June 1913 and 4 June 1914.

T: Among primitive peoples it is thought that Corncrakes hitch lifts because of their apparently weak flight. Certainly Corncrake often migrate with other gallinaceous species, particularly Quail (*Coturnix coturnix*) when sometimes every group of Quail is accompanied by a Corncrake. In ancient times this gave rise to the legend that the Corncrake was the 'King of the Quail'.

> The Corncrake said
> O God of the powers!
> O God of the powers!
> Put food in the field!
> Put food in the field!
>
> From the speech of birds, in *Carmina Gadelica*.[35]

'A comical and absurd belief existed that when uttering its notes the corn-crake does so lying on its back, otherwise the heavens would fall.'[61] Corncrakes were thought to foretell rain with their rasping calls and in the north it was considered a blessed bird which only 'sang' after all threat of frost had passed.

Conversing with Corncrakes using an old credit card and a comb can produce fascinating results... If only from bemused onlookers!

Moorhen
Gallinula Chloropus

(*Gallinula*: Latin, Little chicken or pullet; *Chloropus*: Greek, *chlorus* green, *pous* foot.)

SCOTS NAMES: Marsh Hen, Stank Hen or Stankie [Suth, Per, Loth], Water Hen.

GAELIC NAME: *Cearc uisge*. Hen of the water.

The name Moorhen had been in use since about 1300. Many vernacular names, such as 'stank', which is a shallow pond, refer to habitat.

The Moorhen left traces in the middle Pleistocene and is present throughout Britain and Western Europe. In Britain it has a population of some 300,000 pairs in summer, rising to over a million in winter. This is falling since the bird is prone to predation by feral mink. Moorhens are less common in the Highlands but are widespread throughout lowland areas of Scotland.

Q: 'The Water-Hen may be found almost wherever there are water and aquatic plants of sufficient growth to afford concealment and shelter, for it is naturally of a skulking and wary disposition.'[107]

Coot
Fulica atra

(*Fulica*: Latin, a coot, *atra*: dead black (*niger* is shiny black).)

SCOTS NAMES: Bald Duck, Bald Coot, Bald Duck, Bald Pate, Bell-poote [Loth], Bell Kite, Black Hen [Shet], Bomo [Ork], Cuit or Cute, Queet, Snellie, Sneeshan, Snysin, Snyth, Snythe or Snaith [Ork], Water Crow [Dumf], Whistling Duck.

GAELIC NAMES: *Lach-bhlàir, an dubhlach, Dubh-lachadh, Eunsnàmhach.* Bald duck.

Coot probably goes back to the Middle English word *cote* which is onomatopoeic, resembling the high pitched metallic call (Poot, Cute and Queet are all from the same sound). Many vernacular names refer to the white, featherless shield on the bird's forehead, as in Bald Coot or Pate. The Orkney names Snaithe etc derive from the Norn word *sny*, meaning a white mark or blaze on a horse's head.

Like the Moorhen the coot was present during the Pleistocene but rather later than the Moorhen. It has always been widespread, but numbers would have been reduced during the Little Ice Age. The breeding population is increasing slowly and is estimated at 50,000-100,000, a figure that doubles during winter. Coot are widely distributed throughout lowland areas of Scotland but are less common in north-west Scotland.

Q: According to the *Old Statistical Account* (1791-99) 'Dudingston [sic] Loch is in summer covered with flocks of coots, which when young, form a tolerable variety for the table. They remain till the closing of the ice totally excludes them from the water, when they emigrate to the sea, and return with the first thaw.'[145]

T: These birds are subject to lice, which is so common with them that it has grown into a saying that anything filthy is 'as lousey as a coot'.

Writing in 1927, Loyd observed: 'If a gentleman wishes to have plenty of wild-fowl on his pond, let him preserve the Coots... the reason that all wild-fowl seek the company of the Coots is because these birds are such good sentries to give the alarm by day, when the fowl generally sleep.'[111] There may be other reasons for this observation. Coot feed by diving and in so doing stir up invertebrates towards the surface. Wigeon, and other dabbling ducks, often feed close to Coots in a form of commensalism.

ORDER: CHARADRIIFORMES
WADERS, GULLS AND AUKS

Family: *Haematopodidae,* the Oystercatchers

(*Haimatto*: Greek, stain with blood; *Pous* foot, hence bloodstained feet.)
No. in world, 11; no. in Scotland, 1.

Oystercatcher
Haematopus ostralegus

(*Ostralegus*: Latin, *ostre* oyster, *lego* to pick.)

SCOTS NAMES: Chalder, Chaldro, Cholder or Chaldrick [Ork], Gilliebride, Krocket [Aber], Mussill Picker, Pleep [Mor], Red Neb [Banf, Aber], Scolder or Scottie [Ork], Sea Pilot, Sea Pyot [Aber, For, Per, Gall], Shalder or Shelder [Shet], Sheldro or Skeldrake [Ork], Skelderdrake, Skirly or Skirly Wheeter [Banf, Aber], Tirma, Trillichan or Drilleachan [Heb].

GAELIC NAMES: *Gille-Brighde, Drilleachan, Dolaid.* Servant of St Bridget, onomatopoeic name, *Dolaid* also means impatient.

Oystercatcher species occur all over the world. The name originally came from America where these birds do eat oysters. Pennant[148] took the name Oystercatcher in 1768, writing of the Sea Pie or Oystercatcher, and later dropped Sea Pie, so leading Yarrell[201] to adopt Oystercatcher as the standard name. Scottish names abound for this common bird of the coast. A Norn name *tjald*, meaning piping, has given rise to Chalder, Shalder, Skeldrake etc. Many names relate to the pied plumage or its feeding habits, as in Mussel Cracker and hence Krocket. Martin[126] in his writings on St Kilda (1698) mentioned the 'Tirma', a name which is thought to have come about as a combination of the onomatopoeic sound 'Tir' with ma(w) a gull. Trillichan is clearly onomatopoeic, but serves for other birds of the Hebrides such as Sandpipers and Sanderlings.

The Oystercatcher is a bird of warm climate and its first record in Britain is in the ninth century, since when it slowly spread as a coastal species. By the end of the nineteenth century, when they were widely distributed round the coast, the British population had risen to reach its present approximately 43,000 breeding pairs, of which 70% are in Scotland.

Q: The nineteenth century naturalist Thomas Edward wrote of them: 'Why this bird is called an oystercatcher I cannot understand. Had it been named a "limpetcatcher" I could have understood it. I have crawled amongst the rocks to see them feed, when I have seen the limpet driven from its hold and scooped out of its shell... but I have never seen it attempt to catch an oyster.'[174]

The call is said to resemble the Gaelic '*bi glic, bi glic*' (be wise, be wise), appropriate for a bird under the protection of the patron saint of birds, St Bride.[48]

T: The Oystercatcher is said to have once saved Christ from His enemies by covering Him with seaweed as He lay exhausted upon the shore.[69]

In Uist legend the Oystercatcher left his nest unattended and a Grey Crow robbed it and drank the eggs. On his return the Oystercatcher called out in distress '*Co dh' ol na h-uibhean? Cha chuala mi riamh a leithid!*' 'Who drank the eggs? I never heard the like!' To which the Crow replied with mock sympathy, 'No, nor heard we ourselves that, though we are older in the place.'[35]

Family: *Charadriidae,* the Plovers and Lapwings

(*charadrius*: Greek, a bird dwelling in a mountain cleft or chasm.)
No. in world, 64; no. in Scotland, 5.

Ringed Plover
Charadrius hiaticula

(*hiaticula*: Latin, *cula* or *incola* inhabitant of, *hiatus* a cleft.)

SCOTS NAMES: Lairick [Cai, Aber], Ring Dotterel, Ring Plover, Sandie Lairick or Laverock [Ork and Shet], Sandy Loo or Sandlo or Sinloo [Ork], Sea Lark.

161

GAELIC NAMES: *Bothag* or *Bodhag*, *Tarmachan-tuinne*. Ringed Plover (also used for Common Sandpiper), croaker of the wave.

Ringed Plover derives from the bird's black collar, hence Ring-neck, Ring Dotterel etc. Sand Lark or Laverock are Scottish names used for both Ringed Plover and Common Sandpiper. Loo comes from the Norn *lo* imitating the call.

The Ringed Plover, as a cold weather bird, has a long British history dating from the Middle Pleistocene. As its distribution is largely coastal its numbers probably remained fairly constant until the fashion of seaside holidays started in the nineteenth century, with consequent disturbance of beach nesting sites. The decrease in population continued apart from a respite during World War II when many beaches were out of bounds to all but birds. Numbers have been estimated at about 9,000 breeding pairs with some 35,000 wintering birds. Ringed Plover are the common shore birds of Scotland, particularly on the deserted beaches of the Hebrides.

Q: Writing in the middle of the nineteenth century, MacGillivray declared that: 'This species is found on all our sandy sea-shores and is plentiful in the Shetland and Orkney Isles, as well as in the Hebrides'.[118]

T: Ringed Plover singing near a house warn of a death within.[35]

> The nest of the sealark
> Is on the level shingle-beach,
> My little one shall sleep and he shall have the bird.

> From a lullaby sung to a child.[35]

Dotterel
*Charadrius (*formerly *Eudromius) morinellus*

(*Eudromius*: Greek, *eu* good, *dromos* runner; *morinellus*: Latin, diminutive of *moros*, foolish or stupid, hence 'little stupid thing'.)

SCOTS NAMES: Foolish Dotterel, Moor Dotterel.

GAELIC NAMES: *Amadán móinteach*, *Uiseag riasgach*. Fool of the moorland or mountain plover.

Two explanations compete for the etymology of Dotterel. 'Dot' refers to the calls made by Dotterel. From the onomatopoeic 'dot' with its association with 'dotage' and 'dotard' comes the idea of foolishness. Dotterel are supposedly very good to eat and were much in demand. They are also very tame and easily caught and so are said to be foolish. However one is lucky to see one now, let alone catch it.

The Dotterel was first mentioned in 1450 at the beginning of the Little Ice Age, which suited it, so that it increased during the next four centuries but declined in the subsequent warmer period. It was heavily persecuted during the eighteenth century, among other reasons to provide feathers for fishing flies, and by 1900 was scarce. In the twentieth century there was a slow recovery until 1960, when numbers increased in Scotland and the breeding range increased southwards to the Borders. There is a need for conservation of this uncommon bird, whose numbers are down to about 100 to 150 pairs, almost all in the Central Highlands. Increase in global warming threatens loss of the mountain-top habitat of Dotterel.

Q: Nethersole-Thompson, writing of West Inverness and Argyllshire, described hills with the broad backs and and long ridges that Dotterel love, and advised the seeker after the birds to choose those that look like stranded whales.[140] 'Dotterel occur regularly in Moray only on the Cairngorm/Ben Macdui plateau around Loch Avon and on the highest hills surrounding upper Glen Avon.'[42]

T: Dotterel was used to mean a doting old fool or an old man easily cajoled, because of the ease with which the bird is caught. 'To dor the Dotterel' meant to cheat a simpleton (dor is an obsolete word meaning to cheat).

Golden Plover
Pluvialis apricaria

(*Pluvialis*: Latin, referring to rain, *apricaria*: Latin, golden in the sun.)

SCOTS NAMES: Grey Plover [Ayr, summer only], Hill Plover, Plever Pliver [Ork], Plover [Rox], Pluver, Sea Plover, Whistler, Whistling Plover, Yellow [Loth] or Yella Plover [Mor, For, Fif].

GAELIC NAME: *Feadagh*. Whistle or pipe.

The name Plover comes from the French *pluvier* because of the bird's association with rain. As with many vernacular names there is great overlap between species. Originally known as the Green Plover, a name also applied to the Lapwing, the Golden Plover was so named by Pennant.[148] Many of the other names, though descriptive, might do for either the Grey or Golden Plover. 'Hill Plover' contrasts with 'Strand Plover' and 'Sea Plover', indicating habitat preference of the Golden and Grey Plovers respectively.

163

Early records from the Pleistocene reveal that the Golden Plover has been in Britain for nearly a million years. As a bird adapted to arctic breeding it is likely to have reduced in number during the warmer Holocene and prospered during the Little Ice Age of 1400-1880. From the beginning of this century numbers again dropped and British breeding is limited to high mossy ground (where its plumage offers good camouflage) in the north and west, especially in Scotland, with an estimated breeding population of some 23,000. The winter migration brings in birds from Iceland, Scandinavia and Siberia to boost the population to 600,000.

Q: Pennant (1768) remarked: 'They breed on several of our unfrequented mountains; and are very common on those of the isle of Rum, and others of the loftier Hebrides.'[148]

T: In Scotland the call of the Golden Plover is said to advise farmers 'to plough well, sow well and harrow well.'

> The nest of the plover
> Is in the wooded copse,
> My little one shall sleep and he shall have the bird.
>
> From a lullaby sung to a child.[35]

Grey Plover
Pluvialis squatarola

(*squatarola*: Italian, having a black belly.)

SCOTS NAMES: Sea Plover, Stone Plover, Strand Plover.

GAELIC NAME: *Feadag-ghlas*. Grey plover.

Though there is some overlap with Golden Plover in names, the difference in habitat is indicated by references to sea, strand etc.

The Grey Plover may have bred during the Pleistocene but its first records are at the beginning of the Holocene, about 10,000 years ago. It breeds in the high Arctic, migrating southwards as the nights lengthen in August. In Scotland the Grey Plover is present as a wintering species in numbers of up to 1,000, chiefly in the Eden Estuary in Fife, the Solway Firth and the Firth of Forth.

Q: As far as MacGillivray in the nineteenth century was concerned, 'The Grey Plover, which is pretty generally distributed on the Continent of Europe, seems to be with us merely an annual visitor, appearing in small flocks in autumn and spring, chiefly along the coast.'[118]

164

Lapwing
Vanellus vanellus

(*Vanellus*: French, *vanneau* Lapwing; Latin, *vanellus* diminutive of *vanus*, little ostentatious thing.)

SCOTS NAMES: Chewit [Per], Lappie [Fife], Peesie [For, Per], Peeweep, Peesweep or Peesieweep, Peeweet [For, Per], Scochad or Shouchad [Cai & Suth], Tee Whip, Tee Whippo, Tee-wit or Tee Wup [Ork], Teuchit or Tuchit [For & NE], Tewhit, Teewheet or Teewheep [Kirk], Thievnick [Ork] Tieve's Nacket or Tieves Geit [Shet], Tufit, Wallock, Wallop [NE] or Wallopie Wep [Mor], Wallopieweet [Ork, Aber, Inv].

GAELIC NAMES: *Curracag*, *Feadag-riasgach*, *Adharean-luachrach*. With a bonnet, whistler of the moor or fen, little horned one of the rushes.

'Lapwing' comes from eighth century Old English *lepewince*, in which *lepe* referred to the bird's crest and *wince*, like winch, meant to raise or lower. By the fourteenth century the name had been modified to *Hleapwince* meaning literally 'a leap with a waver in it'. Many names are obviously onomatopoeic. There is a slight catch between the two syllables of the bird's call, which the name Peesieweep captures nicely.

In Britain Lapwing records begin at the end of the Pleistocene. With the marshy open landscape of the early Holocene the Lapwing probably did well until increasing forestation depleted the open grasslands. During the cold period of the Little Ice Age numbers probably fell. Though breeding conditions improved at the end of the nineteenth century the popularity of Plovers' eggs as a delicacy kept numbers down. However the decrease of Lapwings continued after the Second World War due to more machine cultivation, silage production and the use of chemical weedkillers. Lapwings suffered badly in the harsh winter of 1962-3. Monitored populations of grassland waders showed a fall of 30% between 1984 and 1986. The present status is difficult to assess because of huge migration, however the evidence suggests a downward trend which is quite marked in the south, where agricultural changes deleterious to Lapwings have been most pronounced. In Scotland flocking to the major estuaries starts in late summer with many more birds on inland pastures near the coast.

Q: These birds leave Perthshire in winter: Dr Williams[198] noted 'Left Glenalmond by September seventeenth 1913; in low country all winter, returned 24th February 1914.'

'The Changes'

A peewit came
This spring to the island
In snowflakes, daffodils and the wind.

Usually a whole gale of them blow in.
Their voices like children's, their flight
Soft and dipping across the fields.

But this year
only one came back
In the wild sunlight of March.

We watched and waited
We listened in the mornings
But there was just one peewit.

Strange and hopeless
Up on the clay dark of the moorland
Calling and calling without end.

Kenneth C. Steven, Iona 2000.[184]

T: The Lapwing is hated in Scotland, partly because it is alleged to have betrayed the Covenanters in the hills by its restless cries but also because these birds, which habitually call 'Bewitched, bewitched', are the spirits of the dead who cannot rest and have returned to haunt the Earth. For this reason it is associated with the Seven Whistlers (see Curlew). The Lapwing's bad reputation also comes from the legend that as Our Lord was crucified the bird flew over Him crying 'Pine Him!' (make Him suffer) and was evermore accurst.

Maiden ladies were believed in Scandinavian legend to be transformed to Lapwings at death whilst single men became Green Sandpipers. This accounted for the calls of the two birds. Lapwings flew round the place where

the Old Maids lived crying 'Oh why wouldn't you?' to which the Green Sandpipers replied 'Because we dare not', followed by a shout of insulting laughter.

> The nest of the lapwing
> Is in the hummocked marsh,
> My little one shall sleep and he shall have the bird.
>
> From a lullaby sung to a child.[35]

Family: *Scolopacidae,* the Sandpipers and Snipe

(*Scolopax*: Greek, a snipe.)
No. in world, 85; no. in Scotland, 21.

Knot
Calidris canutus

(*Calidris*: Greek, a spotted bird; *canutus*: like Canute, feeding on the
waterline as though daring the waves.)

SCOTS NAMES: Aberdeen Sandpiper, Ebb Cock [Shet], Gnat, Gnat Snap,
Grey Plover or Silver Plover.

GAELIC NAME: *Luatharan gainmhich.* Speeder of the sandy beach.

Traditionally the name Knot derived from Canute who was said to be fond
of them. They may also have acquired this name by their habit of feeding
right up to the incoming tide as though daring it to advance. More prosaic
explanations of the monosyllables Gnat, Knat, Cock, Snap etc. refer to the
bird's call. The similarity with other shorebirds is echoed in Sandpiper and
Plover names.

It is unlikely that it was present in Britain during the Pleistocene. As a bird
of winter estuaries it has been little affected by human interference and in the
1970s the winter population in Britain rose to some 400,000, but this has since
dropped back with a decline of 30% in Western Europe. In Scotland the Knot
is a bird of winter east coast estuaries as a widespread passage migrant.

Q: Saunders in 1899 observed: 'In the Hebrides and down the west side
of Scotland it is comparatively rare until the Solway is reached, where it
becomes plentiful.'[162]

T: Like Canute it is said to forbid the advance of the tide.

167

Sanderling
Calidris alba

(*albus*: Latin, white.)

SCOTS NAMES: Ebb Cock [Shet], Snent, Stint, [Berw] Towillee, Tweeky.

GAELIC NAME: *Luatharan-glas*. Grey speeder.

The characteristic feeding habit of this little shorebird gives rise to names such as Ebb Cock. Other names are onomatopoeic, recalling either its trisyllabic beach call, which could be rendered 'to-will-ee', or its flight call, which sounds like 'twick-twick', hence Tweeky. Stint is a name used indiscriminately for many small waders such as Dunlin and Sanderling; Snent or Stent are versions sometimes used in Berwickshire.

The Sanderling is a bird of the cold, which migrates south during the winter. It is likely to have been present in Britain since the beginning of the Holocene and possibly longer. Arriving in Scotland in late July and August on passage, the migrants concentrate in the Outer Hebrides but spread throughout coastal Britain and are sometimes seen well inland. The majority migrate onwards but some remain to give a winter population of about 2,000 in Scotland, chiefly in South Uist, Orkney and Tiree. On the northern migration large numbers (up to 15,000) pass through Solway in late May.

Q: 'It is a peculiarity of Sanderling that they feed chiefly at the height of the tide... feverishly picking up the minute animal-life which the wave had deposited on the sand.'[69]

T: The toylike movement of this small shorebird has led to a childish, but apt, suggestion that it is powered by clockwork.

Little Stint
Calidris minuta

(*minuta*: Latin, small.)

SCOTS NAMES: None.

GAELIC NAME: *Luatharan beag*. Little speeder.

First called Little Stint by Bewick in 1797.[19] The name Stint, originally used for any small wader, probably meant bill or beak.

There is little early information on the status of this bird in Britain. In Scotland the Little Stint is a scarce passage migrant in the spring with few birds reported from the east coast. It is slightly commoner in autumn from Aberdeen to the Forth.

Q: Saunders, in 1899, declared that: 'In Scotland, it occurs every autumn on the east coast as far north as Aberdeenshire.'[162]

Purple Sandpiper
Calidris maritima
(*maritimus*: Latin, of the sea.)

SCOTS NAME: Blind Dorbie.

GAELIC NAME: *Cam glas. Cam* means crooked, *glas* means grey.

Dorbie is Scottish name for a Dunlin or other small wader, from the verb to dorb or peck. Watching Purple Sandpiper feeding among rocks on Lewis shores they do appear to peer closely at seaweed as if they were more short-sighted than the Turnstones they often accompany.

There is nothing between a single record of this species in the late Pleistocene and the end of the eighteenth century. A few birds are known to remain in northern Scottish islands throughout the summer. It was suspected of breeding there in the nineteenth century but did not colonise Scotland as a breeding bird until 1978.[100] It winters around the coast of the North Sea and numbers are estimated at 20,000; more than 75% of these are in Scotland, especially the Outer Hebrides, the Northern Isles and the east coast.

Q: Coming across winter Purple Sandpipers, Seton Gordon found them so tame that by walking slowly it was possible for him to approach to a few feet from them as they fed where clusters of limpets clung.[73]

Dunlin
Calidris alpina
(*alpinus*: Latin, from the mountains.)

SCOTS NAMES: Boondie or Bundie [Ork], Dorbie [Banf], Ebb Sleeper, Egg Cock [Shet], Horsecock, Jack Snipe [Shet], Peerie [Ork], Pickerel or Pikkerel, Plover's Page [Cai], Sea Lark [Loth, Per], Sea Mouse [Dumf], Sea Snipe [Loth], Sea Peek [For], Snippo [Ork].

GAELIC NAME: *Gille-feadag*. Boy or attendant who whistles.

169

Plumage variations led early naturalists to believe they were dealing with two species and Linnaeus called the Dunlin both *Tringa alpina* (the dun summer bird of the moors) and *Tringa cinclus* (the grey-white shore bird of winter). Pennant[148] showed that there was only one species, which he called the Dunlin. The scientific name was modified to *Calidris alpina*, though the bird has nothing to do with the Alps. There is the usual confusion between species in vernacular names, with Snipe and Plover sometimes prefixed with 'jack' meaning small. Dunlin arrive before Golden Plover, hence the name Plover's Page, and the habitat, call or behaviour is reflected in many names such as Sea, Sand and Ebb Sleeper; Peek or the onomatopoeic names Churre or Purre echo the call, and Sea Mouse, from its scurrying feeding habits. Dorbie comes from 'dorb' to grub or peck. Norn has given rise to Orcadian names such as Boondie.

This bird, probably the most numerous wader on earth, was even more widespread during the Pleistocene. It seems to have flourished throughout history except when human disturbance and drainage reduced its numbers during the late nineteenth and early twentieth centuries. It breeds commonly in Scotland, particularly in the Islands, but Dunlin numbers have shown an alarming drop in the last twenty years. In the 1970s hedgehogs, which take the eggs of ground-nesting birds, were introduced into South Uist and they have increased greatly. Where there are no hedgehogs Dunlin breeding is successful, but on machair that the mammal has colonised, Dunlin numbers are much reduced.[153] In winter the population may reach 600-700,000. On passage Dunlin concentrate in the east coast estuaries, sometimes in huge numbers.

Q: At the end of the nineteenth century, 'In Scotland, where suitable situations abound, the bird is pretty generally distributed on the mainland, though local in Sutherland; and is rather plentiful on many of the Islands as far as the Shetlands.'[162] At the beginning of the twentieth, Williams records that: 'A nest near Tain 2/5/09 contained 4 eggs—warm—sitting but no trace of "setting"—blew easily. A small depression amongst rabbit droppings and other jetsam, on turf just above high water mark. Still incubating 20 May.'[198]

Ruff

Philomachus pugnax

(*Philomachus*: Greek, *philos* lover of, *mache*: fight or battle; *pugnax*: Latin, a fighter, pugnacious.)

SCOTS NAMES: Ruff is male, Reeve is female.

GAELIC NAME: *Gibeagan*. Frilled one.

The name Ruff is often thought to derive from the frill of neck feathers with which the male is adorned in the breeding season. However this name for the neckwear fashionable in the sixteenth century postdated the bird name, which more probably derives from the Old English word *gerofa* which meant commander. This name, with its military connotation, suggests fighting and chivalry.

The first record of Ruff in Britain was in 1465.[59] It is largely a passage migrant in both Scotland and England in autumn, but some 1,400 birds winter in Britain.

Q: 'So named from a frill of feathers on its neck, it is among the most quarrelsome and pugnacious of birds, especially the males.'[61]

Jack Snipe
Lymnocryptes minimus

(*Lymnocryptes*: Greek, *lymnos* reed, *crypto* to hide; *minimus*: Latin, smallest.)

SCOTS NAMES: Dame-ku, Gaverhale, Half Snipe Jedcock, Jetcock, Jid, Judcock, Juddock, Plover's Page [Ork], St Martin's Snipe (see below).

GAELIC NAMES: *Gobhrag-bheag, Croman-bheag*. Little goat, lit. little Hawk.

Many of these names refer to the bird's diminutive size, as in Jack or Half Snipe. Jack is applied to many small, often male, animals and Jud and Jed may have the same derivation, though they also suggest the suddenness with which the birds rise when startled. Plover's Page (see Dunlin) is a confusion with other species. Gaverhale is used for several species of snipe and derives from Celtic words meaning goat of the moor, in reference to drumming. Dame-ku, given by Forbes,[61] is unexplained.

A winter visitor and passage migrant from its breeding grounds in northern Europe. It is a secretive creature and numbers are difficult to estimate but some 10,000 were shot in Britain during the 1980s, so its numbers must be well in excess of that. Occasional birds remain in summer.

Q: 'The Jack Snipe weighs about 2oz, yet its four eggs weigh more than 1½ oz.'[162]

T: The Jack Snipe is sometimes named after St Martin, the patron saint of drunkards and innkeepers, who figures in several bird names. Another St Martin is the St Swithin of Scotland, whose day is 4 July, when, if it rains, the deluge continues for forty days.

Common Snipe
Gallinago gallinago

(*Gallinago*: Latin, *gallina* a hen because of its speckled plumage. Formerly it was *G. coelestis*, meaning hen of heaven, and also *G. Capella* from the Latin for a she-goat, referring to its drumming, as in Gaelic.)

SCOTS NAMES: Heather Bleater, Horse Gawk, Gokk or Gowk [Ork, Shet], Mire Snipe [Aber], Snippack or Snippick [Ork, Shet], Snite, Snyp, Water Pleep [Ork].

GAELIC NAMES: *Gobhar-athair*, *Naosgach*, or *Bog-an-lóin*. Father of the Goat, Snipe or crooked one of the marsh.

Many Snipe names refer to its habit of drumming during the breeding season. This bleating noise has been likened to a horse neighing (hence Horse Gowk) or a bleating lamb. Similar confusion between horse and goat is also seen in Capercaillie names. The other names, Snippick, Snite etc. derive from Middle and Old English as early as the eighth century.

Snipe were present at the end of the Pleistocene and must have increased in the warm wet period of the early Holocene. The species decreased to its lowest numbers during the early part of the nineteenth century (especially in Scotland where forest clearance for sheep reduced many species) before increasing with warmer weather in the early part of the twentieth century. From 1980 onwards it is estimated that some 85,000 Snipe have been shot out of a population of several hundred thousand, of which about a third are in Scotland.

Q: George Lodge described watching drumming Snipe in Orkney, where he could plainly see through his glasses the outside tail feathers on each side widely separated from the rest of the tail, and during the downward swoop the wings were rapidly beating the whole time.[109]

T: It is a sign of good luck for a snipe to rise before cattle being driven to a shieling.[61]

> I saw the snipe while sitting bent
> And I foresaw that the year would not go well with me.[35]

> I heard on Tuesday
> The snipe of the seasons
> Bleating on high
> And calling...
> I knew immediately
> That a flitting there was,
> Blessings there would not be
> After that.[35]

Eunarag from *eun* bird and *gobharag* little goat is the snipe more feared than liked by nightfarers.[35]

Woodcock
Scolopax rusticola

(*Scolopax*: Greek, snipe; *rusticolus*: Latin, living in the country.)

SCOTS NAMES: Cock, Great Snipe.

GAELIC NAMES: *Coileach-coille*, *Crom-nan-duileag*, *Creothar*. Cockerel of the wood, lit. bend of the leaves, Woodcock.

Derived from Old English *wuducocc*, the name goes back to the eleventh century when *coc*, as in cockerel or cuckoo, was echoic of the bird's croaking roding call.

Woodcock occurred during the early Holocene when warm climate produced a combination of bogs and spreading forests. The Woodcock increased after the Little Ice Age (1400–1880), spreading throughout Britain as a breeding bird. This was followed with a slow decline, which has worsened since 1980. There is a considerable immigration from Scandinavia in winter when populations must be much higher, since as many as 200,000 may be shot annually. In Scotland it is widespread on the mainland.

At Christmas 1995, in heavy snow, a large fall of Woodcock occurred at Stornoway (a 'fall' is the collective noun for Woodcock).

Q: Bishop Stanley (1857) refers to the habit of Woodcock of carrying their young: 'In April, near Dornaway Castle, a Woodcock was flushed, which flew as if wounded… the bird was not wounded, but was carrying off a young one in her talons.'[178]

Grahame, writing in the early nineteenth century of the month of November, captured the habitat of the Woodcock:

> Oft at this season, near an oozy spring,
> O'erhung by alder boughs, the woodcock haunts;
> (Sure harbinger, when thus so early come,
> Of early winter tedious and severe);
> There he imbibes his watery food; till, scared
> By man and dog, upward, on pinion strong,
> He springs, and oe'r the summits of the grove
> Flies far...[76]

Charles St John describes the Woodcock's roding flight: 'As early as six or seven o'clock in the evening they begin to fly, uttering their curious cry, which resembles more the croak of a frog than anything else; varied, however, by a short, shrill chirp... they keep up a continual flight, passing and repassing in all directions as if in search of each other.'[161]

T: Some beliefs held that Woodcock arrived together after an easterly wind about All Hallows and that they were guided thither by Goldcrests or Short-eared Owls (hence those birds' vernacular names of Woodcock Pilot and Woodcock Owl).

Black-tailed Godwit
Limosa limosa
(*Limosa*: Latin, favours mud.)

SCOTS NAMES: None.

GAELIC NAME: *Cearra-ghob*. Awkward beak.

Godwit is from the Anglo-saxon *god* = good and *wihta* = an animal, hence one that is good to eat.

Records exist from the end of the Pleistocene, and the Black-tailed Godwit is likely to have flourished in the wet and warm early Holocene. By early in the nineteenth century it declined with drainage, shooting and egg collecting and was much depleted by the middle of that century. Breeding in Britain has been increasingly rare (with a few confirmed reports from Orkney and Shetland) but winter visitors have increased and by the winter of 1970 there were some 4,000 birds concentrated on the Solway and the Eden in Fife.

Q: At the end of the nineteenth century, 'on the east coast of Scotland it is rare to the north of the Firth of Tay.'[162]

174

Bar-tailed Godwit
Limosa lapponica

(*Limosa*: Latin, favours mud; *lapponica*: Latin, from Lapland.)

SCOTS NAMES: Poor Willie [Loth], Prine, Sea Woodcock [Shet], Stone Plover, Yardkeep, Yarwhelp, Yarwhip.

GAELIC NAME: *Cearra-ghob-mhor*. Big awkward beak.

Some names are derived from the more marine habitat of the Bar-tailed Godwit, and others apply to the long, slightly upturned bill of both Godwits (but which is seen more clearly in the Bar-tailed) as in Prine, an old word meaning awl or bodkin.

There is little early evidence of Bar-tailed Godwit in Britain. As an estuarine and coastal winter visitor it has probably escaped much persecution from man though it was shot for food. Winter birds migrate from northern Eurasia to the North Sea, which probably supports 65% of the western European population. In Scotland the winter migrants concentrate in Uist, Orkney, the Solway and the major east-coast estuaries.

Q: Keith Brockie[23] painted Bar-tailed Godwit at Tentsmuir Point in the Tay Estuary.

Saunders (1899) noted that: 'In the west of Scotland it is chiefly seen in autumn and winter but flocks of non-breeding birds frequent the Sound of Harris, and also the Solway, in summer.'[162]

Whimbrel
Numenius phaeopus

(*Numenius*: Greek, New moon (refers to shape of bill); *phaeopus*: grey feet.)

SCOTS NAMES: Little Whaup, May Bird, Peerie Whaup [Shetl], Seven Whistler, Spowe or Spooe, Stone Curlew, Summer or Tang Whaup [Ork & Shet].

GAELIC NAMES: *Guilbneach-bheag*, *Eun-Bhealltuin*. Little lamenting one, Beltane bird.

Whimbrel comes from 'whimpernel', a sixteenth-century word referring to the bird's houndlike whimpering. Whimbrel names either indicate its similarity with the Curlew or are based on its calls. Seven Whistler is echoic because the bird often repeats its call seven times. Spowe and similar names are derived from the Norse word *spov* meaning a Curlew. Other names derived from the bird's resemblance to a small Curlew are little (or Peerie) Curlew or Whaup. In Orkney, Tang Whaup reflects the bird's close association with seaweed. Reference to summer or May (as in Beltane) indicates the earliest arrival of Whimbrel in the Hebrides.

This cool climate species may well have had a wide distribution in the Pleistocene but there is little evidence of this. Occasional breeding has been reported from Scotland (mostly in Shetland, some in Orkney and a few breeding pairs in Sutherland, Caithness and Lewis) during the twentieth century, but for the most part the Whimbrel, though found on all continents but Antarctica, is a winter visitor to Britain when its numbers may reach several thousand.

Q: Writing in the middle of the nineteenth century MacGillivray describes their summer arrival: 'In the beginning of May a few individuals of this species make their appearance on the sandy pastures bordering the west coast of the long range of the Outer Hebrides, from one end to the other. Their numbers daily increase, until in about a week they are in many places very abundant.'[118]

T: Bhealltuin in the Gaelic name literally means 'bright fire' and, as Beltane, was the name given to an ancient Celtic festival, held at the beginning of May, when bonfires were set alight on the hills. It is also one of the quarter-days of Scotland.

Like the Curlew, the Whimbrel was associated with the Gabble Ratchet or Gabriel's Hounds and the Seven Whistlers; both birds were said to foretell death (see pp.12, 177).

Common Curlew
Numenius arquata

(*arquata*: Latin, bow-like (referring to the bill).)

SCOTS NAMES: Collier or Courlie, Faap or Faup, Full Curlew, Great Curlew, Great Whaup [Ork], Guilbinn [W. Isles], Quhap or Quhaip [NS], Stock Whaup, Whaap, Whaip or Whaup [Shet], Whitterick [Fif to Rox].

GAELIC NAMES: *Guilbneach, Crotach-mara*. Curlew (lit. lamenting one), Humpback of the moor.

Curlew itself is onomatopoeic as are so many other attempts to imitate this bird's peculiarly haunting and lovely call, such as Guilbinn. The alternative common name of Whaup (in Old Scots, Quhap) derives from *hwilp* or *huilpe*, which was applied to many seabirds.

There are some traces of Curlew in the late Pleistocene and into the early Holocene, but fossils of the *Numenius* genus date back 65 million years. It was hunted during the Iron Age and also more recently in the nineteenth century. During the twentieth century the range of the Curlew extended to southern Britain. At the same time its breeding range has extended westwards into the Hebrides where it bred for the first time in 1965. The winter population, swollen by immigrants from Northern Europe, may be as high as 200,000. In Scotland it is a widespread breeding bird and in winter concentrates on coasts, especially the estuaries of major rivers, where as many as 15,000 may congregate.

Q: Burns wrote: 'I never hear the loud solitary whistle of the curlew on a summer noon... without feeling an elevation of the soul like the enthusiasm of devotional poetry.'[61]

> The nest of the curlew
> Is in the bubbling peat moss,
> My little one shall sleep and he shall have the bird.
>
> From a lullaby sung to a child.[35]

T: Much superstition surrounds the Curlew because of its eerie lamenting cry. The name whaup is also used in Scotland for a goblin who employed his long beak to carry off evil doers. In many places the cry is said to presage a death, and this also has contributed to the legend of the Seven Whistlers (see pp.12, 176, 210). Curlews are extremely shy and it is difficult to get within shot of them, hence the Scottish proverb 'to kill seven whaups is enough for a lifetime'.

The species was of considerable value, as an old Scottish saying points out: 'A curlew, be she white or be she black, carries tenpence on her back.'[61] Vesey Fitzgerald adds: 'In September it is really good eating... but tastes a bit kippery.'[196]

Redshank
Tringa totanus

(*Tringa*: Greek, white rumped sandpiper; *totanus*: Italian redshank.)

SCOTS NAMES: Ebb Cock [Shet], Clee [Aber], Pellile [NE], Pleep [Mor],

Warden- or Watchdog-of-the-Marshes, Watery Pleeps [Ork].

GAELIC NAMES: *Maor-cladaich, Cam glas, Gobhlan-mara*. Warden or messenger of the shore, Pale bent one, Forked one of the moor or sea.

The most frequent names refer either to the red legs or the calls of this common and delightful wader. It has many calls and hence many onomatopoeic names: Clee, Pellille Teuk or Tuke as well as names indicating but not echoing noise, such as Watery Pleeps or Warden of the Marshes.

The Redshank is thought to have been present in the late Pleistocene. There was a gradual decline in Redshank numbers up to the early nineteenth century when a sharper decline followed changes in farming practice and widespread drainage. Between 1865 and 1940 the species increased slowly, spreading south and west. From 1940 onwards, following a series of hard winters, it again decreased. In Scotland it is a widespread but declining breeding species, with large concentrations along major estuaries. Winter populations, expanded by immigrants from Iceland, probably exceed 100,000, about 20% of the world populations.

Q: One seen on Loch Freuchie near Glenalmond on 19 April 1914 was 'still in very immature plumage: bill almost black and legs not yet red.'[198]

Greenshank
Tringa nebularia
(*Tringa*: see Redshank; *nebularius*: Latin, misty (referring to colour).)

SCOTS NAMES: Greater Plover, Green-legged Horseman or Long Shank, Green-shanked Snipe.

GAELIC NAME: *Deoch-bhiugh*. Drink in the bullrushes.

Unlike the Redshank the Greenshank has few vernacular names in Scotland, probably because it is less often seen.

The earliest record of Greenshank is from the late Pleistocene and early Holocene. After that, with increasing forestation, it is likely to have moved to less wooded areas of Scotland. It is now on the southern edge of its range but there has been a small but steady increase in breeding in the north-west of Scotland and Shetland. Greenshanks winter as far south as South Africa but some remain to winter in Scotland, mainly in the Clyde and Solway.

Q: Seton Gordon 'disturbed a Greenshank from a boggy creek, and he flew off, uttering that wild note of his that cannot be mistaken for that of any other bird.'[72]

His single note—one can't help calling it
piping, one can't help
calling it plaintive—slides droopingly down
no more than a semitone, but is filled
with an octave of loneliness, with the whole sad scale
of desolation.

From Norman MacCaig, 'Greenshank'.[115]

Common Sandpiper
Actitis hypoleucos

(*Actitis*: Latin, moving around, hyperactive; *hypoleucos*: Greek, *hypo* underneath, *leucos* white.)

SCOTS NAMES: Boondie or Bundie (cf Dunlin) [Ork], Fiddler [Heb], Gobarleery [Suth], Heather Peeper [Aber, Per], Killieleepsie or Killie Leepie [Loth], Kittie Needie or Neddy [Aber, Kirk], Land Tripper [Kirk], Otterling, Sand Lark or Sandy Laverock, Sandy Dorbie [Mor, Aber], Sanny [Aber], Shore Snipe [Perth], Skittery Deacon [Stir], Steenie Pouter [Ork], Summer Snipe, Tibbie Thiefie, Water Laverock [Rox], Water Pleep or Watery Pleeps [Ork].

GAELIC NAMES: *Fidhleir bôrd-an-locha, Luatharan bôrd-an-locha, Gobadail-iri*. Fiddler by the loch table or Speeder at the loch table, the nebbed one coloured like the sea.

Many names are onomatopoeic, such as Dickie-di-dee, Kittie Needie, etc. Originally the name Sandpiper applied only to this species, reflecting its habitat and sound. Other names describe its habitat (water, heather) or restless movements, as in Skittery Deacon or Otterling, which means to totter or shake. In Scotland it is called a Fiddler (see Gaelic names) or named for its supposed similarity to a Skylark.

There are no archeological remains and little is recorded before Turner[195] wrote of the Common Sandpiper in 1544. It seems to have disappeared from much of England since the early part of the last century and now breeds north-west of a line from Bristol to York. Though it is widespread in this area it appears to be decreasing, partly, it is suggested, due to acid rain. In Scotland it breeds in all counties, though it is scarce in Lewis, Orkney and Shetland.

179

Q: 'At the present time [1953] the Common Sandpiper breeds in every main-land county; it is well distributed... as a breeding bird on the islands off the west coast'.[13]

Turnstone
Arenaria interpres

(*Arenaria*: Latin, relating to a sandy place; *interpres*: Latin, messenger (refers to its alarm call warning other birds).)

SCOTS NAMES: Ebb Pecker [Shet], Hebridal Sandpiper, Skirl Crake [Loth, Shet], Stanepecker [Shet], Stane Putter [Ork].

GAELIC NAMES: *Drilleachan-beag, Goblachan.* Little piper, Laughing bill.

Almost all its names recall its habit of turning stones or seaweed to peck underneath for sandhoppers and other invertebrates.

Remains are present from the end of the Pleistocene. Now it is a winter visitor, but it is certainly present in the Outer Hebrides in summer and is reputed to have bred there in 1938.[47] It is a common winter bird of most Scottish coastlines.

Q: 'The habits of this bird are singular, more particularly with respect to the method which it adopts to procure food... by turning over small stones in search of the insects beneath them on which it feeds. When the object which it wishes to turn over is too large for the bill to do so, the breast is applied; and it would seem that the birds are willing to assist each other, just as masons or porters will do in turning over a stone or bale of goods.'[174]

Red-necked Phalarope
Phalaropus lobatus

(*Phalaropus*: Greek, *phalaris* a coot, *pous* foot; *lobatus*: Latin, having lobes (both names refer to the coot-like feet).)

SCOTS NAMES: Coot Foot, Half Web, Little Swimmer, Lobefoot, Red-necked Coot, Red Phalarope, Scallop-toed Sandpiper.

GAELIC NAME: *Deargan-allt.* Red one of the stream.

First recorded in Britain in 1768[148] but was not known to breed until 1804.

180

There are records of breeding in the northern and western Scottish islands especially in Benbecula.

Q: 'The Red-necked Phalarope rides with extreme buoyancy, and progresses rapidly. Its neck is long and is held erect, and the russet-red markings on its cheeks and neck are strikingly handsome.'[72]

T: At sea Red-necked Phalaropes may feed on crustacea and minute jelly-fish, and sometimes take parasites off the back of surfaced whales, especially Humpbacks. Martin Martin, the observant seventeenth century chronicler of the Scottish islands, remarked on this: 'The Phalarope picks its food out of the live whale, with which, they say it uses sorrel, and both are found in its nest.'[126]

Family: *Stercorarcidae*, the Skuas

No. in world, 7; no. in Scotland, 4.

Great Skua
Stercorarius skua

(*Stercorarius*: Latin, referring to dung or excrement (they are scavengers feeding on offal); *skua*: onomatopoeic from the call and the Old Norse name of 'skuhr'.)

SCOTS NAMES: Allan, Bonxie [Ork], Dung Hunter [Fou], Hen, Herdsman [Ork], Tuliac.

GAELIC NAMES: *Fasgadair Mór, Tuilleag.* Great one that picks off or destroys vermin, Skua.

Bonxie comes from the Norn word *bunksi,* a dumpy bird, which accurately describes the Great Skua. Skua is a word of mixed derivation, partly ono-matopoeic, partly from a shortened form of the Norse name for the species, *sku,* which became Latinised in the seventeenth century by the addition of the terminal 'a'. Tuliac is thought to be an early printer's error for the Gaelic word *fuliac* or *faoileag,* a seagull. Despite its predatory habits it is believed in Orkney to protect young lambs from eagles and there it is sometimes called Herdsman.

Primarily an Antarctic species, the Great Skua extended into the North Atlantic early in the Holocene, initially in Iceland but spreading to Shetland by the end of the eighteenth century, where they were encouraged by farm-ers because the Bonxies drove off White-tailed Eagles. Ninety percent of the

British birds species now breed in Orkney and Shetland with the remaining ten percent in northern Scotland and the Outer Islands.

Q: Pennant (1768) described the measures that used to be taken against this courageous bird: 'When the inhabitants of the Faeroes visit the nest, it attacks them with great force, so that they hold a knife erect over their heads, on which the Skua will transfix itself in its fall on the invaders.'[148]

A modern-day crofter, miming the diving of the Bonxie, added: 'They're veecious—they'll buzz you... and the Great Black-backed—it's veecious too'.[44]

'The Great Skua, known in Scotland as the bonxie, is notable for its attacks on people who invade its nesting grounds. The birds come in to the attack with great boldness, and strike with their feet.'[180]

Arctic Skua
(formerly Richardson's Skua, see p.51)
Stercorarius parasiticus

(*Stercorarius*: see Great Skua; *parasiticus*: Latin, parasite, referring to its habit of making other birds drop their food.)

SCOTS NAMES: Arctic Bird, Arctic Gull, Alan, Aulin or Auten [Ork, Shet], Black-toed Gull [Mor], Boatswain [NS, Ork], Dirt Bird or Dirtin Allan, Dirty Allen or Aulin [Ork], Dung Bird, Dung Hunter, Dung Teaser [Berw], Fascedder, Feaser, Shite Scouter or Skait Bird, Scooty Alan, Scoutie Aulin [Ork, Shet], Shooi [Shet], Skatie-goo [Ork], Trumpie [Ork], Weese Allan [Ork].

GAELIC NAME: *Fasgadair.* One that picks off, or destroys, vermin.

Allan is a widespread Scottish name for Skuas. Many of this Skua's names refer to its supposed coprophagy (hence Dirt, Dung, Shite, Skait and Scoutie, all of which refer to faeces). This misnomer arose from the observation that the Arctic Skua pursued birds till they disgorged food; it was believed that the birds were defecating and this contributed to the Skua's reputation for unpleasant habits. The name Faskidar, Fascedder or Feaser come from Martin[126] and variants of these names linger on. Trumpie is an onomatopoeic representation of the birds' attacking cry.

A bird of high latitudes, the Arctic Skua may well have been present in Britain during the Pleistocene, but in historic times it has been limited to Scotland. In the warmer period following the end of the Little Ice Age it declined, but since 1940 it has increased, with Orkney breeding populations rising from 80 pairs to 1,000 by 1982.

182

Q: Seton Gordon writes: 'How wild the scream of an Arctic Skua, how dark its swift-flying form that seems always to cleave the air with almost supernatural strength. ...It lives largely on fish which it forces its victims to drop and which the Skua dexterously catches in mid-air.'[69]

Family: *Laridae*, the Gulls

No. in world, 48; no. in Scotland, 9.

Black-headed Gull

Larus ridibundus

(*Larus*: Latin, a sea bird; *ridibundus*: Latin, laughing.)

SCOTS NAMES: Bakie [Shet], Black Cap, Black Head, Brown-headed Gull, Cob, Collachan Gull [Kirk], Crocker or Croker, Hooded Crow or Mew, sometimes Huidie Craw or Heidi Craa [Ork, Loth], Laughing Gull, Masked Gull, Maw, Mire Crow, Moss Donnack, Patch, Perma, Piccatarrie, Pickmire, Pickmaw or Pick Sea or Pictarn, Picktarntie or Pickie Burnet [Rox], Pirr Maw or Perma [Ayr, Wig], Potterton Hen, Rittock [Ork], Sea Maw, Sprat Mew, Swarfarro [Ork].

GAELIC NAMES: *Faoileag-a'chinn-dhuibh, Ceann-dubh, Crann-dubhan.* Gull with a black head (*Faoileag* is the white crest of the waves), Black-head, Flagstaff of black.

This common Gull's accepted name dates from Latham.[103] Many names refer to its plumage (Black Cap, Black Head, etc.). 'Pick', originally from pitch, combines plumage and feeding habits and 'Rittock' refers to the Gull's red legs. Increasingly, Black-headed Gulls are moving inland to fresh water so that terms such as Mire Crow, Pictarn as well as Pick Sea reflect its varied habitat. Mew and Maw are old names for Gulls and Swarfarro is probably from Norn.

No record of this species exists before the tenth century. It appears to have become rare if not extinct as a breeding bird in the south during the last decades of the nineteenth century, partly because of egg harvesting (see below). It now breeds everywhere and is the most numerous inland Gull, especially at roosting sites on reservoirs and gravel pits.

Q: 'The number of eggs collected annually varies from fifteen thousand to twenty thousand, and more might be taken occasionally; for instance, thirty thousand would not have been too large a proportion for this Spring [1837], it having been a wet one'.[178]

T: These birds were believed by people of the Cairngorms to carry the souls of caring people. The black head, which gradually diminishes as autumn approaches, symbolises their fading sin. As they were nearly pure in life, in death they are messengers of the angels.[10]

In 'Queen of Grace' (*Carmina Gadelica*) the Gaelic poet extols the Virgin Mary:

> Mild the expression of her face,
> While her lovely white breast heaves on her bosom
> Like the black-headed seagull on the gently heaving wave.[35]

Common Gull
Larus canus
(*canus*: Latin, white.)

SCOTS NAMES: Blue Maa [Shet], Coddy Moddy, Cullya [Ork], Gow [Aber], Green-billed Gull, Koylie [Ork], Loch Maa or Maw [Ork, Shet], Maa or Mar [Kirk], Mew or Sea Mew, Sea Cob, Sea Gull, Sea Mall, Mell or Maw, Seed Bird [Rox], White Maa [Ork].

This Gull's recognised name was coined by Pennant.[148] The word Gull (derived from a Cornish Celtic word meaning coast) has many synonyms: Cob, Gow, Maa, Mall, Maw and Mew. Blue Gull, Green-billed Gull or White Maa all refer to the bird's colour. 'Seed bird' is used for many species because of their appearance at sowing time.

There is a record of the Common Gull during the later Pleistocene. As a bird of cooler northern climates it is likely to have become scarce during the warm early Holocene. Orkney and Shetland are the principal breeding sites and Scotland holds nearly 90% of the British population, so that in England it is called the 'unCommon' Gull! This is the second most numerous Gull after the Black-headed, especially in north-western Scotland.

Q: MacGillivray (1852) describes their behaviour: 'The fields, having been cleared of their produce, and partially ploughed, to prepare them for another crop, the "Sea Maws", deserting the coasts, appear in large flocks which find subsistence in picking up the worms and larvae that have been exposed'.[118]

T: Faoileag na h-aona chloiche—The seagull of one stone (Gaelic proverb signifying a common but fruitless thing).[61]

184

Lesser Black-backed Gull
Larus fuscus
(*fuscus*: Latin, dark or dusky.)

SCOTS NAMES: Blackback, Greyback, Less Black-backer Gull, Said Fool [Shetland], Saith Fowl, Yellow-legged Gull.

GAELIC NAMES: *Farspach-bheag, Sgaireag.* Lesser black-backed gull, perhaps screamer, from *sgairean* to scream.

Several Gulls, including the Black-backs and Common, attack shoals of young fish, especially Coalfish or Saithe, and have been called Coddy Moddy, Saith Fowl or Said Fool as a result. The name Yellow-legged Gull reminds one that this gull's legs are yellow in distinction from the Greater Black-backed Gull whose legs are grey or pink (see p.187).

The Lesser Black-backed Gull was not distinguished from the similar Great Black-backed Gull until Montagu in 1802;[135] before that there are no records. Egg cropping reduced populations, especially during the food shortage of the Second World War, but Lesser Black-backed Gulls have become a common sight at refuse tips. Though less abundant in Scotland than in England there are large breeding colonies in the Clyde.

Q: Osgood Mackenzie noted in 1921 that: 'The rapid decrease of the Lesser Black-backed Gull is one of the most striking instances of a bird disappearing. They were wont to breed in their thousands in the islands of Loch Maree, and their eggs were a source of food supply, and now there are hardly any'.[119]

Herring Gull
Larus argentatus
(*argentatus*: Latin, silvery.)

SCOTS NAMES: Cat Gull [Kirk], Gray Willie or Grayback, Laughing Gull, Pleengie [imm], Scaurie, Silver Back, Silvery Gull [Ork], White Maa [Ork & Shet], Willie Gow or Willie Goo [Loth, Aber].

GAELIC NAME: *Faoileag-an-sgadain.* Seagull of the herring.

Herring Gull is a misnomer: the species has no association with herrings, but it acquired this name from Ray,[155] which later became standard. Most of its vernacular names describe either its calls (which include a mewing and a hoarse laughing call) or its plumage colours of white and silvery grey. Many common birds acquire diminutive human names such as 'Willie Gow'. Cat Gull is a gamekeeper's name for the species since it causes great depredation on newly hatched game chicks.

There is no fossil evidence of the Herring Gull; its early history is confused with that of the Lesser Black-backed Gull and, like it, it will have been partially controlled by egg-cropping for food. At the beginning of the twentieth century it prospered and its general inland population doubled, reflecting changes in refuse disposal with large open pits, which provided easy pickings for opportunistic Herring Gulls. About half the British population is in Scotland where they are abundant breeders, concentrated in Caithness and the Northern Isles. Since the 1920s Herring Gulls have nested on shore buildings where they block downspouts with droppings and cause increasing annoyance.

Q: A recent handbook states: 'The most abundant of the large gulls.'[192]

T: A Scottish rhyme:

> Sea-gull, sea-gull, sit on the sand;
> It's never good weather when you're on the land.

Great Black-backed Gull
Larus marinus
(*marinus*: Latin, of the sea.)

SCOTS NAMES: Baagie or Baakie or Baukie [Ork, Shet], Black Back, Gull Maw [Loth], Swaabie or Swarbie [Ork, Shet], Swart Back [Ork].

GAELIC NAMES: *Arpag, Farspach, Faoileag-mhor.* Harpy or any ravenous creature, Great Black-backed Gull, Great Seagull.

Many Norn names from Orkney and Shetland derive from Old Norse words such as *svartbakr* (literally black back) and these have led to shortened forms such as Baakie or Swaabie.

See Lesser Black-backed Gull. The Great Black-backed Gull had a reputation for killing lambs and game. This, as well as harvesting for food and eggs, led almost to its extinction between 1850 and 1900. Since then its fortunes have revived and in Scotland it may be seen on all coasts especially in winter, when numbers are boosted by visiting birds. It breeds most commonly northwest of a line from the Moray to the Clyde Firths.

Q: It is often difficult to separate from the Lesser Black backed Gull, but this jingle may help:

Lesser Gulls have *Lemon* legs,
Little wings and smaller size;
Greater Gulls have *Greyish* legs,
Bigger bills and yellow eyes.

Kittiwake
Rissa tridactyla

(*Rissa*: Latin, misspelling of *rissoa* three toed; *tridactyla*: Greek *tri* three,
dactyle fingers or toes.)

SCOTS NAMES: Annet, Cackareer, Cackareen, Chitterweek, Craa Maa
[Shet], Kelt [Aber], Kittick or Kittie, Kishiefaik, Kittiwaako or Kishiefaik
[Ork], Reddag, Rippock, Ritto, Rittock, [Heb, Ork & Shet], Tarrock (imm),
Tirrick, Waeg or Weeg [Shet].

GAELIC NAMES: *Ruideag, Faireag* or *Sgaireag, Tarrach*. Kittiwake, possibly
screamer, from *sgairean* to scream, Tarrock or young Kittiwake.

The name Kittiwake was adopted as standard in 1768.[148] Nearly all the names
of this species are onomatopoeic, copying the bird's trisyllabic cry, hence Kittiwake, Kishiefaik etc. Young Kittiwakes pose identification difficulties and
for a time the Tarrock was thought a separate species. Some Scottish names
derive from Old Norse *ryta* and are probably onomatopoeic. 'Waeg' may be
from Norse but is also used in Cornwall, where it may be a remnant of the
Celtic language of Cornwall.

Present in late Pleistocene remains, the Kittiwake probably succeeded well
as a cliff breeder relatively secure from early man. During the nineteenth
century it must have undergone drastic reduction, since shooting it for both
food and adornment was a common sport. The wings of Kittiwakes were
used extensively in the plumage trade. It was protected at the end of the

nineteenth century and since then, with the decline in the millinery use of plumage and the abundance of fish offal from trawlers, it has recovered considerably. By 1970 the estimated breeding population was 470,000, mostly in Scotland, especially in Orkney, Shetland and on east coast cliffs.

Q: In the *Old Statistical Account* for Shetland (1799) the minister for the Isles of Stenness described the Isles: 'which abound with kettywakes filling every projection and every hole, which can afford them any shelter. The new fledged young, are much esteemed as delicate food, and taken in great plenty.'[145]

T: The souls of dead children are supposed to be transformed to Kittiwakes, possibly because of their innocent, gentle appearance and soulful cry.

Family: *Sternidae,* the Terns

No. in world, 43; no. in Scotland, 6.

Sandwich Tern
Sterna sandvicencis

(*Sterna*: contrived Latin from Old Norse, a tern; *sandvicencis*: refers to Sandwich in Kent.)

SCOTS NAMES: Boatswain, Great Tern.

GAELIC NAMES: *Steàrnag mhór.* Great Tern.

Latham[103] commemorated the Kentish town of Sandwich, from where he had been sent specimens of these birds, by calling them Sandwich Terns. Boatswain is also applied to the Arctic Skua.

The only tern having a Pleistocene record from about half a million years ago, its history is unknown. In the nineteenth century it suffered depredations due to egg collecting and the plumage trade (see p.63). In Scotland, particularly in Orkney, Sandwich Terns nest in colonies, often with other terns and gulls.

Q: In the late nineteenth century, 'Beyond the Solway a few pairs are found on the coast of Kirkcudbrightshire, and birds seem to have occurred on Loch Lomond, as well as on Tiree; on the east coast of Scotland there are breeding places up to the mouth of the Findhorn; and northward a colony was discovered on North Ronaldsay, Orkneys'.[162]

T: Fishermen believe that when Terns are numerous salmon will be plentiful.

Roseate Tern
Sterna dougallii

(*dougallii*, see below)

SCOTS NAMES: None.

GAELIC NAME: *Steàrnag ruiteach.* Roseate Tern.

This species was not discovered until 1812. It was named by Montagu[135] because of the pink flush on its underparts in summer.

Q: This slender and elegant species was discovered on the Cumbraes, in the Firth of Clyde, by Dr McDougall of Glasgow.[129] Montagu[135] named the bird *Sterna dougallii* after its discoverer (see p.51).

Common Tern
Sterna hirundo

(*hirundo*: Latin, a swallow.)

SCOTS NAMES: Pearl, Pease Crow, Piccatarrie [Shet], Picket-a, Pickie-terno [Ork], Pictarnie [Loth, Fife], Pictarntie, Pirr, Sea Swallow, Shear Tail [Ork], Speikintares [Ross], Tarnie, Tarret or Tarrack, Tarrock, Tirrick or Taring [Shet], Willie Fisher [For].

GAELIC NAME: *Steàrnan.* Common Tern.

Until 1812 the Common, Arctic and Roseate Terns had been lumped together under the general name of Great Tern. Common and Arctic Terns were not separated until 1819. Many Tern names are descriptive, as in Sea Swallow, and others derive from the bird's call, as in Purl, Kip, Kirrmew etc. The prefix 'Pic-' in both Arctic and Common Tern names is from pitch, referring to the black head of these birds.

189

After recovering from the demands of the nineteenth century millinery trade Common Terns have increased, benefitting from the warmer weather since 1890. Colonies have decreased in areas where gulls and skuas predate on chicks, but this has been compensated by extension of range and breeding habitats.

Q: In 1909 'Several nested on the small island of Loch Migdale (beyond Bonar School) and on 29th May there were at least nine nests there'.[198]

Arctic Tern
Sterna paradisaea
(*paradisaeus*: Latin, from paradise.)

SCOTS NAMES: Pickieterno [Ork], Piccatarrie, Picket-a, Picktarntie [Ork], Rittock or Ritto [Ork], Sheer tail [Ork], Tarrock [Shet], Tirrick.

GAELIC NAME: *Steàrnal*. Arctic Tern.

The confusion between Common and Arctic Terns has resulted in common nomenclature; this and the differentiation difficulty causes many birdwatchers to refer to the two species collectively as 'Comic Terns'. Pickietarnie combines pick or pitch with tarn to describe the black head.

For early history, see Common Tern. This tern also recovered slowly during the twentieth century. The present breeding population of some 50,000 is mostly in north and west Scotland, especially Orkney.

Arctic terns are among the great commuters of the world, and enjoy more daylight than any other creature. They breed in the Holarctic and though a few may stay in the north, others then make a phenomenal migration, some almost from pole to pole, to winter in the roaring forties of the southern oceans where they may reach the Antarctic peninsula. Some Arctic Terns travel as much as 36,000 km a year, nearly the circumference of the Earth.

Q: Saunders, writing in 1899, states that it 'predominates over the Common Tern in the Orkneys, the Outer Hebrides, and along the west coast of Scotland to the Isle of Skye.'[162]

Little Tern
Sterna albifrons
(*albifrons*: Latin, *albi*: white, *frons*: forehead.)

SCOTS NAMES: Fairy Tern, Little Pickie [Forfar].

GAELIC NAME: *Steàrnal-bheag*. Little tern.

This delightful small tern is well named a Fairy Tern and many of its names refer to its diminutive size.

There is little reference to the species here before the 1670s.[59] Declining in the nineteenth century along with other terns, its numbers increased before falling back when the increased popularity of beach holidays disturbed its nesting sites. In 1970 the population peaked at about 1,800 but has declined since. In Scotland it breeds in small numbers in the Hebrides and on favoured east coast sites.

Q: Seton Gordon observes: 'In South Uist when May is come the Little Tern commences to arrive, moving up the coast from the south, and fishing daintily as it goes.'[71]

Black Tern
Chlidonias niger
(*Chlidonias*: Greek misspelling of *chelidonios*: a swallow; *niger*: Latin, black.)

SCOTS NAMES: None in Scotland.

GAELIC NAME: *Steàrnal dubh*. Black tern.

First mentioned by Turner,[195] the Black Tern suffered as other terns during the nineteenth century and almost disappeared from Britain by 1850. In Scotland it is an uncommon passage migrant in spring and autumn, occasionally numbering 100.

Q: 'Although it has been met with on the Firth of Forth and other parts of the Lowlands of Scotland, as well as on Loch Lomond, it is as yet [in 1899] unknown in the Hebrides or the Orkneys.'[162]

Family: *Alcidae*, the Auks

(Auk comes from the Norse *alka* meaning neck.)
No. in world, 22; no. in Scotland, 5.

Guillemot
Uria aalge

(*Uria:* Greek, *ouria* a water bird; *aalge*: Danish, Guillemot.)

SCOTS NAMES: Aak or Auk [Ork], Foolish Guillemot, Kweet, Langy, Lamhi, Lamy or Lavy or Lavie [Heb], Lary, Loom, Lum, Lungy, Maggie [For], Marrock, Marrot or Morrot [Aber, Fif], Mortoun, Queet or Quit [Aber & NE], Scottock, Scout, Scoot or Skout [For, Ork], Sea Hen [Loth, Cai], Skiddaw or Skuttock [Loth], Willock [EC].

GAELIC NAMES: *Langaidh, Eun-dubh-an-sgadain, Uiseag mhara.* Guillemot, Black fowl of the herring, Sea coot.

Often called the Foolish Guillemot because of the ease with which it could be caught, 'Common' was substituted for 'Foolish' by Yarrell.[201] Guillemot derives from *Guillaume*, the Old French spelling of William from which Willock has arisen. Many names are echoic from the cry of the immature bird. Other onomatopoeic names, including Scout, Scuttock or Skiddaw, may also derive from skite because of the enormous amount of guano left by nesting birds. Langy and variants come from Norse via Gaelic names and are onomatopoeic. Marrot etc., which also echo the call of the adult bird, are probably a corruption of *Mergus*, a diver. Quet or Queet, variants of coot, are Scottish descriptive names for the guillemot.

A race with white facial markings is known as Bridled Guillemot.

Guillemots were present in the early Pleistocene, a million years ago. In the nineteenth century it suffered badly from human predation since adults and eggs have always been an important source of food, which could be gathered at huge communal nesting sites. About 80% of Guillemots breed in Scotland, especially in Orkney and Shetland. Like all Auks, they are vulnerable to oil spillage from supertankers negotiating the difficult waters of the Pentland Firth.

Q: Pennant wrote of them in 1768: 'Foolish Guillemots are found in amazing numbers on the high cliffs of our coasts... They are very simple, for, notwithstanding they are shot at, and see their companions killed by them, they will not quit the rock'.[148]

T: Auks generally are poor walkers on land and this has given rise to the saying 'as drunk as an auk'.

Razorbill
Alca torda

(*Alca*: Italian, an auk; *torda*; Italian, local name for Razorbill.)

SCOTS NAMES: Baakie or Bawkie [Ork], Coulterneb or Coulterback [Ork], Falk or Faik [Heb], Gairfowl, Gurfel, Hellejay or Helligog [Shet], Hiogga [She], Lavie [Heb], Mortoun, Marrot [Loth, Fif, Aber], Razorbill Auk, Scout or Scoot, Sea Craa [Shet], Sea Crow [Ork], Strannie [Ayr].

GAELIC NAMES: *Làmhaidh* or *Coltraiche, Dubh-eunach*. Razorbill, literally Black fowling or hunting.

Known as Auk until Ray suggested Razorbill as the standard name.[155] Bawkie and Faik are variants of the Gaelic word *falc* used as for an auk, Hellejay etc. probably derive from Norn. Coulter is the iron cutter leading a plough-share, which resembles the Razorbill's beak. For Marrot etc see Guillemot. Other names are descriptive of appearance or behaviour or from likeness to other species.

For early history, see Guillemot. The Razorbill suffered badly in the nineteenth century when shooting the massed nesting birds became a popular sport. It breeds colonially on sea cliffs (usually lower down than the Guillemot) especially in Orkney, Shetland and the Hebrides.

Q: Martin Martin encountered the bird on St Kilda in the seventeenth century: 'The bird, by the inhabitants called the falk... It is a size less than the lavy; its head, neck, back and tail are black; the inside to the middle of the throat, white; the throat under the chin of a dusky black.'[126]

T: Auks generally are believed to catch fish for Kittiwakes who then take them off the surface of the sea.

Black Guillemot
Cepphus grylle

(*Cepphus*: Greek, *Kepphos* a sea bird; gryllus: Latin, *grille* a cricket.)

SCOTS NAMES: Dovekie, Greenland Dove or Turtle [Ork], Gret Hen, Jenny or Jinny Gray [Imm. Cai], Dovie or Sea Doo [For], Sea Turtle, Scraber [Loth, Heb], Sinnie Fynnie [Ork], Tinkershire, Toist, Toyste, Teistie, Tystie [Orkney, Shetland], Turtur [Bass Rock].

GAELIC NAMES: *Calltag, Caileag, Eala-bheag an sgadain.* Black Guillemot, *Caileag* literally little girl, little swan of the herring.

Pennant named this species because of its likeness to the common Guillemot.[148] Unlike other auks, Black Guillemots nest on craggy beaches where the devotion between the parents gives rise to names associated with affection, particularly dove, pigeon or turtle. Only in Scotland is the Black Guillemot a Dovekie; elsewhere this name applies to the Little Auk. Tystie and Taister are Norn names for the species still used in Orkney and Shetland. Scraber and Skrabe probably come from *skrabe*, which is Norwegian for scraper (cf. Manx Shearwater). Tinkershire is a seaman's nickname (Tinker) to which -shire is added to make a nonsense name recalling the hue of a tinker.

Black Guillemots date from the end of the Pleistocene. After that there are no records until the seventeenth century. It also suffered at the hand of 'sportsmen' during the nineteenth century and, though it has increased recently, it is still the scarcest breeding auk; its breeding population is estimated at 17,000-25,000 pairs, doubling in winter. More than half of the British breeding birds are in the Northern Isles.

Q: 'At the present time [1953] the Black Guillemot breeds in Wigtownshire... North of Ayrshire there is no definite breeding record on the mainland till the cliffs of Reiff, West Ross. It breeds on the... coasts of Sutherland and Caithness... There is no known nesting place on the east coast of Scotland, south of Caithness, except Kincardine.'[13]

T: The Welsh call this bird *cas gan longw*, or the sailor's hatred, from a notion that its appearance forebodes a storm (cf. Storm Petrel).[148]

Little Auk
Alle alle

(From Swedish *alle* (literal meaning an avenue), a name applied to seabirds in Öland, perhaps because the lines auks form at sea suggest streets.)

SCOTS NAMES: Nor-a-wa-wifie [Banf], Ratch, Rotche or Rotchie [Shet].

GAELIC NAMES: *Falcag, Colcach bheag.* Common Auk, Little Eider.

Rotche is a seventeenth century name derived from the Frisian name for the Brent Goose, *Rotges*, which, imported by visiting Dutch seamen, became applied to the Little Auk. In the early nineteenth century the Little Auk was called the Common Rotche.

Thought to be once the world's most abundant seabird, there are Pleistocene records of Little Auks. They are winter visitors in Scottish waters in variable numbers, mostly in the far north.

Q: A nineteenth century writer on the Arctic commented that it 'frequents the countries stretching far northwards from our latitudes to the regions of perpetual ice.'[7]

Puffin
Fratercula arctica

(*Fratercula*: Latin, little brother, hence a friar, referring to the Puffin's habit of interlocking its feet like hands in prayer; *arcticus*: Latin, of the arctic.)

SCOTS NAMES: Ailsa Cock or Parrot, Bass Cock, Bouger or Bulker [Heb], Cockandy [Fif], Johnny Norie, Lunda or Lunda Bouger or Bonger or Lundi [Far], Lyre or Lyer [Ork], Marrot [Fif], Norie or Norrie [Ork, Shet, Kinc], Rednebbit Pussy [Mor, Banf], Sea Coulter, Tammie Cheekie or Tammie Norie [Ork].

GAELIC NAMES: *Budhaig, Seamus Ruadh, Peata-ruadh*. Bird with a belly, Red Jimmy (for their big red feet), Red spoilt child.

There is confusion with other auk names for this appealing parrot-like seabird. The word 'puffin' or 'puffing' originally applied to obese nestling Shearwaters harvested for food. The word literally means puffed up of fat. It is still used in the scientific names of the Shearwaters and is apparent in the Gaelic name meaning 'bird with a belly'. Some names are from habitat, others are nicknames applied to the Puffin because of its colourful bill, such as Bottlenose, Coulter Neb. Bouger and Bulker are Hebridean names from the Old Gaelic word *bulgair*, meaning a bird with a belly. Norrie is from a Norn word for dwarf, which with the addition of Christian names gives the attractive soubriquets Johnny or Tammy Norie. Lyre (also a name for young Manx Shearwaters) derives from the Norn *liri* meaning fat.

Puffin were recorded in the end of the Pleistocene and there is evidence from Stone Age middens that they were an early food source. The present British population is put at about 700,000 pairs, 90% of them in Scotland, with nearly half of these at St Kilda. In 1889 an explosion of the brown rat population (which had escaped from ships) wiped out the quarter of a million pairs of Puffins that bred on Ailsa Craig.

Q: Martin Martin described it in 1698: 'The bouger, by those in St Kilda so called; coulter-neb by those in the Farn Islands; it is of the size of a pidgeon, its bill is short, broad, and compressed sidewise, contrary to the bills of ducks, of a triangular form and ending in a sharp point, the upper mandible, or jaw, arcuate and crooked at the point... the bill is of two colours; near the head of an ash colour, and red towards the point. They breed in holes under the ground and come with a south-west wind about the twenty-second of March.'[126]

T: In the 'St Kilda lilt', a Gaelic dialogue between lovers, the lady sings:

Thou art my hero, thou art my basking sunfish,
Thou gavest me the puffin and the black-headed guillemot
Dark dusky maid, a cow in the fold!
The birds are a-coming, I hear their tune![35]

In the Northern Islands the name Tammie Norie is used for someone who is shy and gauche, echoing the puffin's solemn monkish appearance. There is a rhyme about such a person:

Tammie Norie o' the Bass
Canna kiss a bonny lass.

Poor Tammie, his neb as well as his shyness may be the barrier!

Where the small burn
spreads into the sea loch
I found the mad, clever clown's beak
of a puffin.

How many times
had it whirled into its burrow
with a six-fold whisker
of tiny fishes?

How many times
had it grunted love
to its parrot-faced lover?

I clack my own beak
by my own burrow
to feel how many little fishes
I've whiskered home, and
I grunt and grunt
before whirling off again
into the huge sea spaces.

   Norman MacCaig, 'Puffin'.[116]

ORDER: COLUMBIFORMES
PIGEONS AND DOVES

Family: *Columbidae*, the Pigeons and Doves

No. in world, 299; no. in Scotland, 4.

Rock Dove
Columba livia

(*Columba*: Latin, *Columba* a dove, or diving bird, from Greek *Kolumbis* a
diver; *livia*: Latin, contrived from lividus meaning blue.)

SCOTS NAMES: Doo, Rock Pigeon, Rock Doo, Rockier, Sod [For], Wild
Dove or Pigeon [Shet].

GAELIC NAMES: *Calman-creige, Smùdan*. Dove of the crag, Dove (lit.
Music of birds).

Most of these names refer to the bird's habit of frequenting sea cliffs. The
wild Rock Dove has retreated in front of the mass invasion of feral Pigeons.
Rock Doves are most commonly found on rocky western Scottish coasts from
the Clyde to Caithness.

This ancestor of the domestic or 'Trafalgar Square' Pigeon is traceable to
the end of the Pleistocene. Domestication may have begun as long ago as
4500 BC, and early man in Britain farmed doves in 'doò-caves', excavat-
ing nesting ledges for them. By medieval times huge numbers were kept
for fresh winter meat. Since then increasing feral populations have spread
throughout Britain. During recent times they have been bred for racing and
ornamental purposes and in World War II were used for secret message
transfer from Europe.

Q: According to Pennant in 1768 they could be a nuisance: 'They swarm
in the Orknies and Hebrides. In the first they collect by thousands towards
winter, and do great injury to the rick-yards.'[148]

T: From a notice in Rendell Doocot in Orkney: 'In 1625 Charles I decreed
that the floors of Doocots should be preserved because of the high concentration of Potassium nitrate which, when mixed with black earth, could be used
to make gunpowder.' (Stone doocots from earlier centuries survive in many
parts of Scotland.)

Pigeon-livered meant timid or cowardly, like a pigeon who has no gall.

198

For sin' the flood of Noah
The dow she has nae ga'.
'Lord of Rorlin's Daughter'.[8]

Stock Dove
Columba oena

(*oenas*: Greek, a wild pigeon the colour of ripening grapes.)

SCOTS NAMES: Craig Doo, Scotch Cushat, Wood Dove.

GAELIC NAMES: *Calman gorm, Fear, Fearain.* Blue pigeon, Dove, Stock-Dove or Woodpigeon.

The name Stock Dove has been known since the fourteenth century and refers to the stocks or stumps of trees in which the bird finds holes to nest. The bird shares the name Cushat with the superficially similar Wood Pigeon; this is a variant of the old English *cuscote*.

A bird of the later Pleistocene, the Stock Dove may have prospered in the warm early Holocene and then declined as the forests were cleared. During the nineteenth and early twentieth century it spread widely throughout Britain. From the late 1950s the use of organochlorine chemicals as seed dressing produced a sharp drop in numbers. In Scotland, which the species colonised in 1866,[100] the Stock Dove is now reasonably common south of the Highland Boundary Fault.

Q: MacGillivray, at the end of the nineteenth century, commented 'It has not been observed in Scotland.'[118]

T: I heard the Stock-dove on the top of the tree
And I foresaw that the year would not go well with me.[35]

Woodpigeon
Columba palumbus

(*palumbus:* Latin, a Wood Pigeon.)

SCOTS NAMES: Croodlin Doo, Cusha [Rox], Cushat, Cushie or Cushie Doo, Cuschet, Ring Dove, Ring Pigeon, Timmer Doo.

GAELIC NAMES: *Calman-coille, Dùradan.* Dove of the wood, *dùrdan* means cooing and is used especially of Blackcock and Doves.

The original name was probably Culver from Old English *culfer* or *culfre*, which in turn arose from Latin, *columba*. The Old German word *duif* was associated with death and became a noa word. This heathen association made the word unacceptable to early Christians who preferred names derived from Anglo-Saxon *cusceote* such as Cushat and Cooscot. By the sixteenth century the newer French word *pigeon* seems to have superseded culver, cushat and dove, but these names hang on in the vernacular.

The Woodpigeon has been traced in the late Pleistocene. It has adapted to climatic and ecological change throughout history and despite much predation by man has maintained high summer populations throughout Britain wherever there are trees.

Q: 'The Wood pigeon has an odd look in its eye that suggests perpetual astonishment'.[80]

T: Legend tells that the Woodpigeon took lessons from the Magpie in nest building but before the teacher was half way through sang out 'That'll doo-oo'. The Magpie was so offended she flew away and forever afterwards the pigeon has built a ramshackle nest compared with the Magpie's.

> The Pigeon said
> Gu-roo! Gu-roo! Gu-roo-oo
> Not of my kin are you!
> Not of my kin are you!
>
> From *Carmina Gadelica*, the speech of birds.[35]

Collared Dove
Streptopelia decaocta

(*Streptopelia*: Greek, *streptos* a necklace, *peleia* a dove; *decaocto*: Greek, eighteen.)

SCOTS NAMES: None.

GAELIC NAME: *Calman a chrios*. A Dove with the wages of a servant.

This recent introduction, though it is known by a Gaelic name, has not collected vernacular names.

This species is a newcomer to the British avifauna from its original breeding zone in Asia. It had reached India and South East Europe by the sixteenth century where it remained static until 1930. Then it suddenly started expanding westwards at a rate of 1,000 miles every twenty years. It arrived in Britain in 1952 and reached the Outer Hebrides in June 1960. This expansion was probably brought about by a genetic mutation, which enabled the species to tolerate colder climates.

Q: 'I was first notified in 1952 of the arrival of a Collared Dove in this country. In those days its rarity meant that only ornithological circles were informed in case, by telling the public, it might be frightened away! Little did we realise that only 25 years later it would be shot quite legitimately as a pest... There has never been such a rapid expansion, both of range and numbers, of a single species in the history of ornithology and no one has a scientific explanation for it.'[53]

T: The scientific name *decaocto* echoes the cooing of the Collared Dove. The name comes from Greek mythology. A servant girl who was paid 18 pence a year complained to the Gods about such meanness and they created a dove who would say *decaocto* for ever. This myth is reflected in the modern Gaelic name for the bird.

ORDER: CUCULIFORMES
CUCKOOS

Family: *Cuculidae*, the Cuckoos

No. in world, 139; no. in Scotland, 1.

Cuckoo
Cuculus canorus

(*Cuculus*: Latin, a cuckoo; *canorus*: Latin, melodious.)

SCOTS NAMES: Gokk [Ork], Gock, Gouk, Gowk or Gowkgoke.

GAELIC NAMES: *Cuach, Cubhag* or *Cuthag, Caolag*. These are onomatopoeic but *cubhag* also means a silly woman.

Both Cuckoo and gowk are old names, present at least from the thirteenth century. Cuckoo was brought to Britain by the Normans, as the Old French word *cucu*, and Gowk came with the Vikings, either from Old Norse or from Icelandic *gaukr*, a fool or simpleton.

This bird is first recorded in Britain at the end of the seventh century.[59] Though this bird is less common than it used to be south of the Tweed in Scotland, it is widely heard even as far north-west as the Outer Hebrides, where the hillsides still ring with the familiar cry in early summer. The Meadow Pipit is the common host in Scotland.

Q: On St Kilda Martin records the cuckoo 'being very rarely seen here, and that upon extraordinary occasions such as the death of the proprietor Mack-Leod.'[126]

T: In Aristophanes' *The Birds* several species built Utopia and called it *Nephelokokkygia* from *nephele*, a cloud, and *kokkyx*, a Cuckoo. Since then an

impractical idea or plan has been called 'cloud cuckoo land'.[11]
  In *Carmina Gadelica* it appears as a bird of ill omen.

> I heard the cuckoo with no food in my stomach
> And I foresaw that the year would not go well with me.[35]

ORDER: STRIGIFORMES
OWLS

Family: *Tytonidae*, the Barn Owls
No. in world, 14; no. in Scotland, 1.

Barn Owl
Tyto alba
(*Tyto*: Greek, *tuto* a night owl; *albus*: Latin, white.)

SCOTS NAMES: Gillihowlet, Hoolet [Lowl], Hulote or Hullart [Ork], Roarer [Bord], White Hoolet or Owl [Stir to Ayr].

GAELIC NAMES: *Comhachag, Caillach-oidche gheal.* Barn owl (*Comhach* = predatory life), White old woman of the night.

Many of the Barn Owl's names are either directly onomatopoeic, as Hoolet, or describe its voice, as in Roarer. Though this is a generic name for Owls it is inapt for the Barn Owl, which screeches. Others describe its beautifully subtle plumage, which appears white or pale yellow at distance. Gill, which may derive from Anglo-saxon *jil*, meaning night, gives rise to Gillihowlet.

This owl was present in Britain during the late Pleistocene. It is intolerant of cold and did badly during the Little Ice Age. Then, in the nineteenth century, it was persecuted by gamekeepers. After early improvement in the twentieth century a combination of harsh winters in the 1940s, chemical toxins in the food chain, diminished rodent populations and loss of nesting sites (due to destruction of barns) caused severe decline. There are still small populations of Barn Owls in southern Scotland but they are absent from the Highlands and Islands.

Q: The witches in Macbeth used an Owlet's wing in their spell since part, at least, of an owl was considered essential to such incantations.

T: Some superstitions hold that Barn Owls appear when a birth is imminent or that the child will be a girl. Others say the presence of an owl at birth foretells ill luck.

Screech owls, because of their association with the dead, were sometimes called Lich owls after the lich gate, which provided shelter for a funeral cortege waiting for the clergyman to conduct the service.

It is another bird of ill-omen in the Gaelic poem:

> I heard the screech of the owl of the night
> And I foresaw that the year would not go well with me.[35]

Family: *Strigidae,* the Owls
No. in world, 160; no. in Scotland, 4.

Little Owl
Athene noctua

(*Athene*: Greek, Goddess Athene; *noctua*: Latin, a night owl.)

SCOTS NAMES: none in Scotland.

GAELIC NAME: *Comhachag bheag.* Little Owl, from *Comhach* meaning predatory life.

The Little Owl appears to have been present in Britain for about 500,000 years, but only as a vagrant, until it was successfully introduced in the 1870s. Little Owls colonised Scotland as breeding birds in 1958 with limited success.[100] The species is a scarce breeder in Scotland south of the Forth/Clyde line.

Q: Saunders, writing in 1899, describes the earliest sightings of it: 'In 1758 Edwards figured a Little Owl caught alive in a chimney near the Tower of London, and since that date many examples have been obtained in England... As yet it has not been recorded from Scotland.'[162]

T: The owl, named for Athene, the Greek goddess of Wisdom, symbolises wisdom.

Tawny Owl
Strix aluco

(*Strix*: Latin, a screech owl; *alucus* or *ulucos*: Latin, screech owl.)

SCOTS NAMES: Brown Hoolet, Brown Owl, Brown Ullert, Cataface [Ork], Cat Owl, Ferny Hoolet, Golden Owl, Grey Owl, Hoolet, Hoot Owl, Howlet, Ivy Owl, Jenny Hoolet or Howlet, Jinny Oolert or Yewlet, Katogle, Oolit, Ullat, Ullet, Ulnia, Wood Owl.

GAELIC NAMES: *Comhachag, Caillach-oidhche gheal, Corra-sgreuchag.* Brown owl, Bright old woman of the night, Screech-heron.

Tawny Owl became the standard name after Pennant.[148] As with other owls, habitat and plumage give rise to some names, the bird's voice to others and again there is the use of Christian names such as Jenny. Katogle is of Norn origin and literally means 'cat owl' from the bird's appearance, hence Cataface and Cat Owl.

Present from the late Pleistocene, the Tawny Owl probably succeeded well in the period of forestation in the early Holocene. By the nineteenth century it suffered at the hands of gamekeepers. In Scotland the bird is widespread in lowland areas, becoming less abundant in the north-west and scarce in the Hebrides. It is the commonest owl in Perthshire where it is often seen, and heard most nights.

Q: 'Nest in a conifer wood near Glenalmond (beyond top of Sma' Glen) 25th May 1914 contained two young in very white down with very red skin showing below, bills bluish.'[198]

T: 'Like an owl in an ivy bush' is an oxymoron and means to have at one time both a sapient and vacant look like an owl, as some people have when very drunk or when staring into space. Ivy is not only a favourite roosting place of owls but also represented Bacchus, giving the adage double meaning.

Long-eared Owl
Asio otus

(*Asio*: Latin, Long horned Owl; *otus*: Latin, long-eared.)

SCOTS NAMES: Cat Owl, Horn Coot, Hornie Hoolet or Oolet.

GAELIC NAMES: *Comhachag-adharcach, Mulchan, Ullchabhagan.* All mean Horned or Long-eared Owl.

The official name was coined by Pennant in 1768[148] and most of the vernacular names refer to the bird's 'ears' or 'horns' though there is also the same reference to a cat as for the tawny owl.

Like the Tawny the Long-eared Owl was present in the Pleistocene and is likely to have flourished in the early Holocene. In Scotland it breeds in all mainland counties, though least in the north and west, and, in winter, numbers are often boosted by continental birds.

Q: 'At the present day [in 1953] the Long-eared Owl is a common resident from the Borders to the Dee and Moray, but appears to be very scarce in Angus. North of this it becomes less common and is not very abundant in Sutherland and Caithness. In Argyll and the West Highlands it becomes much scarcer.'[13]

T: The Long-eared Owl was believed to be so stupid that if one walked round it enough times it would turn its head until it wrung its own neck.

Short-eared Owl
Asio flammeus

(*Asio*: Latin, Long horned Owl; *flammeus*: Latin, flame coloured.)

SCOTS NAMES: Brown or Grey Yogle [Shet], Cataface [Ork], Cat Ool [Shet], Grass Owl [Banf], Grey Hullet, Horned Oolert, Katogle [Ork], Short-horned Hoolet.

GAELIC NAME: *Comhachag-chluasach*. Owl with ears.

Coined by Pennant[148] the official name contrasts with that of the Long Eared Owl. The bird is quite different in its habitat and behaviour; it hunts by day, frequenting moors and, particularly, coastal marshes, hence 'Grass Owl'. Katogle and Cataface are of Norn origin and derive from Norse *kattugla*, meaning an owl like a cat.

Present from the late Pleistocene, this owl's habit of hunting voles on open heathland by daylight would have rendered it less successful in the forests of the Holocene. In the nineteenth century gamekeepering took its toll. This Owl is highly mobile and opportunistic, and its population fluctuates with that of its chief prey, the Field Vole. Voles' distribution is scattered in the Hebrides but absent in Harris, Lewis and Shetland where the Short-eared Owl is rarely seen. It is commoner in the vole-rich Uists and in Orkney.

Q: Seton Gordon remarked: 'One bird found on the South Uist moorlands, which is met with seldom on the Scottish mainland, is the Short-eared Owl.'[71]

T: The Short-eared Owl is also called the Woodcock Owl, because migrant birds from Europe arrive about the same time as the Woodcock, and also because of its flight and diurnal habit.[61]

ORDER: CAPRIMULGIFORMES
NIGHTJARS

Family: *Caprimulgidae*, the Nightjars

No. in world, 82; no. in Scotland, 1.

Nightjar
Caprimulgus europaeus

(*Caprimulgus*: Latin, milker of goats; *europaeus*: of Europe.)

SCOTS NAMES: Churr Owl [Aber], Goat Chaffer, Moth Hawk [For], Moth Owl [For], Wheel Bird [Stir], Wheeler.

GAELIC NAME: *Gobhar-oidch*. Goat of the night.

Few birds have given rise to so much superstition as the secretive Nightjar. A bird more often heard than seen, its strange, whirring, nocturnal call has given rise to many of its names. Names including churr or jar and their variants are all onomatopoeic, as are references to goats and wheels. When seen the bird is often motionless on a branch, where it dozes throughout the day to become active at night, when its hawklike shape gives rise to a combination of names suggested by its crepuscular pursuit of moths.

The Nightjar is a summer migrant, first mentioned in Britain by Ælfric the Grammarian.[1] It was plentiful in the nineteenth century but started to decline in the early twentieth. Since an optimistic estimate of 6,000 pairs in the 1970s numbers have fallen considerably (though it is often overlooked). In Scotland it is a scarce breeding bird, seen chiefly in Arran and Galloway.[192]

Q: Osgood Mackenzie lamented the bird's rarity in 1921: 'No Nightjars have been for years seen here, though they used in former times to fly about the garden and nest close to my house.'[119]

209

T: Since Aristotle there has been the belief that Nightjars sucked the milk of goats, hence its Greek name *aigothelas* (*aigo*: goat, *-thelas*: sucker). There is no truth in this, but it has given rise to many names including the scientific *Caprimulgus*. Superstition dogs the bird further in that it was associated with death and called the Lich Bird. In the Middle Ages 'lich' was a word meaning body, usually dead, an association which persists in the lychgate to a churchyard, where the bier was rested at funerals. Another name, Flying Toad, continues the unpleasantness, which reaches its climax with Gabble Ratchet (see pp.12, 176, 177).

ORDER: APODIFORMES
SWIFTS

Family: *Apodidae*, the Swifts

No. in world, 92; no. in Scotland, 1.

Swift
Apus apus

(*Apus*: Greek, *apous* without feet.)

SCOTS NAMES: Black Martin, Black Swift [Kirk], Brown Swallow [Renf], Bucharet [For], Cran or Crane Swallow [Loth], Devil Bird, Harley [For], Jack-a-Dells.

GAELIC NAMES: *Gobhlan dubh*, *Gobhlan mór*. Black or Great Martin (from *Gobhlach*, forked).

The Swift is another bird associated with superstition. Black has long equated with the devil and this has given rise to many satanic names. In Jack-a-Dells the unpleasant word Devil is replaced by the noa word Dells, in double superstition so that the dangerous name word could be avoided. Bucharet is an interesting name with its conjectural likeness to Bucharest. This may reflect the suspicion with which south-eastern Europe was regarded during the Middle Ages, when Romania and Bulgaria were often confused. The Albigensian heresy of Bulgaria, whose followers were believed capable of any crime, gave rise to the naming of the unnatural vice of buggery (bugger was a corruption of Bulgar). The name Swift occurred first in 1668[38] and later became standardised by Pennant in 1768.[148]

The Swift is a short-stay summer migrant, which was first mentioned in Britain in the mid-sixteenth century.[195] It probably nested on cliffs, gradually adapting

211

to buildings as increasing urbanisation offered more nest sites. Changes in buildings have depleted its nesting sites and this, with insecticide residues in its preferred food, poses a threat to the species, which appears to be declining. In Scotland Swifts are abundant migratory breeders from April to August.

Q: Thomas Bewick in 1797 was puzzled by practicalities: 'It is difficult to conceive how these birds, which never seem to alight, gather such [nesting] materials; some have supposed that they catch them in the air as they are carried up by the wind.'[19]

T: Swifts were believed not to have feet, hence the family name *Apodidae*. This led to the erroneous belief that they could not take off from the ground. However they are reluctant to come to earth, sleeping, and even copulating, in the air. As Bewick supposed, they do indeed collect nesting material in the air.

In Heraldry the Martlet, as the Swift is known, is the mark of fourth son of the first house because he lacks land on which to set his foot.

ORDER: CORACIIFORMES
KINGFISHERS AND ALLIES

Family: *Alcedinidae*, the Kingfishers

No. in world, 92; no. in Scotland, 1.

Kingfisher
Alcedo atthis

(*Alcedo*: Latin, *Alcedo* a kingfisher; *atthis*: Latin, Athenian.)

SCOTS NAMES: Halcyon, the King's fisher.

GAELIC NAMES: *Crùidein, Biorra-crùidein, Biorr-an-iasgaire*. Kingfisher, Kingfisher with a point, Point of the fishes. (From *Biorra*, a thorn, pin or any pointed thing, which also comes from *Bir* an Old Gaelic word for water.)[61]

Surprisingly, in view of its brilliance, this bird has few vernacular names. The English poetic name of Halcyon, often used in Scots verse, dates from early fourteenth century (see below).

The Kingfisher is recorded among late Pleistocene remains. It was probably constant in numbers until the nineteenth century when it was thought to be a threat to game fish, and its feathers were fashionable for fishing flies and millinery. In Scotland Kingfishers are scarce; however a pair frequents the Tay near Strathtay.

Q: At Traquair in Peeblesshire an eighteenth century clergyman recorded: 'The king's fisher has been frequently seen on the banks of the Tweed'.[145]

T: The name 'Halcyon' derives from classical mythology and the belief that the Kingfisher was a miraculous bird, which built its nest on the sea during

213

a period of calm at the time of the summer solstice. The sea remained so still that the bird could bring off its brood and this tranquillity gave rise to the expression 'halcyon days'.

Kingfishers are reputed not to putrefy and because of this were sometimes hung in linen cupboards to preserve clothes. They were also suspended by the bill to predict changes in winds.

ORDER: PICIFORMES
WOODPECKERS

Family: *Picidae*, the Woodpeckers

No. in world, 198; no. in Scotland, 2.

Green Woodpecker
Picus viridis

(*Picus*: Latin, a woodpecker; *viridis*: Latin, green.)

SCOTS NAME: Specht.

GAELIC NAMES: *Lasaire-choille, Buidhean-na-coille*. Flame or flash of fire in the woods, Yellow bird of the woods (a name it shares with the Yellowhammer).

In England this species, with seventy or more vernacular names, must be one of the world's most nominate birds. By contrast in Scotland it has only the one name, Specht, and that borrowed from Dutch!

The Green Woodpecker is without early records and is first mentioned in the eighth century.[59] In Scotland Green Woodpeckers were occasional visitors until the 1940s when they started to spread throughout the country and, since 1951, it is now recorded as breeding in all mainland counties except Caithness and Sutherland.[100] In heavily wooded areas it is an increasingly common sound but still an uncommon sight.

Q: Though recorded in the parish of Dunkeld in the *Old Statistical Account*,[145] Forbes, writing in 1905, stated 'The Green Woodpecker is said to be almost extinct in Scotland'.[61] The bird can be seen, and more frequently heard, in the woods of Dunkeld to this day.

Great Spotted Woodpecker
Dendrocopos major

(*Dendrocopos*: Greek: *dendron* a tree and *kopos* beating or striking; *major*:
Latin, greater.)

SCOTS NAMES: None.

GAELIC NAMES: *Snagaire daraich, Cnag.* Oak-tree woodpecker, Knocker.

The standard name was conceived by Ray[155] as Greater Spotted Woodpecker
and was shortened to 'Great' by Pennant.[148] Although the species is much
commoner today in Scotland than the Green Woodpecker, it has no specifically Scottish names.

The earliest trace of this woodpecker is from Ireland, where it no longer
occurs, at the end of the Pleistocene. It almost certainly spread with the
increased forestation of the early Holocene but subsequently declined as the
forests were cut. By the mid–nineteenth century it had disappeared from
Scotland, probably as a result of deforestation as sheep farming developed,
but, since 1887, it has made a recovery and now breeds in all Scottish mainland counties. In Perthshire it is the commonest woodpecker and is seen in
small numbers almost every month.

Q: The minister for Killin recorded in the *Old Statistical Account*: 'Some
birds are found in this country, which are reckoned rare; as the Greater Spotted Woodpeckers.'[145]

ORDER: PASSERIFORMES
PASSERINES OR PERCHING BIRDS

Family: *Alaudidae*, the Larks

No. in world, 81; no. in Scotland, 1 (2).

Skylark
Alauda arvensis

(*Alauda*: Latin, a lark; *arvensis*: Latin, *arvum* a field, *ensis* belonging to.)

SCOTS NAMES: Lady Hen [Shet], Lairag, Lairick, Larick, Laverock, Lavrock, Livrock, Lavro or Laveroo [Ork], Lerruck [Ork], Our Lady's Hen [Ork & Shet], Short-heeled Lark.

GAELIC NAMES: *Uiseag* or *Topach, Fosg*. Both are generic for all larks but *Topach* also means tufted. *Fosg* literally means space, so the Lark becomes the bird of space.

Most names derive from *Láwerce*, the Anglo-saxon word for a lark. In Germany it used to be believed that the Lark was under the protection of the Virgin Mary and this seems to be reflected in the Orcadian name. Similarly in Eriskay the Skylark is '*useag Mhuire*' or St Mary's lark.[48]

The Skylark has been present in Britain since the end of the Pleistocene. Early in the Holocene it would have suffered from the increase in woodland but subsequent clearance for farming would have benefitted it. Victorian taste for larks as a delicacy food led to mass netting of newly arrived birds after the winter influx. Reports from the British Trust for Ornithology draw attention to the rapid decline of this species during the early 1990s as a result of intensification of farming practices.

Q:
Bird of the wilderness
Blithesome and cumberless,
Sweet be thy matin o'er moorland and lea!
Emblem of happiness,
Blest is thy dwelling-place—
Oh to abide in the desert with thee!

James Hogg, 'The Skylark'.[88]

Laverock, laverock,
Liltin in the lift,
Singin like a lintie
On a dooble shift,
Never stop a meenit,
Never oot o puff,
Soarin like a jet-plane
Aff to dae its stuff,
Mind ye dinna rush awa
Up high wi sic a speed
Ye dunt your heid agin the sun
And faa doun deid.

J.K.Annand.[5]

T: Lark flesh was supposed to be beneficial for diseases affecting the throat.

As long as a Laverock sings before Candlemas it will greet after it. (Scots proverb.)

According to the Gaelic scholar Forbes, *Fosgag Mhoire*, Mary's lark, augurs good luck, but the bird is capable of uttering as many curses as it has spots on its tongue on anyone who steals its eggs.[61]

The nest of the skylark
Is in the track of 'Dubhag', [Dubhag is a cow's name]
My little one shall sleep and he shall have the bird

From *Carmina Gadelica*: a lullaby sung to a child.[35]

Woodlark
Lullula arborea

This species does not now occur in Scotland and is included here because it was so widely reported in both the New and Old Statistical Accounts. However, according to Baxter and Rintoul 'the Tree Pipit was so often referred to as the Woodlark that faith cannot be placed in these records.'[13] These authorities may well be right, but the observations of ministers, particularly in the *Old Statistical Account*,[145] who mention the Woodlark at least fourteen times, have a ring of first-hand truth about them. For example the minister for Clunie in Perthshire recorded:

'The notes of the wood-lark are heard, delightful along the banks of the Lunan in spring and autumn; its nocturnal song has a dying cadence peculiarly melodious and has often been mistaken for the song of Philomel.'

The most convincing references in the *Old Statistical Account*, such as that above, are to the song of the bird. The Tree Pipit's song is so distinctive with its terminal '*Seee-a, Seee-a, Seee-a*'. The Woodlark, on the other hand, has a mellow, fluty song, often on an interrupted descending scale delivered either from a tree or in circular display flight. It is known to sing at night, which may have given rise to the name 'Nightingale of Scotland' used frequently in the *Old Statistical Account* (though in fairness this name is sometimes applied to the Sedge Warbler). The Tree Pipit is a summer migrant heard and seen in Perthshire from late April to early August, so the fact that the 'Wood-lark' was heard in autumn (it sings throughout the year) at Clunie again suggests that this could have been *Lullula arborea*. Harrison says of it, 'It seems to have been more widespread at times in the past, since it is said to have bred in Lancashire and in Cumbria',[86] and Fisher adds 'In Scotland it is a regular passenger'.[59]

In Europe the Woodlark occurs as far north as southern Sweden and Finland and in the Summer of 1998 the RSPB reported an amazing recovery of this species over the preceding decade, with spread from its southern range as far north as Yorkshire. The verdict for Scottish Woodlarks has to be 'Not Proven', which is at least an advance on that of Baxter and Rintoul.

Perhaps, as the minister for Nielston, in Renfewshire, prophesied, the Woodlark will once again 'be seen every month in the year in some of the woods in this country, and her plaintive notes heard during the greater part of the season.'[145]

Family: *Hirunididae*, the Swallows

No. in world, 81; no. in Scotland, 3.

Sand Martin

(*Riparia riparia. Riparius:* Latin, a bank nester or frequenter of the river bank.)

SCOTS NAMES: Bitter Bank or Bitterie [Rox], Sand Backie [For], Sand or Sandy Swallow [Stir, Rox], Shore Bird, Witchuk [Ork].

GAELIC NAME: *Gobhlan-gainmhich.* Forked one of the sand.

Most names refer to the bird's colonial nesting in sand banks with the additional meaning of sandy colouration. Bitter is a variant of biter, describing the way Sand Martins excavate their nest tunnels. Witchuk is from Norn.

The earliest record of the Sand Martin in Britain is from the eighth century. Increased gravel and sand extraction has improved its breeding opportunities. Sand Martins winter in the Sahel south of the Sahara, where severe droughts in the winters of 1968-9 and 1982-3 produced a drop of some 90% in the population.

Q: 'Though at first one would be disinclined to believe that this weak bird, with her soft and tender bill and claws, should ever be able to bore the stubborn sand-bank without entirely disabling herself; yet with these feeble instruments have I seen a pair of them make great dispatch.'[197]

Dr Williams noted: 'Back at Glenalmond April 11th 1914. 2 nests each with 5 eggs near Glenalmond at Methven Gullery'.[198]

Swallow
Hirundo rustica

(*Hirundo*: Latin, a swallow, *rusticus*: Latin, pertaining to the country.)

SCOTS NAMES: Latower, Red-fronted Swallow, Swalla, Swallie.

GAELIC NAME: *Gobhlan-gaoithe.* Forked one of the woods.

Most names are variants on Swallow, which derives from Norse *Svala* or *Svalwõ* (literally a cleft stick: cf. Gannet, p.95.) 'Red-front' refers to the throat patch of this species and 'Latower'comes from 'lath over', a wooden structure over an aperture or doorway; the sort of place Swallows like to nest.

The Swallow has left traces in the middle Pleistocene of some 500,000 years ago. It probably did poorly in the Holocene, but as man increased his settlement, providing nesting sites, the bird prospered. Though it suffered badly in the Sahel droughts of 1968-9 and 1982-3, populations in Britain now reach up to a million pairs in summer.

Q: The bird was well known to Aristotle who originated the aphorism 'Two swallows do not make a summer'.

T: According to Scandinavian tradition the swallow hovered round Christ's cross calling 'Svala! Svala!' (meaning console! console!) whence it was called *svalow* the bird of consolation.

An old legend has it that the Swallow introduced Adam and Eve by taking some of his hair to her. 'Since the Swallow carried on as internuncio between Adam and Eve it is allowed to nestle in the dwellings of men'.[61] To this day it is considered good fortune to have Swallows nesting on one's property.

House Martin
Delichon urbica

(*Delichon*: this is an anagram of *chelidon* which is Greek for swallow, *urbicus*: pertaining to the city.)

SCOTS NAMES: Black Martin, Martin Swallow, Mairtin, Martlet, Swallow [Rox], Window Martin, Wunda Swalla.

GAELIC NAME: *Gobhlan-taighe*. Forked one of the house.

Swainson[190] states that this bird is named after St Martin (the patron saint of innkeepers and drunkards) but St Martin's bird is really the goose, and Brewer's *Dictionary of Phrase and Fable* attributes the name Martin to the bird's arrival in March (the Martian month) and its disappearance about Martinmas (11 November, however, seems late for Martins).

This species occurred in Britain at the end of the Pleistocene as a summer migrant from its wintering zones in the southern hemisphere. As man increased his building so the House Martin thrived as it found additional nesting sites. It was reduced during the industrial revolution by air pollution, particularly in large cities, but has recovered with improvement in air quality since 1965.

Q: This guest of summer,
       The temple-haunting martlet, does approve
       By his loved mansionry, that heaven's breath
       Smells wooingly here: no jutty frieze,
       Buttress, nor coign of vantage but this bird

Hath made her pendent bed, and procreant cradle:
Where they most breed and haunt, I have observed,
The air is delicate. *Macbeth* I, vi.[169]

T: Martins, like Swallows, are considered a sign of good fortune, and harming them tempts fate to wreak disaster.

The Martin and the Swallow,
God Almighty's birds to hallow.

Family: *Motacillidae*, the Pipits and Wagtails

No. in world, 58; no. in Scotland, 6.

Tree Pipit
Anthus trivialis

(*Anthus*: Latin, a small bird inhabiting grasslands, *trivialis*: ordinary.)

SCOTS NAMES: Field Lark or Lesser Field Lark, Field Titling, Grasshopper Lark, Pipit Lark, Short-heeled Field Lark, Wood Lark [SS] also Wode, or Wudd Lark (see under Woodlark p.218).

GAELIC NAME: *Riabhag-choille*. Pipit of the woods.

This species, with its superficial similarity to Larks and other Pipits, has long been confused with them.

Present from the later part of the Pleistocene, its population probably increased as birch woods proliferated from about 10,000 years ago. It is a summer visitor to Britain, wintering in Africa. Recently numbers of Tree Pipits have declined somewhat with a breeding population of some 50,000-100,000 pairs. In Scotland they are seen and heard frequently in wooded counties.

Q: To add to the Woodlark/Tree Pipit confusion Burns wrote:

Oh, stay, sweet warbling Woodlark, stay,
Nor quit for me the trembling spray;
A hapless lover courts thy lay
Thy soothing, fond complaining.[27]

Loyd,[111] who quotes this stanza, emphasizes that *this* Woodlark *was* a Tree Pipit! The Tree Pipit 'sits high in a tree descending like a parachute singing as it comes down. The song is loud and ends with notes that are very emphatic and determined.'[72]

Meadow Pipit
Anthus pratensis

(*pratensis*: Latin, of the meadow.)

SCOTS NAMES: Banks Teetick, Earth or Field Titling [Loth], Gray Cheeper [Per], Ground Lark, Heather Peeper [Banf], Hill Sparrow or Teetick [Ork, Shet], Moss or Muir Cheeper [Per], Moss Cheeper, Moss-creeper, Peep [For], Pipit Lark, Teetan or Teeting [Ork], Teetik or Tietick [Shet], Titlin or Titling [Ork, Cai].

GAELIC NAMES: *Mioneun, Snathag or Didig, Tacharan cuthaig.* Meadow pipit, Grey bird, Cuckoo's attendant or page.

Most of these names refer to this very common bird's moorland habitat or to its weak piping call. The species is so often foster parent to Cuckoos that it has earned the name 'Cuckoo's Page' in Gaelic.

Present from the late Pleistocene when it must have been limited to upland heaths, this species is the commonest British passerine above 500 metres. It is locally migrant with many breeding in Scotland, from where, in winter, flocks move south. In summer there may be as many as 3,000,000 breeding pairs, mostly in the north, with about half this in the winter. There is no historical evidence for change in the status of this species until the early 1980s when it started to decline; there have been noticeably fewer Meadow Pipits in Scotland since then.

Q: 'Meadow Pipits attract pointers on grouse moors'[80] and I have seen this happen with my own Labradors.

Pipit identification is difficult, as Pat Hall, an expert from the British Museum, pointed out in verse:

> It's a pity that the pipits have no diagnostic features,
> Specifc'ly they are the least distinctive of God's creatures,

223

For naming any one you need five measurements together
With a drawing of the wing tip and the length of every feather.

Count the spots on breast and back, be sure of which the sex is;
Make a picture of the pattern of the one-but-outer retrix.*
Pay extravagant attention to the hind claw's conformation;
Note 'weak and long' or 'curved and strong'. (Or 'snapped in
      preservation.')

And when you've marshalled all the facts,
No matter what their sense is,
If the bird was caught in Europe
It is, ten to one, *pratensis*.[84]

T: In Ireland it is said that the Pipit is forever trying to get into the Cuckoo's mouth and that if it should succeed the end of the World would come.

Meadow Pipits signify the death of a child; three of them singing near a house are singing requiem for a child within.[35]

Tacharan cuthaig, the page of the Cuckoo, is the Meadow Pipit. When the Cuckoo sings, the Pipit emits a hissing sound resembling *tach! tach! tach!* and this gave rise to the name.[35]

Rock Pipit
Anthus petrosus

(*petrosus*: Latin, of the rocks)

SCOTS NAMES: Gutter or Shore Teetan [Ork], Rock Lark, Rock Lintie [Aber], Shore Sparrow or Teeting [Ork], Sea Lintie [Ayr], Sea Mouse, Shore Pipit, Tangle Sparrow or Tang Sparrow [Ork, Shet], Teetan or Teetuck [Shet].

GAELIC NAME: *Glas-eun.* Grey bird.

These names refer to habitat and similarity with species such as Sparrows and Linnets.

Until 1986, when they were split by the British Ornithological Union, Rock and Water Pipits were considered conspecific. Though probably present in the latter part of the Pleistocene the earliest records of these Pipits are Holocene. Rock Pipits have been little affected by man apart from disturbance

*Retrix: one of the tail feathers of a bird; there are usually 12 retrices.

224

due to increased leisure use of beaches during the twentieth century. The breeding population is about 50,000 pairs, with up to three times this in the winter as birds migrate from Scandinavia. Most Scottish rocky shores are inhabited by Rock Pipits.

Q: There is a Hebridean race, which Cunningham describes as being very dark.[48]

Grey Wagtail
Motacilla cinerea

(*Motacilla*: Latin, possibly derived from *motum* to move and *cilium* an eyelash, referring to the wagging tail; *cinereus*: Latin, ashy.)

SCOTS NAMES: Yella or Yellow Wagtail.

GAELIC NAMES: *Bricein-an-uillt, Breacan-baintighearna.* Chequered one of the mountain stream or Lady's tartan.

Originally from Ray,[155] the name Grey Wagtail is a misnomer, since the predominant colour of this beautiful bird is yellow and many, on seeing it for the first time, question the name Grey Wagtail. It is only grey in comparison with the more brilliant yellow plumage of the Yellow Wagtail (which is seldom seen in Scotland) accounting for the confusion of vernacular names. The Gaelic names suggesting plaids are better.

The Grey Wagtail also has left traces in the late Pleistocene. During early agriculture many small watermills were constructed which provided breeding habitats for this species (this is especially true of the Hebrides where Norse invaders brought mill technology quite early). To this day Grey Wagtails are often seen near watermills. They have a curious habit of tapping on windows, possibly in response to their own reflections. They move south during winter when they are seldom seen in Scotland.

Q: The Italians call this beautiful species *Ballerina gialla*, Yellow Ballerina; how much better than the prosaic standard misnomer.

225

T: The grey washer by the ford, the *bean-nighe* of Celtic mythology, was a wraith who appeared to travellers to be washing clothes in a stream. When the viewer approached she held up the clothes, which were seen to be a phantom of the spectator complete with the death wounds he was later to suffer. 'In Perthshire the washing woman is described as small of stature and rotund, and clad in a muslin green garment. In Skye she is squat and resembles a shrunken, rather disagreeable child. If caught while at her labours she is bound to reveal the circumstances of her captor's fate, so long as he truthfully responds to her questions in turn.'[176] (See pp.13, 227.)

The window-tapping habit of Grey Wagtails has been seen as foretelling disaster or sudden death.

Pied and White Wagtails

Pied (or British Isles race): *Motacilla alba yarrellii*
White: *Motacilla alba*
(*Motacilla* (see under Grey Wagtail); *albus*: Latin, white; *yarrellii* from Yarrell.)

SCOTS NAMES: Devil's Bird or Deviling [Ireland], Seed Lady [Peeb, Selk], Wagtail, Waggie or Waggitie [Fif, For, Loth], Waggatie wa, Wagster, Washdish, Washerwoman, Washtail, Water Pie, Water Wagtail, Wattie Wagtail, Waterie [For], Willie Wagtail [Ork].

GAELIC NAMES: *Breac-an-t-sil, Glaisean-seilich, Glasag.* Chequered, or tartan, one of the rain, Sparrow of the willows, Water Wagtail.

This attractive and readily visible bird has many names often associated with water; its movement suggests business at the water and gives rise to washer-woman names. The dark patterning of Pied Wagtails recalls the association between Satan and black birds and this lies behind Irish Devil names. In Scotland Pied Wagtails are partly migratory and arrive at seed-time, hence Seed-lady.

The two races of this species are both seen in Scotland. *M. alba yarrellii* is confined to Britain as a breeding bird. The silvery continental race, *M. alba*, is widespread throughout western Europe except Britain, where it occurs on migration especially in the Hebrides. There is evidence of Pied or White Wagtails in the Pleistocene when the differentiation between the races occurred; the White race occupied the European mainland when glaciation had lowered the North Sea; later warming separated the races.

Q: The White Wagtail has a grey back and very white face.[48] It is a fairly common passage visitor to Outer Hebrides.[153]

And sittin' chirpin' a' its lane
A water-waggy on a stane...
    J. R. Selkirk, 'A Border Burn'.[168]

Wee Wullie Waggletail, what is a' your stishie?
Tak a sowp o' water and coorie on a stane:
Ilka tree stands dozent, and the wind without a hishie
Fitters in atween the fleurs and shogs them ane by ane.

What a whigmaleerie gars ye jowp and jink amang the duckies
Wi' a rowsan simmer sun beekin on your croun
Wheeple, wheeple, wheeplin like a wee burn owre the chuckies,
And wagglin here, and wagglin there, and wagglin up and doun.
    William Soutar.[175]

T: It has been suggested that a white wagtail was the legendary caladrius, a dazzling white bird which could foretell death by gazing into a sick man's eyes. Sometimes the caladrius absorbed the patient's sickness and flew towards the sun, either to die itself or to have the poison burned away.[101]

Nigheag bheag a bhroin, the little washer of the sorrow, is the water nymph who presides over those who are about to die, and washes their shrouds by a ford. She is also called the *Luideag,* a little hairy female who wailed piteously as she washed the shroud. She was reputed to have been seen at *Lochan nam Breac Dubh* (the lakelet of the black trout) between Broadford and Sleat in Skye. As she washed she sang:

I am washing the shrouds of the fair men
Who are going out but in shall never come,
The death-dirge of the ready-handed men
Who shall go out and fall in the peril.[35]

Family: *Bombycillidae*, the Waxwings

No. in world, 8; no. in Scotland, 1.

Waxwing
Bombycilla garrulus

(*Bombycilla*: from Greek, *bombukos* silk, and Latin, *cilla* a tail; *garrulus* from Latin, meaning garrulous or chattering.)

SCOTS NAMES: Black-throated Waxwing, Bohemian Chatterer, Bohemian Jay, Carolina Chatterer, Chatterer, Pest or Plague bird, Silktail.

227

GAELIC NAMES: *Caifean* or *Gabair*. Chatterer.

It is possible that in the late Pleistocene Waxwings nested in Britain, since there are records of the species from the last glaciation. The bird is known as a winter visitor since 1662 and in recent years it may have become an annual visitor. They occur infrequently in Scotland during winter irruptions.

Q: There are several references to Waxwings in the *Old Statistical Account*: 'The Bohemian chatterer, a bird of a most beautiful plumage and striking conformation, was taken, last season, in this country' (Argyll).[145]

T: Waxwings appearing in Scotland early in winter foretell harsh weather.

Family: *Cinclidae*, the Dippers
No. in world, 5; no. in Scotland, 1.

Dipper
Cinclus cinclus
(*Cinclus*: Greek, water ouzel.)

SCOTS NAMES: Benny Ducker, Bessie Ducker or Bessy Dooker, Bobby, Brook Ouzel, Ess Cock [Aber and NE], Piet or Water Piet or Pyot [Per, Ayr], Water Blackbird, Water Bobbie, Water Cock, Craw or Crow [Loth, Lan], Water Crake, Water Ouzel, Water Peggie or Meggie [Loth, Lan, Dumf].

GAELIC NAMES: *Gobha uisge, Gobha-dubh-an-uisge, Feannag uisg*. Water Smith, Blacksmith of the stream, Water Crow.

The Dipper was known as the Water Ouzel to Pennant[148] and only acquired its standard name in 1825.[163] Most of the names refer to water, its black and white plumage or to its characteristic bobbing motion.

A bird of the latter part of the Pleistocene, the Dipper probably did well in the wet postglacial period but later was persecuted because of its undeserved reputation for taking trout and salmon ova. A bird of rapidly flowing streams of the north-west, it is also in the area most affected by acid rain, which may pose a new threat to it.

Q: Samuel Smiles records the nineteenth century persecution of the dipper: 'Every means has been put in requisition to destroy this little bird. It was abundant thirty years ago; but it is now rarely to be seen. It was supposed to destroy the young salmon, hence it has been shot down wherever found. But I have never as yet found anything appertaining to fish in its stomach, and I have dissected about forty—water insects and their larvae being what I have most frequently observed.'[174]

'A big black Wren with a white bib'.[61]

> No webbed feet,
> but a water bird for all that.
>
> And a gentlemanly one—
> he walks on the bottom
> of his helter-skelter stream
> wearing a white shirt front
> and a brown cummerbund.
>
> He hates dry land.
> Flying up a twisty stream
> he follows the twists
> all the way.
>
> When he perches on a stone
> it's a wet one.
> He stands there, bobbing and bobbing
> as though the water's applauding him.
>
> He likes his nest
> to be behind a rippling tapestry—
> a tapestry? Well,
> a waterfall.
>
> Naturally.
>
> Norman MacCaig, 'Dipper'.[113]

Family: *Trogloditidae*, the Wrens

No. in world, 69; no. in Scotland, 1.

Wren
Troglodytes troglodytes

St Kilda Wren
Troglodytes troglodytes hirtensis

Shetland Wren
Troglodytes troglodytes zetlandicus

Hebridean Wren
Troglodytes troglodytes hebridensis

(*Troglodytes*: Greek, one who creeps into holes; *hirtensis*: Latin, of St Kilda; *zetlandicus*: Latin, of Shetland; *hebridensis*: Latin, of the Hebrides.)

SCOTS NAMES: Jenny Wren, Katie Wren or Kitty Wren [Aber, Berw, Loth], Kitty-me-wren [Loth, Dum, Rox], Our Lady's Hen, Wirran [Ork], Wran, Wrannie, Wrannock [Ork].

GAELIC NAMES: *Dreathan-donn, Drean.* Brown wren. *Drean* literally means the lascivious one, and probably comes from *Draoi-eun* or Druid bird.

Most names derive from the Anglo-Saxon name of *Wrenna*, as in Wranny etc. The Scottish name 'Our Lady's Hen' refers to the legend that the Wren brought moss to cover the infant Jesus in the stable. Many names are from small children, as in Kitty or Jenny.

The Wren is originally a North American species which spread across the Bering Straits into Eastern Asia at some time during the Pleistocene and then slowly spread westwards, reaching Britain at the end of the Ice Age. Since then it prospered to become Britain's commonest bird during the 1960s. Though the British Wren differs subtly in voice and behaviour from its American forbears it is the same species. Some forty races are recognised, including the St Kilda, The Shetland and the Hebridean Wrens.

Q: Malisons, malisons more than ten,
       Who harries the queen of heaven's Wren. (Borders Proverb)

According to a South Uist saying, *Cha dig ugh mór a tòn an dreathain.* (A big egg will never come from the wren's backside: which signifies that nothing small will achieve greatness.)[172]

T: The Wren is a bird of augury, hence the name *drui-eun,* the Druid bird. In Druidic divination many birds were used to foretell the future. In Ireland the Wren was domesticated for this purpose and it seems that this use of the bird was brought to Ireland by Pictish settlers from Scotland.[176]

    The hunting of the wren in Ireland, the Isle of Man and Scotland is a surviving Celtic ritual. On 'wrenning day', St Stephen's day, it was customary to stone a wren to death in commemoration of the saint's martyrdom. Forbes suggests that this comes from an early Christian attempt to destroy pagan ideas.[61] Another explanation for this massacre of Wrens lies in the story that Irish soldiers were about to surprise enemies when a Wren perched on a drum and woke the sentinels with its loud song. Even today Wrens are hunted and their bodies preserved until St Stephen's Day to decorate holly boughs.

      The nest of the wren
      Is in the rock thicket,
      My little one shall sleep and he shall have the bird.
      From *Carmina Gadelica*: lullaby sung to a child.[35]

    The Wren was portrayed on the obverse of the farthing, which ceased to be legal tender in January 1961.

Family: *Prunellidae*, the Accentors
No. in world, 12; no. in Scotland, 1.

Hedge Sparrow or Dunnock
Prunella modularis
(*Prunella*: French, *prunelle* a sloe; *modularis*: Latin, modulator or director of music, referring to its high pitched song.)

SCOTS NAMES: Blind Dunnock, Blue Dickie [Renf], Blue Jannie, Blue Jig,

Blue Sparrow or Blue Tom, Bush Sparrow [Stir], Bushock, Creepie, Field Sparrow or Fieldie [Rox], Hedge Spurdie or Spurgie [Aber, Per], Hempie, Titlene or Titling [NS], Whin Sparrow [Kinc to Wig].

GAELIC NAMES: *Gealan-gàraidh*, *Gealan-nam-preas*, *Donn-eun.* Noisy Sparrow, Sparrow of the thicket, Brown bird.

Many names describe its sparrow-like appearance or its habitat. Its plumage is bluish-brown, giving rise to a number of names such as Smokey and Dunnock, which is a diminutive of dun. In habit it is a skulking, creeping bird, seen often hopping in hedge bottoms, and this is reflected in the nomenclature. Prunella is a worsted material used for making clergymen's gowns and the uppers of ladies' boots; like the bird it was prune or sloe coloured; a parallel wth the Dunnock's scientific name. 'Blind' refers to its apparent inability to distinguish a Cuckoo's egg laid among its own bright blue clutch.

The Dunnock was present in the late Pleistocene as a bird of scrub woodland, and it is likely to have increased with the afforestation of the early and middle Holocene. It has probably increased with the popularity of garden shrubberies in suburban Britain.

Q: Grey mentions it singing in January and February and describes it as 'apologetic'.[80]
  Victorian writers often extolled the Dunnock for its celibacy and sexual rectitude. Recent research has shown that the female mates with two or more males but that the dominant male removes his rival's semen from her cloaca to ensure that his progeny survive. Queen Victoria would not have been amused!

T: The nest of the cuckoo
         Is in the hedge-sparrow's nest,
         My little one shall sleep and he shall have the bird.

             From *Carmina Gadelica*: a lullaby sung to a child.[35]

Family: *Turdidae*, the Chats and Thrushes

No. in world 329; no. in Scotland 12 [13]

Robin
Erithacus rubecula

(*Erithacus*: Latin, a winter bird that changed into the Redstart in summer: now used specifically for species with red breasts; *rubecula*: diminutive from Latin, *ruber* red.)

SCOTS NAMES: Bob Robin [Stir], Mason's (or Painter's) Ghost [SS], Red Rab [Loth, Selk], Redbreast, Robin Ruck or Ruddock, Robinet, Robin Redbreast.

GAELIC NAMES: *Brù-dhearg*, *Pigidh*, *Bruin-deargan*. Red Belly, Robin Redbreast.

Most names relate to plumage but the odd name Mason's Ghost is related to the bird's love of haunting old masonry, where it may have been likened to the spirit of the mason who built the wall. It is sometimes called the Painter's Ghost as 'it is much in evidence when painters cannot work because of inclemency of the weather'.[61]

Present from the Pleistocene, the Robin is ubiquitous in Britain apart from Shetland and high Scottish mountains. In winter northern birds migrate to the south and in autumn there are occasional influxes of Scandinavian birds. The British population is estimated at about 3 to 5 million pairs.

Q:
        Holy, Holy, Holy,
        A wee brown bird am I
        But my breast is ruddy
        For I saw Christ die.

    Fiona MacLeod (William Sharp), 'The Birth of Christ'.[122]

233

(William Sharp (1856-1905) was born in Paisley and educated at Glasgow University. He published under his own name and also as Fiona MacLeod, whose identity he concealed until his death).

T: The marriage between Wren and Robin is a tradition extending back for centuries: in one version Robin asks what happened to the ring he gave the Wren and she replies 'I gied it till a soger' (I gave it to a soldier).

This bird is held to be so sacred that a decoction of the very bark of a rose-briar in which a Robin's nest is, is said to be a cure for some ailments.[61]

The Robin was believed to cover the dead, and this belief was immortalised in the story of the Babes in the Wood where an old ballad describes that after the death of the children:

> No burial this pretty pair
> From any man receives,
> Till robin redbreast piously
> Did cover them with leaves.[8]

Other legends tell that the Robin had its breast singed bringing primeval fire from Hell. This has led to a Scottish belief that if a Robin is killed the murderer's cows will yield bloody milk.

Christmas cards came into popular use in the mid-nineteenth century and among many birds that they feature, the Robin is the commonest. Christmas cards date from the time when postal deliveries began. The uniform of early postmen included a red waistcoat and they were nicknamed Robins. Christmas cards, became popular at about the same time and, because they were delivered by Robins, acquired the same nickname. Later this led to the frequent use of pictures of this bird on the cards.

Nightingale
Luscinia megarhynchos

(*Luscinia*: Latin, nightingale; *megarhynchos*: Greek, *Megas* large, *rhunkos* bill.)

GAELIC NAME: *Spideag*, Nightingale, also spiteful, any slender creature, melodious.

This species is not found in Scotland (apart from a single record by Baxter and Rintoul from the Isle of May).[13] However no less a person than Sir John Sinclair, editor of the *Old Statistical Account of Scotland*, sought to rectify this deficiency:

A gentleman who was very desirous of introducing these birds [in Scotland], commissioned a person in London to purchase as many Nightingale eggs as he could procure at a shilling each. This was done accordingly; they were carefully packed in wool, and forwarded by the mail. In the meantime men had been employed to find and take care of several Robin Redbreasts' nests, in places where they might hatch securely. The eggs were then placed under the Robins, by whom the young Nightingales were successfully reared, and remained in the neighbourhood till the usual time for migration; when it is supposed they went away, as they were not seen again after that period, and not one was known to return to the place of its birth.[178]

Redstart
Phoenicurus phoenicurus
(*Phoenicurus*: Greek, *phoinix* dark red, *oura* tail.)

SCOTS NAME: Red tail

GAELIC NAMES: *Ceann-deargan* , *Deargan*, *Èarr-dhearg*. Red stain or Red Tail.

The Redstart has records dating from the Pleistocene and flourished during early Holocene afforestation. It has undergone wide fluctuations of fortune, culminating in severe losses during the Saharan drought of the early 1970s, since when it has partially recovered. It is a summer visitor to Scotland.

Q: The Redstart is well distributed in Scotland, breeding in every mainland county.[13]

Dr Williams noted: 'Nest near Crieff 10/6/1914 in a hole in a low wall by roadside two feet above the ground; a cup of coarse grass with a little moss and a feather or two. Four young, spotted like young Robins and within two or three days of flying.'[198]

Whinchat
Saxicola rubetra
(*Saxicola*: Latin, living in rocks; *rubetra*: Latin, mispelling of *rubeta* bramble thickets.)

SCOTS NAMES: Bush Chat, Chackart [Aber], Fern Lintie [Aber], Fun Chackert or Lintie, Whin Chacker or Chackert, Whin Clocharet [For], Whin Lintie [Aber].

GAELIC NAMES: *Gocan*, *Fraoichean*, *Conasag*. Whinchat, Heather Chatterer, of the furze. *Gocan* also means a pert conceited little person or a little attendant.

Whinchat was coined by Ray.[155] It shares names with the Stonechat, especially when onomatopoeic. 'Fun' is a nineteenth century Scots name for Whin. Clocharet comes from Gaelic *cloich* a stone.

Differentiation between bones of Whinchat and Stonechat is extremely difficult and early history of the species is confused. Certainly there are traces of either or both from the end of the Pleistocene. Later both species would have been inhibited by afforestation but later profited from clearance as it occurred. Today the Whinchat occurs sporadically, with its main strongholds in the northern and western uplands of Scotland.

Q: 'Whin-chats and stone-chatters stay with us the whole year.'[197] For once Gilbert White was wrong; Whinchats are summer visitors!

Stonechat
Saxicola torquata
(*Saxicola*: Latin, living in rocks; *torquata*: Latin, *torquatus* adorned.)

SCOTS NAMES: Black-a-top, Blackcap, Bushchat, Chackart [Banf], Clockwret, Stane Chacker or Chapper [For & S], Steenchack or -chacker, Stone Chack or Chatter, Stonechart, Stone Clocharet [For].

GAELIC NAMES: *Clacharan*, *Cloicheran*, *Fearna Fèill-Padraig*. Literally stone-runner (used for both Stonechat and Wheatear), Follower of St Patrick (Stonechats appear in northern Scotland around St Patrick's day).

Named Stonechat by Pennant,[148] this bird has many vernacular names which it shares with both the Whinchat and Wheatear. Others refer to its black head or habitat, and possibly to its habit of sitting high on a bush or stem where it is easily visible.

For early history, see Whinchat. Stonechats suffer badly in harsh winters and are found in the milder western part of Scotland from the Borders to Orkney.

Q: 'This bird has been named the Stonechat, but very inaptly, for it does not frequent stony or rocky places, its usual haunts being similar to those of the Whinchat. It is generally distributed, and although nowhere abundant, is to be seen here and there on commons, heaths, and hill pastures, overgrown with whins, juniper, and other low shrubs.'[118]

T: To see the first Stonechat on grass is good luck, but bad luck if the first is seen on rocks or a road.[35]

Northern Wheatear
Oenanthe oenanthe

(*Oenanthe*: Greek, *Oenos* wine; *anthos* flower; hence a bird that appears when the vine is flowering.)

SCOTS NAMES: Chack, Chacker, Chackbird or Chacks [Ork], Clocharet [For], Clockwret, Dyke Hopper [Stir], Joctibeet [Cai], Stanechack or -chacker [Aber], Steinkle, Stinkle or Stenkle [Shet], Stenshik, Stinkiebeul [Ork], Stone Chatterer [Banf], Stonechipper [SW].

GAELIC NAMES: *Brù-gheal*, *Clacharan*, *Crithneachan*. White belly (cf Robin), shared with Stonechat, Trembling one.

The name Wheatear is a probable corruption of the Old English White Arse (arse did not become vulgar until seventeenth century). It is suggested that the name became bowdlerized in Victorian Britain because its old and more descriptive name was considered impolite. Joctibeet is probably onomatopoeic and northern names such as Stinkiebeul are Norse.

This summer visitor is represented in Pleistocene remains. As a bird of open heathland it probably suffered from increase in afforestation during the early Holocene. When sheep farming in Scotland led to clearance of much upland during the nineteenth century the Wheatear flourished, despite widespread slaughter of the species for Victorian restaurants. In England there has been a marked reduction in Wheatear populations resulting from changed agricultural practice. Myxomatosis in rabbits also contributed, through loss of burrows used as nest sites and overgrowth of vegetation on heaths. Breeding is now on upland moors of the north and west. The Northern Wheatear is but one of many species of Wheatear, several of which may occur as vagrants in Scotland.

Q: According to Pennant in 1763, 'They grow very fat in autumn, and are esteemed a delicacy… The season is in July and August'.[148]

'As a boy', wrote Charles St John in the 1840s '…I used to be an adept at catching them in horsehair nooses as we used to consider them particularly good eating.'[161]

T: Wheatears were considered unlucky in Scotland because of supposed connections with the Devil and with toads, which were supposed to hatch its eggs. To hear a Wheatear calling was a sign of bad luck, even a death omen, especially if seen perched on a stone; however if the observer happened to be sitting on grass then good luck was to be anticipated!

> On the fair evening of Tuesday,
> I saw on the smooth stone.
> The snail, slimy, pale,
> And the ashy wheatear
> On top of the dyke with holes...
> And I knew from these
> That the year would not go well with me.
>
> From *Carmina Gadelica*.[35]

Clacharan, the Wheatear or stone-bird, is called *fear na Feill Padruig*, bird of the feast of St Patrick, because he appears then. The Wheatear was believed to lie dormant underground during the winter.[35] (There are several clear accounts of such 'dormant' birds being found in winter. One can only suppose that such birds had been trapped in some naturally occurring landslide or that they were a late brood which had been abandoned by their parents, as sometimes happens with Swallows and Martins.)

Ring Ousel
Turdus torquatus

(*Turdus*: Latin, a thrush; *torquatus*: Latin, adorned with a neck chain or collar.)

SCOTS NAMES: Chackart [Lan], Ditch Blackie [Loth], Flitterchack [Ork], Heath Throstle, Heather or Hedder Blackie [Aber], Hill Chack [Ork], Moor or Mountain Blackbird, Mountain Ouzel or Thrush [Kirk], Oswald, or Oswat [For], Ring Blackbird or Thrush, Rock Blackbird [Stir], Rock Starling [Rox].

GAELIC NAMES: *Gobha-dubh-a' mhonaidh, Dubh-chreige, Lon-cheilearach.* Blacksmith of the mountain, Black one of the rocks, Warbling Ouzel.

Indistinguishable from the Blackbird in fossil remains, the early presence of the Ring Ousel is unproven. Its first mention, according to Fisher,[59] was in 1450. In Scotland it is a mountain bird rarely seen below 300 metres and so limited to remote places.

Q: At Tannadice in Angus the minister noted in the *Old Statistical Account*[145] 'Besides other common birds, they have one called the oswald, or oswat, very much resembling a blackbird.'

Dr Williams records finding a nest 'in the Sma Glen near Glenalmond College on 14th June 1914. It had 4 young, two with rings, and the nest was of coarse grass lined with fine grass and a little wool and moss. It was in heather seven feet up on a ledge of a big piece of rock'.[198]

Blackbird
Turdus merula

(*Turdus*: Latin, a thrush; *merula*: Latin, a blackbird.)

SCOTS NAMES: Blackie, Chucket [Ork], Garden Ouzel, Grund Blackie, Lintoo, Merl or Merle, Merlie or Merlin, Osill, Ouzel or Ouzel Cock, Skitterie Mavie.

GAELIC NAMES: *Lòn dubh*, *Thein-dubh*, *Rear* or *Rearg*. Black one of the meadow or lawn, Black one of the furze or Blackbird.

Until the seventeenth century Ousel was the usual name for this species. In Scotland, and in poetry, it was Merle. Its similarity to the Songthrush gave it Mavis names to which the addition of Skitterie encapsulates the bird's habit of skittering dry leaves. Lintoo is an anglicised form of Gaelic *Lòn-dubh*.

Blackbird or Ring Ousel remains have been found among Middle Pleistocene deposits. It probably benefitted from afforestation during the Holocene and seems to have adapted to clearance of forests, first by colonising coppiced areas and, in the nineteenth century, the shrubberies of Victorian Scotland.

Q: David Millar mentions the species in his poem 'The Tay' of 1850:

'And hush! the notes of the lintoo.'[132]

T: Once all white, the blackbird took refuge from a storm in a warm chimney; too late it realised that this was the Devil's lum and that it would forever be black.[10] In Scotland the Blackbird was a Jacobite symbol referring to Charles II, who, as a boy, was of swarthy complexion and nicknamed 'Black Boy'.

239

Fieldfare
Turdus pilaris

(*Turdus*: Latin, a thrush; *pilaris*: Greek, hair.*)

SCOTS NAMES: Blue Back, Feltie [Loth, Dum], Feldifare [Fif], Feltifer [Fif], Feltiflier [Loth], Feltifare [Kirk], Grey Thrush, Hielan Paddy or Hielan pyat, Hill Bird, Monthly Bird [For], Redshank (see *T*), Screech Bird or Screech Thrush [Stir], Skittery Feltie [Stir & SW], Storm Cock.

GAELIC NAMES: *Liath-truisg, Uiseag sneachda*. Grey truss, Lark of the snow.

Most names refer to the Fieldfare's colours or to its harsh 'chack–chack–chack' call. Monthly Bird is probably a corruption of Mountain Bird.

This winter migrant from breeding grounds in Scandinavia and Russia was present during the Pleistocene, probably as long as 500,000 years ago. Its population has probably been stable throughout its history but in recent times it has extended its range with a few birds remaining to breed in Scotland.

Q: Fieldfares have bred in Shetland only since the early 1970s.[44]
   Dr Williams recorded their arrival at Glenalmond on 12 November 1913 and departure on 26 April 1914.[198]

T: The Fieldfare, according to a Scottish nursery rhyme, coloured its legs reddish when, in an attempt to domesticate itself with man, it got too near his fire.
   Grahame warns of October Fieldfares:

> If, 'mid the tassels of the leafless ash,
> A fieldfare flock alight, for early frosts
> Prepare...[76]

Song Thrush
Turdus philomelos

(*Turdus*: Latin, a thrush; *philomelos*: Greek, *philos* loved, *melos* song.)

SCOTS NAMES: Mavie [SW Scotland], Mavis (lit), Thissel Cok, Thristle or Thristle Cok (lit), Throstle.

GAELIC NAMES: *Smeòrach, Ciarsach, Smòlac*. Songthrush, Dusky one, Ember.

*This is probably an error: *Trikhos* also means a hair but is easily mistaken for *trikhas* which is the Greek for thrush. It appears that at some time in history a translator made a slip which has been perpetuated.

Mavis, now largely used poetically, goes back to the fourteenth century and stemmed from the Old French *mauvis*. Throstle comes from Middle English *throstel* and has led on to several Scottish names.

Song Thrush remains date back some 500,000 years to the Middle Pleistocene. Less tolerant of cold than the Blackbird, it probably was more successful during the early Holocene, but later with the clearance of forests it declined. It may have benefitted from the planting of copses for game protection during the early nineteenth century. During the harsh winters of the 1940s and of 1962-3 numbers dropped dramatically. In 1972 the population was estimated at 3,500,000 pairs, but there has been further decline since. Increased use of garden molluscicides has reduced the Song Thrush's favourite food of snails. They also take marine molluscs and may be seen in company with Purple Sandpipers collecting winkles which they then bash on rocky anvils. The species is now in serious decline, however there seemed to be plenty of Song Thrushes in Perthshire in 2000.

Q: The Mavis also said:
Little red lad!
Little red lad!
Come away home!
Come away home!
Come away home
My dear to your dinner.

From *Carmina Gadelica*: the speech of birds.[35]

T: It was once believed that Thrushes cast their legs and acquired new ones when ten years old.

Redwing
Turdus iliacus

(*Turdus*: Latin, a thrush; *iliacus*: Greek, genitive of *ilias* a thrush.)

SCOTS NAMES: Norway Nightingale, Redwing Mavis [For].

GAELIC NAMES: *Deargan sneachta*, *Sgiath-dheargan*. Red stained bird of the snow, Wing of red.

Most names refer to the bird's plumage. Redwings in Scandinavia sing well, hence the name Norway Nightingale.

The Redwing is a winter visitor from Scandinavia and Siberia. It has been traced in deposits from the late Pleistocene. It suffers in severe winters and Scotland is at the northern limit of its winter range. Redwing began to colonise Scotland as breeding birds in 1925,[100] since when breeding has been recorded regularly with up to 300 pairs remaining through the summer. Winter numbers may be larger locally, but birds often pass rapidly through on southern or northern migration.

Q: Writing in the middle of the nineteenth century, MacGillivray noted the bird's migratory habits: 'The Red-winged Thrush arrives in the northern and eastern parts of Scotland in the end of October or beginning of November... It is not until the end of April, or the beginning of May that they take their final departure for the season; and in the island of Harris I have seen individuals remain so late as the 25th of May, although I never observed one in July or August, and should not have supposed that any breed there, had not Mr Bullock stated that he had found a nest in the neighbourhood of Rodhill.'[118]

T: The nocturnal flights of migrating Redwings in the North Sea sometimes cause such a rushing sound that they are called 'the herring spear or piece'. This sound, heard with awe by fishermen, is believed to be a portent of good fishing.

Mistle Thrush
Turdus viscivorus

(*Turdus*: Latin, a thrush; *viscivorus*: Latin, *viscum* mistletoe, *voro* to eat.)

SCOTS NAMES: Bell Throstle, Big Mavis [Loth], Feldifare, Feltiflier, Feltifare or Feltifer, Highland Pyot, Hillan Piet [Aber], Muzzel Thrush [Rox], Stormcock, Thrice-cock, Thristle Cok, Thostle-cock, Wood Thrush [Dumf].

GAELIC NAMES: *Smeárach-mhor, Sgraicheag-ghlas.* Big thrush, Grey Screecher.

Mistletoe berries pass through the gut of the Missel Thrush and so the bird is responsible for its propagation. But other explanations of the name hold that it stems from mizzle, an old word for speckled. It shares several names with other members of the Thrush family, especially the Fieldfare.

This Thrush was present at the end of the Pleistocene. As a bird of open woodland it would have done poorly in the dense forests of the early Holocene but it is likely to have become more numerous as clearances produced more suitable habitats. Despite this it was scarce until 1800 when it began an unexpected recovery, spreading widely so that by 1950 it was present through most of Britain. In the hard winter of 1962-63 it lost 75% of its population, but recovered in the next five years and is now abundant in Scotland.

Q: In Renfrew in the 1840s 'The Missel-thrush, which was rare in this country perhaps twenty years ago, is now so abundant as to cause great annoyance where there is small fruit'.[142]

T: It was once believed that the Mistle Thrush spoke seven languages.

Family: *Sylviidae*, the Old World Warblers

No. in world, 376; no. in Scotland, 9.

Grasshopper Warbler
Locustella naevia

(*Locustella*: Latin, diminutive of locust or grasshopper, so-named because of its call; *naevia*: Latin, having moles (referring to the spotted underparts).)

SCOTS NAMES: None in Scotland.

GAELIC NAME: *Ceileiriche leumnach.* Frog Warbler.

The first British record of this warbler, which is more often heard than seen, was by Ray in 1678.[155] In Scotland it is rare, but 'reeling' birds are reported annually in small numbers from many areas.

Q: The song 'is like the whispering noise of a grasshopper or of a small soft-running reel. He sits in a dwarf willow bush and "reels" turning his head from one side to another, which makes the sound appear now more, now less distant, to the listener'.[80]

Sedge Warbler
Acrocephalus schoenobaenus

(*Acrocephalus*: Greek, *acron* top, *kephale* head; *schoeobaenus*: Greek, *schoinos* reed, *baino* to walk or step.)

SCOTS NAMES: Scotch Nightingale or Nichtingale [Rox, Stir].

GAELIC NAMES: *Glaisean, Uiseag-oidche.* One who is grey, Lark of the night.

Most of the names arise from the bird's habitat. It sings long after dusk and has been given the name of Nightingale in Scotland, which was also applied to the Woodlark.

First recorded in Britain by Pennant[148] it has almost certainly been present since the Holocene, but drainage of marshes between the seventeenth and nineteenth centuries reduced its habitat considerably. Though it increased during the first half of this century, severe drought in its wintering area of the Sahel caused numbers to drop sharply and they are still falling. In Scotland it is a fairly common reedbed warbler.

Q: 'The only bird we have [in Banffshire] that attempts to give music at the dead hours of night, is the Sedge-warbler.'[174]

Whitethroat
Sylvia communis

(*Sylvia*: from Latin, *silva* a wood; *communis*: Latin, common or general.)

SCOTS NAMES: Beardie, Blethering Tam, Caperlinty [Jed], Charlie Muftie [Stir], Churr, Churr Muffit, Jack Straw, Jennie [Rox], Meg Cut-throat [Rox], Meggie or Muggy [N], Nettliecreeper, Wheetie, Whishie, Whitebeard, White Lintie [For], Whusky Wheybeard.

GAELIC NAME: *Gealan-coille*. White bird of the wood.

The descriptive name, like Redbreast, is very old and probably dates from the fourteenth century. The bird's names describe its habitat (straw, nettles etc.), its colouration (whey, white etc.) and its song (Blethering Tam and Churr). It has a number of familiar names such as Meggy, Jenny and Charlie and shares Whitebeard with the Willow Warbler.

This was the commonest of warblers at the end of the nineteenth century. Since World War II it has suffered major habitat loss because of removal of hedgerows. In 1968 and 1983 there were serious sub-Saharan droughts affecting the Sahel, where these warblers winter, leading to a huge loss in the Whitethroat population. It is thought that during this period the population fell from five million to a tenth of that figure. From being the commonest Warbler it is now quite a rarity.

Q: Dr Williams noted: 'Glenalmond July 10 1913. Young out. A nest found (in June) by some boys (and robbed). Not common in the neighbourhood.'[198]

Garden Warbler
Sylvia borin
(*Sylvia*: from Latin, *silva*, a wood; *borin*: derivation uncertain.)

SCOTS NAME: Billy Whitethroat [Loth].

GAELIC NAME: *Ceileiriche-garaidh*. Warbler of the garden.

This rather undistinguished-looking warbler left traces in the late Pleistocene. Despite minor fluctuations in numbers over the centuries Garden Warblers are widespread as far north as lowland Scotland. The songs of the Blackcap and Garden Warbler are so similar that confusion is easy. The Garden Warbler's song tends to be sustained and less varied than the Blackcap's and lacks the watery cadences of the latter.

Q: The rule 'that if you can see it, it's a Blackcap and if you can't, it's Garden Warbler' sometimes helps.

Blackcap
Sylvia atricapilla
(*atricapilla*: Latin, *ater* black, *capillus* hair of the head.)

SCOTS NAMES: No specifically Scottish names.

GAELIC NAME: *Ceann-dubh*. Black head.

Pleistocene deposits in Devon and Derbyshire have yielded traces of Blackcap. Present since the Holocene, the Blackcap seems to be altering its habits and range. Formerly fairly uncommon in Scotland during the twentieth century, this Warbler has extended its range northwards and it now frequently overwinters in Scotland. From about 20 records of overwintering in Britain during the 1940s it is now thought that some 3,000 birds do so now. If, as some predict, climate change produces warmer winters, this trend is likely to increase.

Q: At the end of the nineteenth century: 'In Scotland it becomes scarce as a breeder beyond the Firths of Clyde and Forth, but its nest has been found as far north as Ross-shire'.[162]

245

Wood Warbler
Phylloscopus sibilatrix

(*Phylloscopus*: Greek, *phullion* a leaf, *skopos* searching; *sibilatrix*: Latin, hissing or whistling.)

SCOTS NAMES: No specifically Scottish names.

GAELIC NAME: *Ceileiriche coille.* Warbler of the wood

First recognised in Britain by Ray in 1678[155] this warbler requires open woodland, especially of beech and oak. Its population has varied with different forestry techniques but has always been somewhat scarce and localised.

Q: In 1899 Saunders wrote that in Scotland it is fairly distributed and has apparently spread northward of late years, being recorded as breeding in the south-east of Sutherlandshire and as having been identified in Caithness, Wester Ross and the Outer Hebrides.[162]

Chiffchaff
Phylloscopus collybita

(*collybita*: Greek, corruption of *Kollubistes* money or change, referring to the call which sounds like money being counted.)

SCOTS NAMES: No specifically Scottish names.

GAELIC NAME: *Caifean.* A trifling, diminutive fellow or a Chiffchaff.

Bones which may be either Chiffchaff or Willow Warbler are known from the end of the Pleistocene. In the 1960s the Chiffchaff increased four-fold, before falling back by about half to the present number of about 300,000 pairs. Whilst in England this warbler is common, it is far less so in Scotland where the Willow Warbler greatly outnumbers it.

Q: Edward in 1877 commented on the rarity of this species in Banffshire: 'The only bird of this kind that I have seen, is the one I took myself.'[174]

Willow Warbler
Phylloscopus trochilus

(*trochilus*: Greek, a small bird, possibly a wren.)

SCOTS NAMES: Muffie Wren [Renf], Scotch Wren, Smeu or Smeuth or Smooth [Stir], Wheelie Oe [Ayr], Whitebeard (also Whitethroat, see above), White Wren, Willie Muff, Muftie or Muffitie, Willow Wren.

GAELIC NAME: *Crionag-ghiuthais*. Wren of the pines.

Willow Warbler names describe the habitat and colouration, but do not refer to its greatest distinguishing feature from the Chiff-chaff, the difference in song.

For early history, see Chiff-chaff. In this century Willow Warblers have spread to colonise almost the whole of Britain except the Fens. The population is thought to exceed 3 million pairs.

Q: In Scotland 'the Willow Warbler is our commonest breeding warbler, nesting in all the mainland counties and... on many of our islands.'[13]

Goldcrest
Regulus regulus

(*Regulus*: Latin, a small bird, also a small king from the gold crown on its head.)

SCOTS NAMES: Gold-crested Wren, Golden Crestie [Loth], Golden Wren [Stir], Miller's Thumb [Rox], Moon or Moonie or Muin [Rox], Woodcock Pilot.

GAELIC NAME: *Crionag-bhuidhe*, Wren with gold.

Most names refer to the crown colour or size of this wren-like bird. Miller's Thumb is really a reference to the size of this, the smallest British bird. The same name is used of other small creatures such as the Long-tailed Tit and a tiny freshwater fish called a Bullhead (*Cottus gobio*).

The Goldcrest, Britain's smallest bird, is likely to have been present throughout the Holocene but was not mentioned until 1544.[195] Its distribution depends on trees, especially conifers. The population rose four-fold during the 1960s and 70s but suffered badly in the harsh winters at the end of the 1970s. It then rose again and the breeding population is estimated at 1.5 million pairs with migration from the continent boosting this to 5 million in winter. The species is quite common in Scotland but often overlooked because of its size.

Q: In the Parish of Jedburgh, Roxborough 'In the winter of 1788, during a severe fall of snow, a golden crested wren made its appearance. The size of it was much smaller than the common wren; the colour of the body nearly the same; but the head was adorned with feathers of a beautiful orange colour and gold'.[145]

T: Goldcrests are supposed to lead migrating continental Woodcocks to their winter quarters, arriving there two days in advance of the first Woodcock, and so have gained the name of Woodcock Pilot in the Borders.

Family: *Muscicapidae*, the Flycatchers
No. in world, 147; no. in Scotland, 2 + vagrants.

Spotted Flycatcher
Muscicapa striata
(*Muscicapa*: Latin, *musca* fly, *capio* sieze; *striatus*: striped.)

SCOTS NAME: Beam Bird.

GAELIC NAMES: *Breacan-sgiobalt*, *Glac-nan-cuileag*. Tartan of the granary, Seizer of the fly.

Spotted Flycatchers build their nests on flat rafters or beams, hence the name Beam Bird.

The Spotted Flycatcher is present in remains from the late Pleistocene and it probably flourished throughout the Holocene when it would have found adequate nesting sites. In the last century it has become closely associated with man, and it was often seen around old buildings, especially farms, where there is a good fly population. In recent years it has undergone a serious decline with other Sahel wintering birds. The population is of the order of 100,000 pairs, however in the summer of 2000 they were abundant in Perthshire.

Q: This bird arrives late in the north, but is noted for the speed with which it builds its nest.[61]

T: Spotted Flycatchers are considered lucky, hence the couplet:

> If you scare the Flycatcher away
> No good luck will with you stay.

Pied Flycatcher
Ficedula hypoleuca

(*Ficedula*: Latin, small garden bird; *hypoleuca*: Greek, *hypo* below, *leukos* white; *Muscicapa*: Latin, *musca* fly, *capio* sieze.)

SCOTS NAMES: No specifically Scottish names.

GAELIC NAME: *Breacan-glas*. Grey chequer or tartan.

First recorded in Britain by Ray[155] in 1676, the Pied Flycatcher with its requirement for open, broad-leaved woodland is largely limited to Western Britain and Wales. During the latter part of the nineteenth century there were large spring influxes and Pied Flycatchers extended their British range. Similar increases seem to occur in cooler years, but the population remains small and localised and is estimated at 20,000 pairs. It is increasingly common in Southern Scotland with a number of sightings most years in Perthshire, where it has a liking for streams and open water and often nests in old oak and birch woodland, gardens and parkland in hilly country near water.

Q: 'Pied Flycatchers are African birds, which pass along the eastern coast of Britain on their way to nest in their preferred breeding grounds further north, but many of them will stop in this country if they find a suitable site'.[53]

Family: *Aegithalidae*, the Long-tailed Tits

No. in world 7; no. in Scotland 1

Long-tailed Tit
Aegithalos caudatus

(*Aegithalos*: Greek, *aigithalus* titmouse; *caudatus*: Latin, *cauda* a tail, *-atus* provided with.)

SCOTS NAMES: Bellringer [Kirk], Bottle Tit, Feather Poke, Fuffit or Juffit [Loth], Millithrum, Oven Bird or Builder [Stir].

GAELIC NAMES: *Cìochan, Cìochan-fada, Cailleach-bheag-an-earbaill.* Long-tailed Tit, Little old woman with a tail.

Titmouse is a misnomer and has nothing to do with mice. Tit is Scandinavian and means small (as in titbit); mouse is derived from Old English *mäse*, which was used of several small birds. Many of the names for this bird refer to its exquisite domed nest woven from moss and lichen. The nest expands as the brood grows, a considerable feat of engineering, when as many as 22 eggs have been found in a single nest. Millithrum comes from Miller's Thumb (see under Goldcrest, p.247).

There is a Pleistocene record of a Long-tailed Tit but no other early account of the species until the eighth century. Cold weather in the latter half of the twentieth century has reduced the population considerably and it was estimated in 1972 that the numbers were of the order of 150,000 pairs. They are now generally distributed, but formerly were less common north of the Clyde.

Q: Saunders, writing at the end of the nineteenth century, describes two races of Long-tailed Tit, adding, of the northern race: 'Our form... although somewhat partial in its distribution in Scotland, it is by no means uncommon there; ranging as far west as Skye, and wandering to the Shetlands.'[162]

T: A very descriptive children's name for this species is 'Flying Crotchet'.

Family: *Paridae*, the Tits
No. in world, 50; no. in Scotland, 5.

Willow and Marsh Tits
Willow Tit
Parus montanus

(*Parus*: Latin, a Titmouse; *montanus*: Latin, of the mountain.)

Marsh Tit
Parus palustris

(*palustris*: Latin, of the marsh.)

SCOTS NAMES: None.

GAELIC NAME: *Ceann-dubh*. Black head (also used of Marsh Tit). I am informed that *Conan-coille*, *Conan-conuisg*, *Conan-crion* and *Crionag-ghiubhais* are all used for the Willow Tit, though Dwelly gives different translations for these names.*

The Willow Tit does not seem to have collected local names that distinguish it from the Marsh Tit.

The two species are so similar that it was not until 1897 that the Willow Tit was recognised as occurring in Britain. Willow Tits extend further into Scotland (reaching from the Borders to localized areas of the Lowlands) than Marsh Tits, which, in Scotland, are only found in Berwickshire.

Q: Saunders says that the Marsh Tit was not known to nest in Scotland until 1893 when a nest was found in Strathspey, but makes no mention of the Willow Tit.[162]
   Dr Williams refers to 'the much disputed so-called Willow Tit.'[198]

---

*Dr Sheila Kidd supplied this information from a twentieth century manuscript dictionary by Charles Loch.

Crested Tit
Parus cristatus

(*Parus*: Latin, a Titmouse; *cristatus*: Latin, having a crest.)

SCOTS NAMES: None.

GAELIC NAMES: None.

Crested Tits are birds of conifer forests of central and south-eastern Europe, but which also occur in eastern Scotland, particularly in the Spey Valley in Aberdeenshire where there are extensive Scots Pine forests. There is possible evidence of the species in the late Pleistocene and it is likely to have been present in southern Britain of about 8,000 to 10,000 years ago. The first reference to Scottish Crested Tits is from Willughby and Ray of 1678.[155] The small isolated population of the species has remained in Scotland for centuries. Numbers may have increased with commercial planting of conifers but are susceptible to hard winters and fluctuate considerably. In 1982 the population was estimated at 900 pairs.

Q: In the nineteenth century, Smiles observed that 'This rare British Tit is an inhabitant of the higher and middle districts of the country, where it breeds occasionally.'[174]

One feature of the Spey Valley forests is the presence of so many juniper bushes, the berries of which are eaten by the Crested Tit, in addition to the seeds of ripe pine cones and insects and larvae.[109] 'This is the most famous small bird of Strathspey and the emblem of the Scottish Ornithologists' Club.'[141]

Coal Tit
Parus ater

(*ater*: Latin, black.)

SCOTS NAMES: Black Cap [Stir], Black Ox-eye [For], Coal head, Coal or Coaly Hood, Coal Hooden [Loth].

GAELIC NAME: *Cailleachag-cheann-dubh*. Little old woman with a black head.

Evidence of either this or the Blue Tit (the species being indistinguishable from bony remains) goes back to the middle Pleistocene, some 500,000 years ago in the Old Stone Age. Ælfric[1] mentioned the Coal Tit in 998. It favours conifers and probably increased in Victorian times with the planting of these trees in woodlands and ornamental gardens. Formerly absent in Northern Scotland, it spread there in the latter years of the nineteenth century and though it has fluctuated with cold winters, its present population is estimated at 1,000,000 pairs.

Q: Valerie Thom[192] describes it as 'widespread and abundant on the mainland. Breeding regularly on some islands of the Inner Hebrides it has bred in the Outer islands but is absent from Orkney and Shetland'.

Blue Tit
Parus caeruleus
(*caeruleus*: Latin, sky blue.)

SCOTS NAMES: Blue Bonnet or Cap, Blue Ox-eye [For], Blue Tomtit, Blue Yaup, Oxee, Ox-eye [Loth], Yaup [Renf].

GAELIC NAME: *Cailleach-ghorm*. Blue old woman.

Many names relate to the bird's size and colour. Yaup is a Lallans word meaning clever, well applied to the thief who opens milk bottles.

For early history, see Coal Tit. The first British record of Blue Tits, other than fossil remains (which may be Coal Tit) of 500,000 years ago, dates from the eighth century. In the early Holocene the Blue Tit probably decreased with reduction of woodland but it proved more adaptable to environmental change than the Great Tit. During the twentieth century it has expanded its range, reaching Northern Scotland and breeding in the treeless Western Isles. It is now widespread throughout Scotland except for Orkney, Shetland and more mountainous regions.

Q: Dr Williams noted: 'Nest with fully fledged young, 2½ feet up in a hollow tree, Glenalmond 10/7/13. Very common here and resident.'[198]

253

Great Tit
Parus major

(*major*: Latin, greater.)

SCOTS NAMES: Black-headed Tomtit [Stir], Big Ox-eye [For, Loth, Rox], Oxee [Fif], Saw Sharpener [Rox], Tomtit.

GAELIC NAME: *Currac-bhain-tighearna*. Superior white cap.

There is overlap with names for other tit species; Saw Sharpener refers to the chiming bell-like call which is such a feature of the species in spring.

Like other Titmice the Great Tit has a history dating back some 500,000 years. It probably suffered as trees were cut in the Holocene but adapted well, especially when land enclosures led to the development of hedgerows. More recently it has spread widely through gardens to become a bird of suburbia as well as woodland. Though breeding in the Hebrides it is not present in Orkney and Shetland.

Q: This distribution was indicated by Saunders in 1899: 'Present in the greater part of Scotland; but in the northern and western portions it becomes uncommon; being only a rare visitant to the Isle of Skye, Sutherland, the Orkneys and, perhaps, the Shetlands.'[162]

Family: *Sittidae*, the Nuthatches

No. in world, 21; no. in Scotland, 1.

Nuthatch
Sitta europaea

(*Sitta*: Greek, *sitte* a bird like a woodpecker mentioned by Aristotle and now applied to the Nuthatch. Latin, *europaea* of, or belonging to, Europe.)

SCOTS NAMES: Jobbin, Nutjobber, Woodcracker.

GAELIC NAMES: *Gobach, Gob-sgoltan, Sgoltan. Gobach* means a scold and is used of the Hawfinch; *gob* is a beak and *sgoltan* is specifically the Nuthatch.

Though the Nuthatch has records extending back to the Middle Pleistocene in England it has only recent history in Scotland. Despite single and controversial entries in the Old and New Statistical Accounts for the parish of Killin it was unknown as a breeding bird in Scotland until 1989. Since then its numbers have increased in the Borders, where I first saw Scottish Nuthatches at Mellerstain.

Q: According to the *Old Statistical Account*: 'Some birds are found in this country, which are reckoned rare; as the nuthatch...';[145] the *New Statistical Account* added: 'The following, which are found in this country, are reckoned rare; as the nuthatch'.[142] But MacGillivray in 1837 stated: 'the Nuthatch is not generally distributed in Britain, being of rare occurrence in the northern parts of England, and not hitherto observed in Scotland.'[118]

Family: *Certhidae*, the Creepers
No. in world, 7; no. in Scotland, 1.

Treecreeper
Certhia familiaris

(*Certhia*: Greek, *Kerthios* little creeping bird; *familiaris*: Latin, familiar, because of its familiarity with man to whose company it seems indifferent.)

SCOTS NAMES: Tree Sheeler, Tree Speiler [Loth], Woodpecker [Perth].

GAELIC NAME: *Snaigear*. One who creeps.

The earliest record in Britain is from the eleventh century. The Treecreeper inhabits broad-leafed woodland rather than coniferous woods. Its population is likely to have been reduced by clearance of forests. In recent times a succession of hard winters of the 1960s reduced its numbers but it has since made dramatic increases and its population is now of the order of 300,000 pairs. It is common throughout Scotland but absent from Orkney, Shetland and the Outer Isles.

Q: It was reported at Penicuik in the *Old Statistical Account*: 'A very small and beautiful bird, the creeper, like a little mouse running up the trees for insects...'[145]

Family: *Emberizidae*, the Buntings

No. in world, 284; no. in Scotland, 4.

Yellow Bunting or Yellowhammer
Emberiza citrinella

(*Emberiza*: Latin, *Emberiza* a Yellowhammer or Bunting; *citrinella*: Latin, *citrinus* yellow, *ellus* diminutive.)

SCOTS NAMES: De'il, De'il, De'il, tak' you, Gold Spink, Little-bit-of-bread-and-no-cheese, Scotch Canary, Skite [NE], Yaldie, Yalla Lintie, Yite or Yorlin, Yallock, Yellow Lintie, Yarldrin, Yarlin, Yeldrick, Yellow, Yella or Yelly Lintie [Aber, For, Ayr], Yellow or Yella Yite, Yellow Yarling [Ork], Yellow Yeldock, Yellow Yoit [Wig, Kirk], Yellow Yeldrin, Yeldring, Yoldrin, or Yoldring, Yellow Yorling [Berw, Loth].

GAELIC NAMES: *Buidheag-bhuachair*, *Buidhean-na-coille*, *Buidheag-bhealaidh*. Yellow one bedaubed with dung, any small yellow bird, yellow of the broom.

Few birds have so many Scottish vernacular names, probably because it has so much folklore connected with it and because the bird is easily identified both visually and audibly. Hammer comes from Old English *amore*, a small bird, or German *Ammer* a bunting. Many names reflect its striking, bright yellow plumage. Others reflect its song or the bizarre patterning of its eggs.

There are traces of Yellowhammers in the late Pleistocene. It is a bird of woodland margins and probably increased with forest clearance in the Holocene. As farming became widespread and enclosure led to the development of hedges the Yellowhammer population would have risen. In the twentieth century there has been a decline in its numbers due to loss of hedges and increased use of toxic chemicals in farming. It is now widespread throughout Scotland but is sparse in mountain areas and in the Scottish islands.

Q: MacGillivray wrote of it in the first half of the nineteenth century: 'The Yellow Bunting is very widely distributed, but does not occur in those parts of the country which are destitute of wood.'[118]

T: The Yellowhammer is a bird of very evil repute in the Highlands, where it is called the Devil's bird because its call is said to sound like 'Deil'. In Scotland the song is sometimes interpreted as 'whetil te, whetil te, whee! Harry my nest and the De'il tak ye' or 'The de'il tak' ye a' and leave me'. It is also supposed to drink a drop of the Devil's blood every May Day.

Many of these ideas stem from the 'writings' on the Yellowhammer's egg, which have been taken for cabbalistic signs. Some believe that the initals of a future lover may be found among the scrawled symbols on this bird's egg. Tradition recounts that the Yellowhammer fluttered about Christ's cross, getting its plumage stained with blood. In punishment its eggs were ever after to bear the marks of blood. Because it was cursed, boys were taught that it was right to steal its eggs and to sing:

> Half a paddock, half a toad
> Half a drop o' de'il's blood,
> Horrid yellow yorling.

However even to look at the Yellowhammer was enough to cure one of jaundice.

Snow Bunting
Plectrophenax nivalis

(*Plectrophenax* comes from two Greek words: *plektron* a cock's spur and *phenax* an impostor. This refers to the long hind claw of the Snow Bunting. *Nivalis*: Latin, of the snow.)

SCOTS NAMES: Mountain Bunting, Lesser Mountain Finch, Northcock [Aber], Oatfowl [Ork], Pied Finch, Sea Linnet, Snawfowl or Snawful [Shet], Snowbird, Snawflake or Snowflake [Ork].

GAELIC NAMES: *Gealag-an-t-sneachd, Bigein-sneachda, Eun-an-t-sneachda.* White one of the snow, Chirper of snow, Bird of the snow.

The official name of Snow Bunting was coined in 1771 and was applied to the bird in North America. Many of its names are derived from its favoured mountain or shore habitats and there is confusion with the Brambling or Mountain Finch with which, in winter plumage, Snow Buntings have similarities. Snow Flake or Fleck is a common Scottish form and in Orkney and Shetland this becomes Snaw Fowl or Snawful derived, via Norn, from the Old Norse *snaefugl*.

The Snow Bunting was known as a breeding bird in the Scottish Highlands in the mid–eighteenth century, and probably flourished in cooler periods before that. During the twentieth century its range shrank, with a few birds breeding in the higher Cairngorms but, even there, breeding was sporadic until the 1960s.

Q: Captain Burt observed them in 1730: 'Snow sends down from the mountains large flights of small birds about the size of a lark or something bigger, and very white, which they are not in summer. These have no other name but snowbirds.'[33]

'Seen in large flocks during the winter, and exhibiting a motley mixture of pure white, jet black, dull tawny and deep chestnut, a beautiful band across the wings being conspicuous only in flight. They arrive about the beginning of November, and depart about the first of April.'[174]

Reed Bunting.
Emberiza schoeniclus

(*schoeniclus*: Greek, *schoiniklos* waterbird (*schoinos* = reed).)

SCOTS NAMES: Black Bonnet, Coaly Hood, Chink, Colin Blackhead [Renf], Moss Sparra, Reed Sparrow, Ring Fowl [Aber].

GAELIC NAMES: *Gealag-dubh-cheannach*, *Ceann-dubh-fraoich*. Whitethroat with a black head, Blackhead of the heather.

Most of the Reed Bunting's vernacular names derive from the black head and throat of the male bird and others from the white neck ring. Other names derive from its habitat.

There are traces of Reed Buntings from the late Pleistocene, and as a marsh bird it would be likely to have prospered in the lowland marshes of the early Holocene, only to suffer as land was drained in the sixteenth and seventeenth centuries. In the twentieth century it has adapted to environmental change, and since the 1930s has colonised drier areas and so has increased despite loss of marsh. Noticeably it seems to like oil seed rape and the increased cultivation of this crop in recent years may help its population growth.

Q: Although sedentary in England, this species is migratory in most parts of Scotland, departing in October and reappearing about the beginning of April.[118]

The Song of the Reed Sparrow

Where the waters gently flow,
There I always love to go:
As the waters gently glide ,
Sweet I sing in all my pride.

Mounted on a bended reed,
Chanting as my fancies lead,
Tender tales I oft repeat,
Clear, harmonious, soft, and sweet.

Be the weather foul or fine,
Let it rain, or hail, or shine;
Prove the weather how it will,
I can sing about it still.

Anonymous, late eighteenth century.[9]

Corn Bunting
Emberiza calandra

(*calandra*: Greek, *Kalandros* a lark.)

SCOTS NAMES: Buntling Lark or Buntlin, Bountain, Grattie Lavro [Ork], Skitter Brottie [Ork], Sparrow [Heb], Stocking Weaver, Thistle Cock [Ork].

GAELIC NAMES: *Gealag-bhuachair, Eun-ballach-a'-ghar.* Cowdung White-throat, Speckled bird with a big belly.

The name Bunting originally applied only to the Corn Bunting and has done since about 1300. Literally the word means a plump or thick-set person. Most of the names refer to a rather nondescript brownish larklike bird as in Grattie Lavro, a weeping Lark. Skitter Brottie literally means one who shits on the braithes, or cross ropes, of a corn stack. The name Stocking Weaver is unexplained, but may have something to do with the bird's habit of flying with its legs dangling. Bountain, presumed to be Bunting, is commonly used in the *Old Statistical Account.*[145]

Though there are traces of the Corn Bunting in the late Pleistocene it was probably not until late Neolithic and Bronze Ages when man was beginning to clear the forests and to establish farming that the Corn Bunting flourished. From then until the twentieth century the species appears to have thrived. Since 1930 however Corn Buntings have become progressively scarcer throughout Britain. Reports from the British Trust for Ornithology draw attention to the rapid decline of this species during the 1990s, probably as a result of intensification of farming practices. The Corn Bunting has lost 60% of its range in Scotland between 1972 and 1997 and is now virtually extinct in Ayrshire and most of NE Scotland. Pockets of population concentrations occur, such as at Balranald in North Uist.

Q: Lord Grey, statesman turned ornithologist, is less than complimentary about the Corn Bunting: 'The carthorse of the buntings, of slovenly disposition and clumsiness of body. He grinds out the noise that is his song. He even seems to *like* barbed wire.'*[80]

In North Uist (where the species is still common) 'from dawn to dusk the bunting never ceased from "jingling his keys"…I grew almost to hate his relentless "wheezing": as ruffling up the feathers of his big head and body he hastened alone, or with his mate, over the broad strips of corn.'[149]

Family: *Fringillidae*, the Finches
No. in world, 144; no. in Scotland, 11.

Chaffinch
Fringilla coelebs
(*Fringilla*: Latin, *fringilla* a small bird; *coelebs*: Latin, *caelebs* unmarried, single.)

SCOTS NAMES: Apple Sheelie, Applie, Binkie [Ros and Crom], Blue Cap [Aber], Boldie [Kinc], Beechfinch, Brichtie, Briskie or Brisk Finch [Wig], Chaffie or Chilfie Chay [Mor], Chy or Chye [Aber], Prink Prink [Inv], Roberd or Robinet, Scobb or Scobbie, Shelfie, Shellifaw, Sheelfa, Shilfer or Shilfa [Cai], Shell Apple, Shelly [Cai], Shillie, Sheltie or Shiltie [Fif], Shoufall, Shuilfie or Shulfie [Fif], Skelly, Snabbie [Dumf, Fif], Spink or Spinkie, Treack or Tree Lintie [Mor], Twink, Wet Bird [Stir], Wet Chaff [For], White Finch, White Wingie [Lan].

*A bête noir of Lord Grey's.

GAELIC NAMES: *Breacan-beithe, Breac-an-t-sil, Uiseag a chàth*. Tartan of the birches, Chaffinch (also Pied Wagtail), Lark of the chaff.

Linnaeus gave the Chaffinch the name *coelebs* because he noticed that females migrated from Sweden in autumn while the males did not and hence were 'celibate'. Many names echo the Chaffinch's call—Bink, Prink, Chy etc. Others mention colour or shell, meaning variegation (but it also borrows the name Apple Sheelie from the Crossbill). Shoufall or Shuffle refer to its movement.

Until the arrival of toxic agricultural chemicals this was Britain's commonest bird and, in Scotland, it probably still is. Paleontologically inseperable from Bramblings, it is difficult to be sure which species or both is found among late Pleistocene remains. Throughout history the Chaffinch has adapted well to man's manipulation of the environment, profiting by woodland clearance and grain culture. More recently it has adapted to suburban gardens, thriving until about 1950. Since then the species has declined coincidentally with the dressing of grain seed with toxic chemicals.

Q: 'So-called, it is supposed, from its liking for chaff.'[61]
  In winter, according to Saunders in the nineteenth century, 'large flocks arrive from the continent on our east coast'.[162]

T: In Scotland the Chaffinch's call is regarded as a sign of impending rain, and boys imitate it saying 'Weet, Weet, Dreep, Dreep', since they expect rain if the bird calls. It is sometimes called a drunken sow because it advises its listeners to 'drink till fou'.

Brambling
Fringilla montefringilla
(*montefringilla*: Latin, *Mons* mountain and *fringilla*.)

SCOTS NAMES: Bramble Finch, Cock o' the North [E & S Scotland], Tartan Back.

GAELIC NAME: *Breacan-caorainn.* Tartan of the rowans.

For early history, see Chaffinch. First mentioned by Turner in 1544,[195] this species may have bred in Britain at cooler periods of history but is now a winter visitor to beech forests. A few Bramblings breed in Northern Scotland.

Q: Thomas Bewick remarked on its culinary qualities: 'The flesh of the Mountain Finch, though bitter, is said to be good to eat, and better than that of the Chaffinch.'[19]

Baxter and Rintoul describe its incidence in the middle of the twentieth century: 'It now and then appears in different parts of the country during winter, and searches for food in the open fields, generally in company with Chaffinches and Yellow Buntings.'[13]

T: The Scottish name of Cock o' the North was also given to the Duke of Gordon (1770-1836) who raised the Gordon Highlanders in 1795.

Greenfinch
Carduelis chloris

(*Carduelis*: Latin, *cardus* thistle, hence thistlefinch; *chloros*: Greek, green.)

SCOTS NAMES: Greenie or Green Linnet or Lintie.

GAELIC NAME: *Glaisean-daraic*. Greenfinch or Greyfinch (lit. Grey-headed one of the oak tree).

Present from late Pleistocene, the Greenfinch probably flourished with woodland clearances but it is vulnerable to cold weather, and suffered during the Little Ice Age. In the present century it has increased and is widespread throughout Britain. It is now one of the commoner species in Scotland.

Q: In the middle of the nineteenth century MacGillivray noted: 'Green linnets... are met with in all cultivated parts of the country, excepting the western and northern islands of Scotland; and in most districts the green linnet is very abundant.'[118]

Goldfinch
Carduelis carduelis

SCOTS NAMES: Goldie [Lan] or Gooldie [Arg], Goldspink, Goud- or Gowdspink [Per], Gowdie [Lan], Sweet William, Thistle Finch [Stir], Thistle Warp.

GAELIC NAME: *Deargan-fraoich*. Red stained one of the heather.

Goldfinches love thistles, giving rise to their scientific, and some vernacular, names. Sweet William is an interesting name, presumably taken from the flower, which, in Scotland, is called Stinking Billy after 'Butcher' Cumberland of Culloden.

Present in later Pleistocene remains, the Goldfinch is likely to have flourished when early forest clearing encouraged growth of thistles and other food plants. In the nineteenth century its beauty caused reduction in its numbers because of trapping for the Victorian cage bird craze. Caged Goldfinches were often made blind with red-hot needles, as it was thought this improved their song. Trapping was finally banned in 1888 with an immediate improvement in numbers of Goldfinches. In winter 80% of British Goldfinches migrate to Continental Europe, but its breeding population is of the order of 300,000 pairs.

Q: MacGillivray[118] said of it 'although not uncommon about Aberdeen and Elgin, it is very rare in the neighbourhood of Edinburgh' and Saunders added in 1899 'it has almost disappeared from the Lothians owing to the influence of high farming'.[162]

T: The Goldfinch, because of the bird's partiality for thistles and thorns, was adopted by the early church as a symbol of Christ's Passion, and features frequently in Renaissance paintings of the Holy Family.

> Beauteous yellow Goldfinch,
> I will spend a Sunday
> Sweeping out thy chamber
> Said the foolish yellow Hen.
>
> Gaelic nursery rhyme.[35]

Siskin
Carduelis spinus
(*spinos*: Greek, small bird.)

SCOTS NAMES: Aberdevine, Barley Bird, Blackheaded Thistlefinch, Golden Wren.

GAELIC NAME: *Gealag-bhuidhe*. Golden-yellow whitethroat.

Siskin derives from the Swedish name *siska* meaning chirper. Aberdevine is a fancier's name for the Siskin because, in Victorian times, it was a popular cage bird. Most authorities state that the name is of doubtful etymology, though Swainson[190] claims it to mean Alder-finch.

Though likely to have been present in the late Pleistocene and early Holocene when food plants such as conifers and alders were commonplace, its first British record comes from Chaucer in 1369. Formerly it was largely confined to the remnants of the old Caledonian Forest, but it has increased recently in parallel with increased conifer planting in Scotland where it succeeded in breeding in 1840. Since then Siskins have become widespread.[100] It has spread rapidly since the 1940s. In winter it moves south, when its numbers are boosted by large influxes from Europe, possibly increasing its numbers tenfold.

Q: 'They feed wholly on the alder and looked beautiful, hanging like little parrots, picking at the drooping seeds of that tree.'[190] 'Lively, restless and gymnastic, you often hear Siskins before you see them in the canopy of conifers.'[141]

T: Like the Swallow Siskins were reputed to discover magic stones. In the Siskin's case the stone was believed to make one invisible.

Linnet
Acanthis cannabina
(*Acanthis*: Greek, *acantha* a prickle; *cannabinus* of hemp (referring to diet not drug abuse!))

SCOTS NAMES: Brown Lintie [Ork], Grey Linnet (imm) [S. S], Heather Lintie, Linlet (imm), Linnet Finch, Lintick [Ork], Lintie-whitie, Linwhite or Lint-white [Ork], Lintie [Ork], Rose Lintie [NE], Whin Linnet [Stir], Whin Lintie.

GAELIC NAMES: *Didig, an Breacan-beithe, Bigein Brighde*. One who peeps, Tartan of the birch, St Bridget's little bird.

Linnets' plumage varies considerably with season and for some time it was thought that there were several different species; this gave rise to many vernacular names mentioning different colours. The name Linnet derives from *Linum*, flax, which is the bird's common food plant.

Traces of Linnets have been found in late Pleistocene remains. The species is unlikely to have thrived in the early Holocene forests but would recover with their clearance. In the nineteenth century it declined because of extensive trapping. From the late nineteenth century it recovered substantially only to suffer badly from 1940 onwards because of increasing cultivation of marginal land and the use of weedkillers which destroy its food. In the decade 1975-85 numbers of Linnets fell by about 45% and the position has worsened since then. Linnets are absent from north-west Scotland where they are replaced by Twite.

Q: At Kilsyth in Stirling during the eighteenth century the minister recorded 'The red breasted or rose linnet with all the varieties of small birds, are common here.'[145]

T: The Linnet is called '*bigein Bride*' the little bird of Bride.[35]

Twite
Acanthis flavirostris
(*flavirostris*: Latin, *flavus* golden, *rostrum* a beak.)

SCOTS NAMES: Grey Linnet, Heather Lintie [Shet. to Bord], Hill or Heather Lintie [Ork, Cai to For], Lintick, Lintie [Ork], Mountain Linnet, Rock Lintie or Rockie [For], Yellow or Yella Neb Lintie [Wig].

GAELIC NAME: *Gealan-beinne*. Linnet of the mountains.

The name Twite is onomatopoeic, from the bird's strange nasal call note. It is the northern counterpart of the Linnet, often replacing it in Scotland. There is much overlap of names. Yella Neb Lintie draws attention to a distinguishing field mark of this rather dowdy 'Little Brown Job'.

According to Fisher[59] the Twite was first recognised as a British breeding species in 1562, though it is likely to have been present from the late Pleistocene. It may also have flourished during cooler periods of history such as the Little Ice Age of 1400-1890. It is now a bird of the north-west of Scotland, particularly in the Outer Hebrides and St Kilda, where it is described as the upland analogue of the Linnet.

Q: 'The most striking characteristic of the Twite, in the Outer Hebrides at all events, is its remarkable fearlessness.'[71]

Redpoll
Acanthis flammea
(*flammeus*: Latin, fiery red.)

SCOTS NAMES: Red-headed Linnet, Rose Linnet or Lintie [Lowl].

GAELIC NAME: *Deargan-seilich*. Red stained slaverer.

Most names arise from the bird's rose-red crown (an impossible diagnostic feature for the colour blind).

Though the Redpoll is likely to have been present in the Pleistocene, no record exists before in 1678.[155] The principal winter food plant of Redpolls is birch seed, and winter produces flocks of Redpolls where Birch is prolific. Numbers are very variable, with large irruptions occurring in some autumns (particularly those of 1959, 1964 and 1977).

Q: Valerie Thom noted it widely distributed on the mainland and fairly regular on Inner Hebridean islands, but very rare in the Outer Hebrides and Northern Isles.[192]

Crossbill
Loxia curvirostra
(*Loxia*: Greek, *loxos* slanting or crosswise; *curvirostra*: Latin, *curvus* crooked, *rostrum* a beak.)

SCOTS NAMES: European Crossbill, Robin Hawk, Sheldapple, Shell Apple.

GAELIC NAME: *Cam-ghob*. Crossbill.

Crossbill remains date from the Pleistocene. In the Holocene the species spread across Europe following westward colonisation of the spruce some 6,000 years ago, reaching northwest Europe 3,000 years ago. Crossbills follow food plants, especially conifers, occurring in irruptions in years of plentiful cones, as in 1985. Crossbills breed in winter and overproduction of young may lead to irruptions of birds to distant areas.

In the Highlands of Scotland there is found the Scottish Crossbill (*L. scotica*), which was promoted to specific status in 1977. There is also the rare

Parrot Crossbill (*L. pytopsittacus)* a vagrant from Scandinavia and Russia with a much heavier bill.

Q: According to Lodge in the middle of the twentieth century, 'Ross-shire is the headquarters of the Crossbill in Britain... Crossbills are very sociable in their habits and during the time that they are not nesting may be seen in flocks feeding on the cones of various fir trees.'[109]

T: The red plumage and the curious bill of this bird are accounted for by a medieval fable which explains that these were bestowed on the bird by Christ at the crucifixion, as a reward for trying to pull out the nails from the cross with its beak. Swainson[190] tells us that the crossbill hatches its eggs at Christmas and that the young birds fly in full plumage at Easter: that it obeys its master's orders and awakens children sleeping in baleful moonshine. Sleeping in moonlight was thought to cause lunacy and a service the Crossbill performed was to protect children so sleeping by waking them.

It also warns the household against outbreaks of fire, and watches over the mistress in childbirth.[190]

Bullfinch
Pyrrhula pyrrhula
(*Pyrrhula*: Greek, *purroulas* a red coloured bird.)

SCOTS NAMES: Alp, Awp, Bullie, Coallyhood.

GAELIC NAMES: *Deargan-coille*. Red stain of the woods.

The Bullfinch is so called because of its large head and short neck. Alp was the old name used, among others, by Ray[155] and has given rise to Hoop, Olf, Mope etc. elsewhere in Britain.

Present among late Pleistocene deposits, the Bullfinch, a species of Southern Eurasia, is at its northern limit in Scotland. As a woodland species it was probably widespread during warmer periods of the Holocene, gradually decreasing with woodland clearance and colder climate to a low at the end of the eighteenth century. Since 1940 the Bullfinch has increased and has tended to move from woodland areas into more open areas and orchards where it damages fruit trees. This led to persecution of the species, permitted by law, which has decreased its population.

Q: In the *Old Statistical Account* the minister for Moffat recorded that 'The bullfinch has appeared within the last 7 years, and seems to multiply fast.'[145]

T: The nest of the bullfinch
        Is in the wood of the dell,
        My little one shall sleep and he shall have the bird.
           From *Carmina Gadelica*: a lullaby sung to a child.[35]

Hawfinch
Coccothraustes coccothraustes

(*Coccothraustes*: Greek *Kokkos* kernel, *thrauo* to break into pieces, *istes* suffix for one who acts.)

SCOTS NAMES: None

GAELIC NAME: *Gobach*. Snouty or beaky.

Earliest records of Hawfinches date from the late Pleistocene. As a bird of woodland dependent on seeds of cherry, beech and other trees it probably was limited at first in the Holocene until suitable food bearing trees became plentiful about 6,000 years ago. From then it probably increased in the warmer parts of southern Britain until woodland clearance and the colder weather of the Little Ice Age (1400-1880) again limited its numbers. From the end of the Little Ice Age it has spread sparsely in south-eastern England. The Hawfinch first colonised Scotland in 1903 where it has succeeded in establishing itself.[100]

Q: According to Saunders, writing in the nineteenth century: 'A young bird obtained near Edinburgh was, in the opinion of Mr W.E. Clarke,* bred in the neighbourhood, and the species has been taken in winter in the Solway district, whilst said to have been seen in Sutherland.'[162]

At about the same date, Forbes noted: 'This bird is said to be peculiar to Sutherland, but as woods must be plentiful, that is now questionable, as it lives chiefly on wood insects.'[61]

*Eagle Clarke, see p.**.

Family: *Passeridae*, the Sparrows

No. in world, 32; no. in Scotland, 2.

House Sparrow
Passer domesticus

(*Passer*: Latin, a sparrow; *domesticus*: Latin, of the house.)

SCOTS NAMES: Lum Lintie [Loth], Philip, Spadger, Sparra, Sparry, Speug [Ayr, Lan, Stir], Sporrow [Ork & Shet], Sprog [Ork], Sprong [Cai], Sprug [Loth], Spug or Spurg (child), Spurdie [Aber, Banf], Spurg or Spurgie [Aber], Spying [Kirk].

GAELIC NAMES: *Glaisean, Gealbhonn.* Sparrow.

Many of these names derive from Anglo-Saxon *spearwa*, a flutterer. The familar name Philip is onomatopoeic, from the bird's incessant cheeping, and other names refer to the Sparrow's liking for chimneys, eaves and thatch.

This familiar and ubiquitous species originated from western Eurasia and has British records in the late Pleistocene. Probably at that time it was scarce, but increased as a commensal with man as his settlements and farming increased. It has also been linked with horses, whose grain and droppings provided an urban food supply. Noticeably the House Sparrow has become more suburban than it was during the heyday of city horse transport. There was a steady slight increase in numbers of House Sparrows up to about 1970, after which the species declined. This decrease became sharp at the very end of the twentieth century when its population was estimated at 7 million pairs and falling.

Q: Bishop Stanley in 1857 tells of a pair of Sparrows who nested in the rigging of a coal-vessel from Newcastle, which had put into Nairn in Scotland. After the vessel sailed the Sparrows followed her and resumed incubation

269

when they were fed on bread by the crew. The voyage lasted several days but, on returning to the Tyne, the nest, with four chicks, was taken down, and in the presence of the old birds, put into the crevice of a ruined house where they continued to rear their brood.[178]

T: The Sparrow is believed to have betrayed Our Lord in the Garden of Gethsemane; when all other birds were silent the Sparrow chirped, leading the soldiers to Jesus. Later when Swallows flew away with nails from the cross the Sparrows brought them back. The Swallows flying round the cross mourned 'He is dead', but the sparrows contradicted them saying 'He is alive', leading to yet more cruelty from the tormenting soldiers. In consequence the Sparrow is forever cursed; its legs are bound together invisibly, so that it cannot run but must always hop.

In some beliefs the souls of the dead are incorporated in Sparrows and they must not be killed. Yet others claim that if a Sparrow is caught it must be killed immediately otherwise the captor will die.

In *Carmina Gadelica* the *Glaisean* or sparrow is not lucky but blessed and is a sign of death.[35]

A bird proverbial for lewdness.[61]

Tree Sparrow
Passer montanus
(*montanus*: Latin, of the mountain.)

SCOTS NAMES: None.

GAELIC NAMES: *Gealbhonn-nan-craobh.* Sparrow of the trees.

This Eurasian species replaces the House Sparrow in many countries. Its first mention in Britain was by Ray[155] though it was probably present long before that but never as abundant as the House Sparrow. Since the nineteenth century it has undergone decline but recovered in the early 1970s when its British population was estimated at 250,000 pairs. Since then it has again steadily declined with a loss of perhaps three quarters of its numbers. Reports from the British Trust for Ornithology draw attention to the reduction of this species during the 1990s as a result of the intensification of farming practices, especially weed spraying. In the last 30 years 90% of Britain's Tree Sparrows have been lost. In Scotland, they are down by 80% because of changed agricultural practice; only altered farming policies can help them to recover.

Q: Saunders (1899) observed: 'On the mainland of Scotland its settlements are mostly along the eastern side, from the border to Sutherland.'[162]

Family: *Sturnidae*, the Starlings
No. in world, 108; no. in Scotland, 1.

Starling
Sturnus vulgaris

(*Sturnus*: Latin, *sturnus* a starling; *vulgaris*: Latin, common.)

SCOTS NAMES: Black Felt, Black Starling [Loth], Scootie [Ork], Sheepster, Sheeprack. Stare [Ork], Starn [Shet], Stirling or Stroling [Ork], Stuckie or Stushie.

GAELIC NAME: *Druid*. Starling.

The name Starling derives from the Anglo-saxon word *stare*, which also gives rise to Starn, Staynil etc. The birds often sit on the back of sheep to seek ticks, hence Shepster and Sheeprack.

Records exist of Starlings in the Middle Pleistocene of about 500,000 years ago. With its adaptability to almost any habitat it is likely to have prospered throughout history, apart from the end of the eighteenth century when, during exceptionally cold weather, the species was practically exterminated, especially in the north and west of Britain.

In the 1970s its population was estimated at 4-7 million pairs, rising to nearly 40 million birds in winter due to massive migration of continental birds.

Q: A recent writer comments: 'A hundred years ago the starling was little known except in the Western and Northern Scottish islands and there is a special race whose young are dark called the Shetland Starling, *S.v.zetlandicus*. During the nineteenth century the continental starling *S.v.vulgaris* colonised the whole of Britain exploiting artificial nesting sites in buildings.'[47, 48]

271

T: In the Hebrides fowlers always pull the head off a shot Starling owing to a belief that the blood in its head is poisonous.

> The nest of the starling
> Is under the wing of the thatch,
> My little one shall sleep and he shall have the bird.

From *Carmina Gadelica*: a lullaby sung to a child.[35]

Family: *Corvidae*, the Crows

No. in world, 113; no. in Scotland, 8.
(Crow, from Old English Crawe, is based on an Indo-european root
meaning to cry hoarsely.[112])

Jay
Garrulus glandarius

(*Garrulus*: Latin, talkative; *glandarius*: Latin, pertaining to acorns.)

SCOTS NAMES: Blue Jay [Lin], Gae, Ja or Ja Pyot, Jay Piet [Per], Kae [Rox], Oak Jay.

GAELIC NAMES: *Sgraicheag choille*. Screecher of the woods.

Most of these names derive from the Old French *gai*, which means speckled or pied. Oak Jay, and the Latin name *glandarius* (acorn), refer to the Jay's partiality for acorns.

Pleistocene deposits from about 500,000 years ago contain Jay fossils, but it was probably rare in Britain until the arrival of the oak about 8,000 years ago, after which its numbers expanded. It later decreased as woodlands were cleared and its reduction became marked with the preservation of game, to reach a nadir at the turn of the nineteenth century. The reduction in game preservation during two World Wars allowed it to recover partially and by the 1980s its population was estimated at 100,000 pairs.

Q: A Banffshire minister recorded: 'Jays are the greatest enemies to the pigeon-houses. In times of scarcity, they enter them and destroy the young.'[145]

At the time (1899) when Saunders was writing, 'In Scotland the Jay is very local, and its numbers have decreased, though its range has extended northward with the spread of plantations, and now reaches Glengarry, Inverness-shire. Messrs Harvie-Brown and Buckley have not found it in

Sutherland or Caithness; and Saxby is the sole asseverator of its occurrence in the Shetlands.'[162]

T: In fable a Jay is supposed to have attempted to make herself beautiful by decking herself out in Peacock feathers which are a mark of rank. The Jay's supposed behaviour made her ridiculous and has given rise to the literary use of the term 'peacocks' feathers' meaning to insert borrowed ornaments of style into one's composition.

The Jay is said to line its nest with magical stones, causing invisibility, and this accounts for the cryptic nature of their nests, which are difficult to find.

Magpie
Pica pica

(*Pica*: Latin, a Magpie.)

SCOTS NAMES: Maggie [Aber], Maggot Pie, Peyet, Piet, Pyat, Pyet or Pyot, Pye Mag.

GAELIC NAME: *Pioghad*. Magpie or a talkative young woman.

Most of these names stem from the Latin, name *Pica*. Formerly Maggot Pie came from mag as in Margaret and pie as in pied. The name probably is a shortened form of Margot or Marguerite, as the bird's chattering was said to resemble a scolding or chattering woman.

A bird of woodland margins, known from late Pleistocene deposits, it became commoner as dense forests were cleared. Persecuted to the point of near extinction in some parts of Britain during the heyday of game preservation, it recovered with the two World Wars and then increased enormously after 1945, spreading to colonise urban areas. By the 1980s the Magpie population was estimated at half a million pairs and must have increased considerably since then. In Scotland it is limited to the central belt and the fertile north-east; in the Highlands it is a rarity.

Q: Campbell Steven hints at the scarcity of the species in the Highlands in an account of a successful bid to see 100 species in Perthshire in the month of May 1989: 'One still to go... We did make a detour past Gleneagles, hoping that we might perhaps surprise a Magpie foraging for a cast-off tiara in one of the hotel dustbins... Of course we had no such good fortune...'[182]

T: Eating the leg of a Magpie is said to be a cure for one bewitched. They were called *Gille-ruith nan Caimbeulach*, the messengers of the Campbells, and it is unlucky, except for the Campbells, even to see one.[61]

> I saw a magpie, to me luck then did die,
> I once saw two and they troubled me,
> Great joy was on me when I once saw three,
> But four forever let me not see.[48]

Chough
Pyrrhocorax pyrrhocorax
(*Pyrrhocorax*: Greek, *purrhos* red, *korax* crow.)

SCOTS NAME: Red-legged Crow.

GAELIC NAME: *Cathag-dhearg chasach*. Chough, or Red-legged crow.

The cave-dwelling, largely coastal, Red-billed Chough has left fossil remains in the late Pleistocene. However the bird's later history is confused by the name Chough also being used for Jackdaws. It was known to breed on the Berwickshire coast but disappeared from there in the late nineteenth century. It is now rare apart from localised colonies in some Scottish islands, notably Islay. In 1982 its total British population was put at no more than a thousand birds, but there has been a slight increase since 1982. Most of these Choughs are in Islay and Colonsay with small populations in North Wales and the Isle of Man.

Q: 'Being much taken with glitter... it is very apt to catch up bits of lighted sticks, so that there are instances of houses being set on fire by its means; which is the reason that Camden calls it *incendiaria avis*'.[148]

T: The Chough has always had great significance in all Celtic religious beliefs. Its red bill enhanced the bird's incendiary reputation and, though it was also considered a thief, was protected in Cornwall because it was believed that the soul of King Arthur migrated to a Chough. It was therefore sacrilegious to kill one. This belief is referred to in an unattributed verse quoted by Swainson:[190]

And mark you bird of sable wing,
Talons and beak all red with blood,
The spirit of the long-lost king
Passed in that shape from Camlan's flood.

Jackdaw
Corvus monedula

(*Corvus*: Latin, a crow; *monedula*: Latin, a Jackdaw.)

SCOTS NAMES: Caw [Banf, Kirk], Daw, Grey Head or Neck [Loth], Jack, Jackie, or Jaikie [Loth, Berw], Ka, Kadder, Kae [Ork], Ka wattie, Kyaw [Mor, SW esp.Wig], Pate or Paiet [Kirk].

GAELIC NAME: *Cathag*. Jackdaw.

Many names are onomatopoeic: 'jack' is a common sharp ejaculation of the bird as is its more reflective 'daw'. Other names refer to its grey head and neck, which, in a good light, is reminiscent of a judge's wig.

The Jackdaw's Pleistocene records date from about 12,000 years ago. As a bird of open grassland it probably suffered during the extensive afforestation of the early Holocene, later increasing with clearance and the growth of farming. It is susceptible to cold and declined during the Little Ice Age (1400-1880) but suffered less at the hands of gamekeepers than others of its genus. It is an abundant species in Scotland.

Q: 'The habits of a Jackdaw are known to everybody; wherever found, he is the same active, bustling, cheerful, noisy fellow… He seems to know neither care nor sorrow—ever satisfied—always happy! Who ever saw or heard of a moping, melancholy Jackdaw?'[178]

T: Jackdaws, like Magpies, are associated with misfortune. To see a single Jackdaw is unlucky, especially if to one's left. A Jackdaw down the chimney is an omen of death and if they flutter and caw round the house rain is on the way. In many parts of Britain a Jackdaw on a weather vane presages rain.

275

Rook

Corvus frugilegus

(*frugilegus*: Latin, fruit gathering (referring to diet).)

SCOTS NAMES: Barefaced Crow, Corbie or Corby [Ork], Ruik or Ruke, White-faced Crow.

GAELIC NAME: *Ròcas.* Rook.

Rook, as a verb, means to fleece and, as a noun, a simpleton. In the fifteenth century Corbie meant a Raven, but by the nineteenth was a Carrion or Hooded Crow and by the twentieth it was also used of the Rook. The names Bare- or White-faced refer to the cere of naked skin of the adult Rook's cheek.

Apart from the skull, Rook bones resemble those of Carrion Crows, so that precise identification among Pleistocene remains is difficult. Its first clear reference in British literature shows that it was known from the eighth century. Rooks have long been regarded as a pest because they eat newly sown cereals. The young themselves were esteemed for eating well into the twentieth century and were shot leaving the nest. Up till 1960 they were steadily increasing, since when there has been a decline attributed to seed dressing. The British population may be about a million and a half pairs, very many of which are in Scotland.

Q: 'In the northern parts of Scotland... extraordinary meetings of Crows are occasionally known to occur. They collect in great numbers, as if they had all been summoned for the occasion; a few of the flock sit with drooping heads, and others seem as grave as judges while others again are exceedingly active and noisy: in the course of about an hour they disperse, and it is not uncommon, after they have flown away, to find one or two left dead on the spot... These meetings will sometimes continue for a day or two, before the object, whatever it may be, is completed. Crows continue to arrive from all quarters during the session. As soon as they have all arrived, a very general noise ensues, and, shortly after, the whole flock fall upon one or two individuals, and put them to death; when this execution has been performed, they quietly disperse.'[178]

T: Rooks, unlike crows, are usually considered as friendly to man and it is said they only build near houses where the inmates are of a kindly, generous disposition. They build high in trees (formerly especially in elms) and their desertion of a tree indicates that it will soon fall or portends some calamity about to befall the tree's owner. Building high in the tree foretells a good summer. In Scotland Rooks tumbling up and down in flight were said to be ominous of approaching gales.

Perhaps the most endearing superstition is that of telling the Rooks (as in many places people talk to bees) of their owner's death. The new owner is supposed to stand under the trees and tell the rooks about the death and promise that only he and his friends will shoot them.

Carrion Crow
Corvus corone

(*corone*: Greek, *korone* a crow.)

SCOTS NAMES: Black-nebbed Crow [Rox], Corbie or Corby [Loth], Cra, Craa or Craw [Aber], Gor Crow, Hoddy Craw or Huddy or Huidie Craw [SS] Ket Crow, Midden or Minden Crow, Mussel Crow.

GAELIC NAMES: *Starrag, Feannag*. Used for Carrion or Hoodie Crow and also Rook.

Most of the names for this species derive from its habit of feeding on carrion: Gor and Ket are names for carrion and a midden is a dung-heap. This bird frequently scavenges on the shore, hence Mussel Crow; other names come from its black plumage or harsh call.

The Carrion Crow occurs in two forms: the all black and the grey and black, or Hooded Crow. These two forms are slowly diverging to become separate species. Virtually indistinguishable from Rooks in Pleistocene deposits, the archetypal 'crow' has been present for some 12-15,000 years. Persecution by man throughout its history reached a climax in the nineteenth century, when game preservation was at its height and when every effort was made to wipe it out. It recovered in the gamekeeperless years of the two World Wars to the extent that it has reached a population of the order of a million pairs. This is increased in winter by influxes of Hooded Crows from Scandinavia and Carrion Crows from southern parts of Europe.

277

Q: Henry Douglas-Home wrote of the depredation caused by Carrion Crows, which will not just discover a partridge nest, but will memorise all the nests in their territory and only rob them when the bird has laid a full clutch.[53]

'*S toil leis an fheannaig a h-isean carrach gorm fhéin.* (The crow likes its own scabby blue fledgling, which signifies that even the least attractive are loved by parents!)[172]

T: In Celtic folklore Crows were associated with terrible goddesses who persisted long after the arrival of Christianity as hags or monsters. An ancient Celtic belief held that war-goddesses, who were collectively described as *badb,** revelled among the bodies of the slain in battle. The memory of the *badb* still survives in the superstitious aversion of some Celtic country-dwellers for their folklore descendants the 'hoodie' crow.[176]

In many places Crows were known as Lich Fowl because they fed on carrion, and a crow on one's left side has been considered a sign of ill-fortune since Roman times. In Scotland a Carrion Crow alighting on the roof of a house indicated that death was hovering over there. Despite this, the ashes of a burnt Carrion Crow were used for treating gout.

King James I of Scotland when riding into Perth in 1437 had his assassination predicted by a Highland woman. When she was asked how she could do this she replied that 'Huthart' had told her. The spirit Huthart seems to have been the Hoodie Crow, from which the Scottish name of Huddy has probably derived.[176]

Hooded Crow
Corvus corone cornix

(*corone*: Greek, *korone* a crow; *cornix*: Latin, a crow.)

SCOTS NAMES: Corbie [Perth], Craa [Shet], Greyback [Cai, For, Per], Hoddy or Hoodie.

GAELIC NAME: *Starrag.* Crow or hoodie crow.

For derivation of names and history, see Carrion Crow.

Q: 'The Hooded Crow is very abundant in the Hebrides, the Shetland and Orkney Islands, and most parts of the northern and middle divisions of Scotland; but is rare in the southern division, and gradually diminishes as we proceed southward.'[118]

---

*Pronounced bive and later modified to banshee or 'Royston Crow'.

T: The Hooded Crow is associated with Cù Chulainn's 'scald-crow' and Odin's Raven.

Crows and Ravens, because they can smell carrion at great distance, are supposed to indicate death.

Raven
Corvus corax

(*corax*: Greek, *korax* a crow.)

SCOTS NAMES: Corbie or Corby, Corbie Craw, Croupie [Fif], Ramna [Ork], Revin, Rive.

GAELIC NAMES: *Fitheach*. Raven.

The name Raven comes from the Anglo-saxon *Hrefn*, from the bird's cry. Most other names derive from *Corvus*. Ramna is possibly from Norn and Revin or Rive comes from a fifteenth century Scots word meaning to tear or lacerate. See Carrion Crow for Corbie.

Like other Corvids the Raven's history dates from the end of the Pleistocene. Ravens were probably common in cities up to about 1800 where, like Red Kites, they served a useful purpose as scavengers. As with other Corvids they suffered badly from persecution by gamekeepers, apart from the war years of the last century. It is now a bird of wild mountainous country, especially in Scotland, where its population is of the order of 5,000 pairs.

Q: The Twa Corbies

As I was walking all alane,
I heard twa corbies making a mane;
The tane unto the tither say,
'Where sall we gang and dine the day?'

—'In behint yon auld fail dyke,
I wot there lies a new-slain knight;
And naebody kens that he lies there,
But his hawk, his hound, and his lady fair.

'His hound is to the hunting gane,
His hawk to fetch the wild fowl hame,
His lady's ta'en anither mate,
So we may make our dinner sweet.

'Ye'll sit on his white hause bane,
And I'll pick out his bonny blue ee:
Wi' ae lock o' his gowden hair,
We'll theek our nest when it grows bare.

'Mony a one for him makes mane,
But nane sall ken whare he is gane;
O'er his white banes, when they are bare,
The wind sall blaw for evermair.'[8]

T: It is most probable that the Raven's supposed prophetic powers, respecting battles and bloodshed, originated in their very frequent presence on these occasions, drawn to the field of slaughter by an attractive banquet of unburied bodies of the slain.[178]

In the west the Raven is an emblem of good luck with stalkers because it appears when a deer is killed, and to hear the Raven's croak when setting out fills the hunter's heart with joy.[69]

'*Tha fios fhitich aige.*' (He has a Raven's knowledge.)

'*Piob mhor air an fhiteach.*' (The bagpipe on the Raven, i.e. an impossibility.) (Old Gaelic sayings.)

Epilogue

This book began with a dedication to my father and to my grandchildren. My father was born in the last month of 1899 and, Isobel, his youngest great-grandchild (so far) a century and a few months later. Much has changed in this time. My father, were he alive, would hardly recognize Britain today, though the changes have been less obvious in the Scotland he so loved to visit on holiday. He might well wonder what would be left for his great-grandchildren. This anxiety is common to all who study changes in our eco-system.

We live in an age where meteorological science makes worrying predictions. Greenhouse gases proliferate leading to global warming, melting of polar ice-caps and a rising sea-level. This is said to explain the unusually heavy rainfall at the beginning of the 21st century, which has caused wide-spread flooding. The Antarctic ozone layer is depleted bringing risks of increased terrestrial irradiation with ultra-violet light threatening plants and human skin. Increased pollution hastens the greenhouse effect and pumps quantities of the oxides of sulphur and nitrogen into the atmosphere which return to earth as acid rain. These are indisputable, measurable changes brought about by human intervention in the intricate balance responsible for climate. What is less clear is the assumption that this will lead to inevitable climate change; science is undecided on this point.

Climate change is not new in geological time, indeed some argue that we are still in the IceAages but benefiting from a prolonged warm interglacial. Pollen analysis of the past shows that huge variations in climate tend to recur with a long time cycle. Taken over such a period climate follows a sine curve of change; from this it may be argued that present trends of extreme climate are but part of the sine curve which, in time, will revert towards normal. That view, held by some meteorologists, offers some comfort compared with those predicting disastrous change resembling that which finished the dinosaurs.

But other changes are taking place, which seem even more threatening to wildlife of in general and to Scotland's in particular. The growth of world population threatens the planet's ecosystem simply by demand for *lebensraum* and change in agriculture to produce enough food. Increasingly wilderness is lost to urban development and intensive monocultural agriculture, which is almost as bad. Colin Liddell illustrates the effect of changes in agricultural practice in Scotland:

> Areas of heather, burnt as part of a muirburn programme, have been grazed by deer and sheep to such an extent that grass, rather than heather, comes back in. Sheep are selective grazers and some areas have become relatively barren of vegetation. Bracken has been marching unchecked up the sides of each strath.[106]

Added to this people, growingly increasingly affluent, have more leisure. Many spend spare time on outdoor pursuits, on beaches, mountains and waterways leading to loss or disturbance of habitat.

In the face of all this gloom one must look back at the past depredations of wildlife. Consider the slaughter of birds to adorn ladies hats, the loss of birds and their eggs taken for private collections or, worse still to make patent leather. Huge numbers have been killed for food, exterminating the Dodo, the Moa and the Great Auk. The annual cull by sportsmen and gamekeeper adds to the loss caused by indiscriminate use of toxic agents in farming. The fact that we still have birds demonstrates their remarkable ability to adapt and to survive despite adversity. In the face of reduction in species such as the Partridge, Corncrake and Corn Bunting among others we must applaud the success of others such as Collared Doves and Little Egrets. The northward spread of Cetti's Warbler and Woodlark is as encouraging as reintroduction programmes for Red Kites and Ospreys.

So how will Edward Hull's great-grandchildren fare in the future? Prognosis is always problematical but I cannot share my father's pessimism. Governments, aware of the problems facing our ecosystem are taking action, though their plans for Scotland are bitterly opposed by some. However Government action will be insufficient to halt destruction of our eco-system unless we all act as individuals. In Scotland, where tourism is so vital a part of the economy, we need to cherish our wilderness which attracts visitors from all over the world. But such tourism must be attuned to the environment, and be sustainable. The in-phrase is eco-tourism. By all means enjoy Scotland's wilderness but it must be respected. The increased litter on our mountains and coastlines is indefensible and irresponsible. (Why do people carry their full beer cans into the countryside but cannot take the empties home?) Fires carelessly started kill wild life and indiscrimate off-path walking and the noisy and thoughtless use of waterways for fishing or boating disturbs nesting or feeding birds.

Anyone who loves the Scottish countryside and who would have others share it must campaign for its preservation, then all our grandchildren may benefit.

Bibliography

1. Aelfric, Archbishop (the Grammarian), *The Glossary* (AD 998)

2 Aldrovandi, Ulisse, *Birds, Insects and Mollusca* (1599)

3. Aldrovandi, Ulisse, *Ornithologiae hoc est de avibus historiae* (1599-1603)

4. Annand, J.K., 'Humphy-backit Heron'

5. Annand J.K., 'Laverock'

6. Angus, Marion 'Alas, Poor Queen'

7. Anonymous, *The Arctic World: Its Plants, Animals and Natural Phenomena* (Nelson, London, ?1880)

8. Anonymous, ballads

9. Anonymous, 'The Reed Sparrow' (late eighteenth century)

10. Archibald, Malcolm, *Scottish Animal and Bird Folklore* (Saint Andrew Press, Edinburgh, 1996)

11. Aristophanes, *The Birds* (circa BC 406)

12. Atkinson, Robert *Island Going* (Collins, London, 1949)

13. Baxter, Evelyn and Rintoul, Leonora, *The Birds of Scotland* (Oliver and Boyd, Edinburgh & London, 1953)

14. Bede, Venerable (673–735), *A History of the English Church and People* (731)

15. Beeton, Mrs Isabella, *Book of Household Management* (various editions, late nineteenth century)

16. Beeton, Mrs Isabella, *Book of Household Management* (1912 edition)

17. Belon, Pierre, *L'Histoire de la Nature des Oyseaux* (1555)

18. *Beowulf* (*circa* AD 597) Old English poem surviving in a tenth century manuscript.

19. Bewick, Thomas *A History of British Birds* (Newcastle, 1797)

20. Boece or Boethius, *A History of Scotland up to the Reign of James III* (1526)

21. Boswell, James, *The Journal of a Tour to the Hebrides* (1786)

22. Bower, Walter, *Scotichronicon* (written in 1440s; modern edition Mercat Press, Edinburgh, 1987-1998)

23. Brockie, Keith, *The Silvery Tay, Paintings and Sketches from a Scottish River* (Dent, London, 1988)

24. Brown, Peter, *The Book of Kells* (Thames and Hudson, London, 1980)

25. Burns, Robert, 'Composed in August'

26. Burns, Robert, 'Composed in Spring'

27. Burns, Robert, 'Address to a Woodlark'

28. Burns, Robert, 'Lament of Mary, Queen of Scots'

29. Burns, Robert, 'Elegy on Capt. Matthew Henderson'

30. Burns, Robert, 'Elegy on Tam Sampson'

31. Burns, Robert, 'On Hearing a Thrush Sing'

32. Burns. Robert, 'The Bonie Moor-hen'

33. Burt, Captain, *Letters from a Gentleman in the North of Scotland to his Friend in London* (written about 1730; published by Ogle, London, 1822)

34. Caie, J.M., 'The Puddock' (*circa* 1950)

35. Carmichael, Alexander, *Carmina Gadelica* (6 vols. in Gaelic and English, 1900-71)

36. Carson, Rachel, *Silent Spring* (Houghton Mifflin, Boston, 1962)

37. *Chambers Concise Scots Dictionary*, Editor-in-chief Mairi Robinson (Larousse PLC, Edinburgh, 1996)

38. Charleton, W., *Onomasticon Zoicon* (Royal Society, London, 1688)

39. Cleveland, John, 'The Rebel Scot' (1644)

40. Coleridge, Samuel Taylor, 'Epigram on a Volunteer Singer'

41. Collett, Anthony, *British Inland Birds* (1906)

42. Cook, Martin, *The Birds of Moray and Nairn*, (Mercat Press, Edinburgh, 1992)

43. Cooper, Derek, *The Road to Mingulay* (Warner, London, 1985)

44. Craig, David, *On the Crofters' Trail* (Jonathan Cape, London, 1990)

45. Crawford, Robert, *Tweedsdale* (*circa* 1700)

46. Crumley, Jim, *The Scots Magazine*, vol. 154, 148-155 (2001)

47. Cunningham, Peter, *Birds of the Outer Hebrides* (Mercat Press, Edinburgh, 1990)

48. Cunningham, Peter, *A Hebridean Naturalist* (Acair Ltd, Stornoway, 1979)

49. Darling, Fraser, *Island Years* (G. Bell & Sons, London, 1940)

50. Darwin Tess, *The Scots Herbal* (Mercat Press, Edinburgh, 1996)

51. De Saint-Fond, *Voyage en Angleterre et en Ecosse* (1784)

52. Dods, Meg, *The Cook and Housewife's Manual* (1826)

53. Douglas-Home, Henry, *The Birdman—Memories of Birds* (Readers Union, Newton Abbot, 1977)

54. Dunbar, William, 'The Thistle and the Rose' (*circa* 1500)

55. Dunbar, William, 'Dirge to the King at Stirling' (*circa* 1500)

56. Dwelly, Edward, *Illustrated Gaelic-English Dictionary* (first edition 1901-11; eleventh edition Gairm, Glasgow, 1994)

57. Edwards, George, *Gleanings of Natural History* (London, 1758)

58. Edwards, George, *Natural History of Uncommon Birds* (1751)

59. Fisher, J., *The Shell Book of Birds* (1966)

60. Fisher, J. (ed), *Thorburn's Birds* (Michael Joseph, London, 1967)

61. Forbes, A.R., *Gaelic Names of Beasts, Birds, Fishes Insects, Reptiles etc* (Oliver & Boyd, Edinburgh, 1905)

62. Fraser, J., *Scottish Gaelic Studies II* (Issued from the Celtic Department of the University of Aberdeen, 1927)

63. Gaius Plinius Secundus (Pliny, AD23–79) *Historia Naturalis*

64. Geddes, Tex, personal communication

65. Gerald of Wales (1146-1223), *The History and Topography of Ireland* (Penguin Classics, Harmondsworth, 1982)

66. Gesner, C., *Historium Animalium* (1555)

67. Glasse, Harriet, (written under the pseudonym 'A Lady' but signed H. Glasse), *The Art of Cookery Made Plain and Easy* (Millar & Co., London, 1757)

68. Goldsmith, Oliver, *History of the Earth and Animated Nature* (Richardson & Co., London, 1774)

69. Gordon, Paul Seton, *A Highland Year* (Cassell & Co., London, 1944)

70. Gordon, Paul Seton, *The Immortal Isle* (Cassell & Co., London, 1926)

71. Gordon, Paul Seton, *Hebridean Memories* (Cassell & Co., London, 1923)

72. Gordon, Paul Seton, *Land of Hills and Glens* (Cassell & Co., London, 1920)

73. Gordon, Paul Seton, *The Charm of Skye, The Winged Isle* (Cassell & Co., London, 1929)

74. Gordon, Robert of Stralloch, *The Story of the Bass* (1654)

75. Graham, Patrick, *Sketches of Perthshire* (Third Edition, John Ballantyne & Co., Edinburgh, 1812)

76. Grahame, James, *Georgics* (1808)

77. Grant, Elizabeth, of Rothiemurchus, *Memoirs of a Highland Lady* (1898)

78. Gray, David, 'The Yellowhammer'

79. Greenoak, Francesca, *British Birds, Their Folklore, Names and Literature* (Christopher Helm, London, 1997)

80. Grey, Lord, of Fallodon, *The Charm of Birds* (Hodder & Stoughton, London, 1927)

81. Grigson, G., *The Englishman's Flora* (London, 1955)

82. Gurney, J.H., *Early Annals of Ornithology* (Minet, Chidhelry, 1972)

83. Hakluyt, R., *Navigations, Voyages, Traffiques and Discoveries* (1589)

84. Hall, Pat, 'Pipits?' (1950s)

85. Harman, Mary, *An Isle called Hirte: History and Culture of St Kilda to 1930s* (Maclean Press, Skye, 1997)

86. Harrison, C. and Reid-Henry, D., *The History of the Birds of Britain* (Collins, London, 1988)

87. Harvie-Brown, J.A., *The Capercaillie in Scotland* (Edinburgh, 1879)

88. Hogg, James, 'The Skylark' (*circa* 1820)

89. Hogg, James, 'Lament of Flora Macdonald' (*circa* 1820)

90. Holland, Sir Richard, 'The Howlat', a satirical poem on James II of Scotland (1453)

91. Hudson, W.H., *The Book of a Naturalist* (Nelson, London, 1919)

92. Hull, Robin, *British Medical Journal* (18 October 1973)

93. Huxley, Julian, *Bird Watching and Bird Behaviour* (Chatto and Windus, London, 1930)

94. Irvine-Robertson, James (ed.), Random Shots, *An Anthology from the First 50 Years of the Shooting Times* (Pelham Books, London, 1990)

95. Jacob, Violet, 'The Wild Geese', *Songs of Angus* (1915)

96. Jobling, J.A., *A Dictionary of Scientific Bird Names* (Oxford University Press, Oxford, 1991)

97. Johns, C.A., *British Birds in Their Haunts* (1861; republished by Routledge & Kegan Paul, London, 1947)

98. Keay, John and Keay, Julia, *Encylopaedia of Scotland* (Harper Collins, London, 1994)

99. Kerr, John (ed.), *Queen Victoria's Scottish Diaries* (Brockhampton Press, London, 1992)

100. Lambert, R.A.L. (ed.), *Species History in Scotland* (Scottish Cultural Press, Edinburgh, 1998)

101. Lambourne, M. *The Art of Bird Illustration* (Wellfleet, New Jersey, 1990)

102. Landsborough, David, 'Arran' (1828)

103. Latham, J. *General Synopsis of Birds* (1785)

104. Leakey, R.E. and Lewin, R., *Origins* (Dutton, New York, 1977)

105. Leslie, J., *Scotiae Descriptio* (1578)

106. Liddell, Colin, *Pitlochry, Heritage of a Highland District* (Perth & Kinross Libraries, 1993)

107. Lilford, Lord, (Powys, Thomas Lyttleton), *Coloured Figures of the Birds of the British Islands* (Porter, London, 1885-98)

108. Lockwood, W.B., *The Oxford Book of Bird Names* (OUP, Oxford, 1993)

109. Lodge, George E., *Memoirs of an Artist Naturalist* (Gurney and Jackson, London, 1946)

110. Logan, John, 'The Cuckoo' (*circa* 1780)

111. Loyd, L.R.W., *Bird Facts and Fallacies* (Hutchinson, London, 1927)

112. Lyman, Darryl, *Dictionary of Animal Words and Phrases* (Jonathan David, New York 1994)

113. MacCaig, Norman, 'Ringed Plover'

114. MacCaig, Norman, 'Dipper'

115. MacCaig, Norman, 'Greenshank'

116. MacCaig, Norman, 'Puffin'

117. Macdonald, Donald, *Lewis—a History of the Island* (Gordon Wright, Edinburgh, 1978)

118. MacGillivray, William, *A History of British Birds*, volumes I-V (Scott, Webster & Geary, London, 1837-52)

119. Mackenzie, Osgood, *100 Years in the Highlands* (1921; reprinted by National Trust for Scotland in 1994)

120. Maclean, Charles, *Island on the Edge of the World* (Canongate, Edinburgh, 1972)

121. MacLennan, Malcolm, *A Pronouncing and Etymological Dictionary of the Gaelic Language* (John Grant, Edinburgh, 1925; reprinted by Acair/Mercat Press, 1982-2001)

122. Macleod, Fiona (aka Sharp, William), 'The Birth of Christ'

123. Major (or Main), John, *De Gesteis Scotorum* (1518)

124. Marquiss, M. and Duncan, K., 'Seasonal switching between habitats and changes in abundance of Goosanders within a Scottish river system.' *Wildfowl* 45 (Wildfowl and Wetlands Trust, Slimbridge, 1994)

125. Martin, B.P., *The Glorious Grouse; A Natural and Unnatural History* (David & Charles, Newton Abbot, 1990)

126. Martin, Martin, *A Late Voyage to St Kilda* (London, 1698)

127. McNeill, F. Marian, *The Scots Kitchen* (Glasgow, 1929)

128. Mearns, Barbara and Mearns, Richard, *Biographies for Birdwatchers* (Academic Press, London, 1988)

129. Mearns, Barbara and Mearns, Richard, *The Bird Collectors* (Academic Press, London, 1998)

130. .Melville, Lawrence, *The Fine Land of Gowrie* (William Culross, Coupar Angus, 1939)

131. Merrett, C., Pinax *Rerum Naturalium Britannicum* (1667)

132. Millar, David, *The Tay: a Poem* (Richardson and Wood, Perth, 1850)

133. Monro, Donald, *A Description of the Western Isles of Scotland Called Hybrides* (1549; first published from the manuscript in 1774)

134. Montgomery, Alexander, *The Cherrie and the Sloe* (*circa* 1590)

135. .Montagu, G., *Ornithological Dictionary* (1802)

136. Moray, Robert, *Proceedings of the Royal Society* (1678)

137. Muir, John, quotation from John Muir Museum in Dunbar.

138. Murray, Charles, *Hamewith* (Constable & Co., London, 1909)

139. Murton, R.K., *Man and Birds* (Collins New Naturalist Series, London, 1971)

140. Nethersole-Thompson, D., *Highland Birds* (Highlands and Islands Development Board, Inverness, 1971)

141. Nethersole-Thompson, D. and Watson, A., *The Cairngorms* (Melven Press, Perth, 1981)

142. *New Statistical Account of Scotland by the Ministers of the Respective Parishes* Vols. I-XV. Edinburgh 1834-45

143. Newton, Norman, *Colonsay and Oronsay* (David & Charles, Newton Abbot, 1944)

144. North, Christopher (John Wilson), *Noctes Ambrosianae* (a series of dialogues in *Blackwoods Magazine* from 1822 to 1835)

145. *Old Statistical Account of Scotland*, ed. Sir John Sinclair, Vols. I-XXI (Edinburgh, 1791-1799)

146. Parker, Eric, *Game Birds, Beasts and Fishes* (The Lonsdale Library, London, 1935)

147. Pennant, Thomas, *Tour in Scotland and Voyage to the Hebrides* (London, 1771-76)

148. Pennant, Thomas, *British Zoology (Birds)* (London, 1768)

149. Perry, Richard, *I Went a-Shepherding* (Lindsay Drummond Ltd., London, 1944)

150. Peterson, Roger Tory and Virginia Marie, *Audubon's Birds of America* (New York, 1925)

151. Plant, Marjorie, *Domestic Life of Scotland in the Eighteenth Century* (Edinburgh University Press, 1952)

152. Pontoppidan, Erik, *Norge Naturlige Historie* (1755)

153. Rabbitts, G.B., *Outer Hebrides Bird Report* (1999)

154. Rackham, James, *Animal Bones* (British Museum Press, London,1994)

155. Ray, John, *The Ornithology of Francis Willughby* (1678)

156. RCAHMS (Royal Commission on the Ancient and Historical Monuments of Scotland), *Pictish Symbol Stones; An Illustrated Gazeteer* (1999)

157. Renfrew, Jane, *Food and Cooking in Prehistoric Britain; History and Recipes* (English Heritage, 1985)

158. Robson, Michael, *Rona, The Distant Island* (Acair, Stornoway, 1991)

159. Rogers, Charles, *Social Life in Scotland* (Paterson, Edinburgh, 1884)

160. Routh, Shelagh and Jonathan, *Leonardo's Kitchen Notebooks* (Collins, London, 1987)

161. St John, Charles, *Wild Sports and Natural History of the Highlands* (London, 1846)

162. Saunders, Howard, *An Illustrated Manual of British Birds* (Second Edition, Gurney & Jackson, London, 1899)

163. Selby, P.J., *Illustrations of British Ornithology: I Land Birds* (1825) *II Water Birds* (1833)

288

164. Scot, Alexander, 'The Eagle and the Robin Redbreast' (*circa* 1550)

165. Scott, Sir Walter, *Marmion* (1808)

166. Scott, Sir Walter, *The Heart of Midlothian* (1818)

167. Scott, Sir Walter, 'Melrose Abbey by Night'

168. Selkirk, J.R., *A Border Burn* (*circa* 1900)

169. Shakespeare, William, *Macbeth*, I, vi

170. Shakespeare, William, *Winters Tale*, IV, iii

171. Sharpe, Charles Kirkpatrick, *A Historical Account of the Belief in Witchcraft in Scotland* (London and Glasgow, 1884)

172. Shaw, Margaret Fay, *Folksongs and Folklore of South Uist* (Aberdeen University Press, 1955)

173. Sibbald, Robert, *Scotia illustrata sive Prodromus historiae naturalis* (Edinburgh, 1684)

174. Smiles, Samuel, *Life of a Scotch Naturalist: Thomas Edward* (Fourth Edition, John Murray, London, 1877)

175. Soutar, William, *Wullie Wagtail* (*circa* 1930)

176. Spence, Charles, 'Linn-ma-Gray' (*circa* 1820)

177. Spence, Lewis, *The Magic Arts in Celtic Britain* (Constable, London, 1945)

178. Stanley, Edward, *A Familiar History of Birds* (London, 1835)

179. Steel, Tom, *The Life and Death of St Kilda* (National Trust for Scotland, Edinburgh, 1965)

180. Stephen, David, *Watching Wildlife* (Collins, London & Glasgow, 1963)

181. Steven, Campbell, *The Island Hills* (Hurst & Blackett, London, 1955)

182. Steven, Campbell, *Enjoying Perthshire* (Perth & Kinross Libraries, 1994)

183. Steven, Maisie, *The Good Scots Diet* (Aberdeen University Press, 1985)

184. Steven, Kenneth, *Iona* (St Andrews Press, Edinburgh, 2000)

185. Stevenson, Robert Louis, 'Ross of Mull'

186. Stevenson, Robert Louis, 'Good and Bad Children'

187. Stevenson, Robert Louis, 'The Pentland Hills'

188. Stevenson, Robert Louis, *Kidnapped* (1885)

189. Stewart, Alexandra, ed. Innes Macbeath, *Daughters of the Glen* (Leura Press, Aberfeldy, 1986)

190. Swainson, Charles, *The Folk Lore and Provincial Names of British Birds* (Elliot Stock, London, 1886)

191. Swinton, W.E., *Fossil Birds* (British Museum, London, 1958)

192. Thom, Valerie, *Birds in Scotland* (Calton, published for Scottish Ornithologists Club by Poyser, 1986)

193. Thomson, James, *The Seasons* (1730)

194. Tomkies, M., *On Wing and Wild Water* (Jonathan Cape, London, 1987)

195. Turner, W., *Avium precipuarum, quarum apud Plinium et Aristotelem mentio est, brevis et succincta historia* (1544)

196. Vesey-Fitzgerald, Brian, *British Game* (Collins New Naturalist Series, London, 1946)

197. White, Gilbert, *The Natural History of Selbourne* (1789)

198. Williams, C.L., manuscript notes in Saunders (1899 to 1914)

199. Wilson, Alexander, 'Lochwinnoch' (*circa* 1784)

200. Wilson, Edward, ed. Brian Roberts, *Birds of the Antarctic* (New Orchard Editions, Poole, 1987)

201. Yarrell, W., *History of British Birds* (1843)

202. Zealand, Gillian, *William MacGillivray—Deeside's forgotten Naturalist* (Book of the Braemar Gathering and the Scottish Annual, Arbroath Herald, 2000)

Bird Index

General Index

Raasay 35, 43
Raeburn, Sir Henry 37
Rat, Brown 196
Ray, John 31, 42, 95, 107, 111, 115, 118, 122, 123, 126, 128, 136, 148, 150, 151, 152, 155, 185, 193, 216, 225, 236, 243, 246, 249, 252, 268, 270
Renfewshire 219
Renfrew 138, 243
retina ix
Reynolds, Sir Joshua 37
Richardson, Sir John 51
Rintoul, Leonora 66, 218, 219, 234
River Bran 127
River Clyde 8, 51, 152, 178, 185, 186, 189, 198, 205, 245, 250
River Dee 127, 207
River Forth 8
River Phasis 153
River Tay 59, 68, 86, 119, 150, 174, 175, 213, 239
River Tweed 55, 202, 213
Robert the Bruce 18, 104
Robert of Avenel 18
Robson, Michael 93
Rodhill 242
Romans 7, 8, 153
Rome 7
Rona 45, 93
Ross and Cromarty 66, 111
Ross, James Clark 51
Ross, John 51
Rossend Castle 26
Rosshire iv, 127
Rossie Priory 15
Ross-shire 67, 245, 267
Rousay 6
Roxborough 99, 248
Roxburgh 65, 119
Royal Society 23, 28, 36
RSPB 64, 219
Rum 3, 88, 132, 164

Ruskin, John 67
Russia 129, 240, 267

Sahel 220, 221, 244, 248
Salmon 63, 127, 128, 188, 229
Sandwich 188
Satan 13, 140, 226; see Devil
Saunders, Howard 69, 70, 110, 115, 116, 119, 122, 128, 167, 169, 190, 205, 246, 250, 251, 254, 263, 268, 270, 272
Scandinavia 1, 78, 79, 81, 82, 85, 121, 129, 142, 164, 166, 225, 240, 241, 250, 267, 277
Scone 23
Scot, Alexander 16
Scott, Caroline, Marchioness of Queensberry 37
Scott, Robert Falcon 71
Scott, Sir Walter 20, 54, 55
Scotti 8
Scottish Enlightenment 34, 50
Scottish Ornithologists' Club 252
Selkirk, J.R. 227
Shakespeare ix, 11, 38, 136
Sharp, William, see Macleod, Fiona
Sharpe, Charles Kirkpatrick 104
Shaw, Margaret Fay 98
Shetland 14, 18, 36, 67, 77, 80, 82, 85, 87, 89, 93, 97, 122, 123, 124, 125, 142, 155, 162, 170, 174, 176, 178, 179, 181, 184, 185, 186, 188, 193, 194, 207, 230, 231, 233, 240, 251, 253, 254, 255, 258, 271, 273, 278
Sibbald, Sir Robert 132, 147
Siberia 106, 109, 164, 241

Sigurd 13
Sinclair, Sir John 35, 66, 234
Singh, Maharajah Duleep 59
Skara Brae 6, 98
Skelmorlie Aisle 26
Skye 58, 82, 88, 106, 132, 190, 226, 227, 251, 254
Sleat 227
Slimbridge 129
Sloane, Sir Hans 36
Sma' Glen 206, 239
Small, William 35
smallpox 43
Smiles, Samuel 229
Smythe, Robert & James 53
Soay 27, 82
Solnhofen 1
Solway 105, 108, 111, 112, 164, 167, 168, 174, 175, 178, 188, 268
Somerset 7
Soutar, William 227
Spain 97, 129
Spence, Charles 55
Spittal 36
Spitzbergen 111
St Abb's Head 43
St Andrew 22
St Andrews 11, 51, 53
St Bride 13, 144, 161, 265
St Columba 8, 9, 68
St Cuthbert 9, 124
St David's 10
St Giles 10, 23
St John 15, 25
St John, Charles 53, 87, 174, 237
St Kentigern 13
St Kevin 9
St Kilda 18, 27, 28, 30, 31, 32, 43, 45, 46, 51, 60,.61 89, 90, 92, 93, 94, 95, 96, 160, 196, 202, 230, 231, 265
St Maddoes 18
St Martin 9, 171, 221